...icnising
and the

Two week
loan

Please return on or before the last
date stamped below.
Charges are made for late return.

© Longman Group UK Ltd 1991

ISBN 0 85121 748 6

Published by
Longman Law, Tax and Finance
Longman Group UK
21–27 Lamb's Conduit Street, London WC1N 3NJ

Associated offices
Australia, Hong Kong, Malaysia, Singapore, USA

A CIP catalogue record for this book is available from
the British Library

Phototypeset by Intype, London
Printed in Great Britain by Biddles of Guildford

Preface

This book considers the impact of European Community Law on the practice of franchising, in the twelve Member States, with particular reference to the implications for franchisors and franchisees of the EC Commission's block exemption regulation on franchise agreements. Two aims above all have been pursued. The first is to explain the objectives of European Community law, as it applies to franchising and indeed to commercial activities generally. The second is to look especially at the terms in which franchise agreements are drafted; that is, at the clauses of franchise agreements which are either going to ensure a smooth passage for the agreements or certain to create difficulties. This is in fact intended to be a practical handbook for franchisors, franchisees and their advisers, and to be helpful to those responsible for the efficient operation of franchise networks in Member States of the European Community, whether the franchisor is from Europe, the United States, Canada or elsewhere.

Bryan Harris
Martin Mendelsohn
March 1991

Contents

Table of Cases

EC Cases

(*Note*: Cases which do not show full citations were not reported at the time this book was published)

Table of Statutes

EEC Regulations

EC Treaties

Chapter 1

The meaning of franchising

A: Background: 'the economic context'
B: Definition: what franchising is
C: Substance: the business format

A: Background: 'the economic context'

In its judgment in *Pronuptia* (161/84) (which is described more fully in Chapter 4), the Court of Justice of the European Communities noted that the case was the first opportunity which the Court had had to review the legality of franchise agreements. The Court took note of the French Government's view that, while it was possible to apply art 85(1) of the EEC Treaty to franchise agreements, it did not necessarily apply 'having regard to the positive aspects of these agreements'. The Court further noted that 'the compatibility of distribution franchise agreements with art 85(1) cannot be assessed in an abstract way but only by reference to clauses contained in these agreements'. In answering the first question referred to it, the Court added to this phrase the words 'and on the economic context in which they have been included'. This seems to be an implicit acknowledgment of the view expressed by the French Government. At the same time, it is hard to see how the principle of taking into account the economic context has in practice been applied either by the Court or by the Commission in deciding whether franchise arrangements, of which the agreements between the franchisor and franchisees are only a part, conform with the EEC rules on competition.

While *Pronuptia*, which was heard by the Court in 1985 (although the judgment did not appear until 28 January 1986), may have been the first case in which the Court had franchise contracts brought to its attention, franchising had been evident in many Member States for a considerable period of time.

It is not necessary to trace the distant origins of franchising since one finds that there are many who lay claim to the origins of franchising having first seen the light of day in their country at some time during the last millennium.

The indisputable fact is that the late 1940s and 1950s saw immense growth in the use of this marketing technique in the United States, during which time many of the now household names first emerged. These included ServiceMaster, Holiday Inn, McDonalds, BurgerKing and Budget Rent-a-Car. The indigenous growth of systems in the US has been striking and now there are in excess of 350 US franchise systems operating in one or more foreign territories. In domestic US terms franchising in all forms is reckoned to account for 34 per cent of all retail sales at which level it has been for some 15 years, during which time the business format franchise content has increased while the content comprising other forms of franchise has declined.

The growth of franchising on a world wide basis has been rapid and extensive and franchising can be found in some 80 countries. There are probably between 8,000–10,000 franchise systems worldwide with between 800,000–1,000,000 franchised outlets. In most countries where there is a significant franchise community, while there are a number of foreign franchisors, the development of indigenous networks provides the major growth pattern which emerges.

Franchising, which is a method of marketing goods and services, has created new business areas, stimulated the growth of existing business categories and generally provoked businesses into introducing competing networks. In addition many have become business owners and successful entrepreneurs through the intro-duction to business provided by the franchise method.

During the years of franchise development there have been problems with the application of competition laws. In the USA there were many early problems which assumed a considerable magnitude. Some of the anti-trust problems went so far as to result in the destruction of networks to the detriment of franchisor, franchisee and consumer. More recently anti-trust problems have become less of a difficulty for franchise systems. This owes something to the changes in legal approaches by the Courts and regulatory authorities as well as to the greater refinement in technique which franchisors have developed.

B: Definition: what franchising is

Before examining the impact of competition laws on franchising it may be helpful to explain in essence what franchising is and why it works. It is a marketing method which has been used to good effect at and between all levels in the chain from manufacturer to consumer, although the block exemption regulation does not apply to all types of franchise arrangement. It does not apply to what are described as 'manufacturing licenses based on patents and/or technical know-how, combined with trade mark licences'. Nor does it apply to industrial franchise agreements, 'ie those which govern relationships between producers (which) present different characteristics than the other types of franchise'.

Franchise arrangements exist between:

>   Manufacturer and Wholesaler
>   Manufacturer and Retailer
>   Wholesaler and Wholesaler
>   Wholesaler and Retailer
>   Retailer and Franchised retailer
>   (of goods and/or services).

The arrangement between manufacturer and wholesaler, of which soft drink bottlers are a good example, would be considered industrial franchises. The arrangement between a wholesaler who establishes a franchised wholesale network will not benefit from the block exemption regulation since the franchisee will invariably not be serving the end user, which is a requirement of the Regulation.

The business format franchise to which the Regulation does apply covers the other three relationships.

The definitions, of franchising which have been coined around the world are not helpful in establishing an understanding because a definition is always created with an objective in mind. Many definitions make sense only to those who already understand the subject matter.

There are more definitions of franchising for legal purposes in the USA than anywhere else, and the main elements which all those definitions have in common are:

- —a trade mark, trade name or other branding;
- —the use under licence of the mark, name or other branding and the franchisor's system by the franchisee; and
- —a payment by the franchisee to the franchisor.

The British Franchise Association (founded in 1977) has the following definition in its Memorandum and Articles of Association:

A contractual licence granted by one person (the franchisor) to another (franchisee) which:

(a) permit or requires the franchisee to carry on during the period of the franchise a particular business under or using a specified name belonging to or associated with the franchisor; and

(b) entitles the franchisor to exercise continuing control during the period of the franchise over the manner in which the franchisee carries on the business which is the subject of the franchise; and

(c) obliges the franchisor to provide the franchisee with assistance in carrying on the business which is the subject of the franchise (in relation to the organisation of the franchisee's business, the training of staff, merchandising, management or otherwise); and

(d) requires the franchisee periodically during the period of the franchise to pay to the franchisors sums of money in consideration for the franchise or for goods or services provided by the franchisor to the franchisee; and

(e) which is not a transaction between a holding company and its subsidiary (as defined in Section 154 of the Companies Act 1948) or between an individual and a company controlled by him.

The equivalent franchisors' association in the USA — the International Franchise Association — has adopted the following definition:

> A franchise operation is a contractual relationship between the franchisor and franchisee in which the franchisor offers or is obliged to maintain a continuing interest in the business of the franchisee in such areas as know-how and training; wherein the franchisee operates under a common trade name, format and/or procedure owned or controlled by the franchisor, and in which the franchisee has or will make a substantial capital investment in his business from his own resources.

The European Franchise Federation, a federation of national franchise associations, has just adopted a new code of ethics and rather than follow the Regulation's definition has prepared its own:

> Franchising is a system of marketing goods and/or services and/or technology, which is based upon a close and ongoing collaboration between legally and financially separate and independent undertakings, the Franchisor and its individual Franchisees the right, and imposes the obligation, to conduct a business in accordance with the Franchisor's concept. The right entitles and compels the individual Franchisee, in exchange for a direct or indirect financial consideration, to use the Franchisor's trade name, and/or trade mark and/or service mark, know-how, business and technical methods, procedural system, and other industrial and/or intellectual property rights, supported by continuing provision of commercial and technical assistance, within the framework and for the term of a written franchise agreement, concluded between parties for this purpose.

However, know-how is given the same meaning as that attributed to it in the Regulation.

C: Substance: the business format

The business format franchise involves the following six characteristics.

First, the franchisor develops a successful business format which is operated under a trade mark, service mark, trade name or other form of branding.

Second, the franchisor grants a licence to the franchisee permitting the franchisee to trade using that business format under the trade mark, service mark, trade name or other form of branding.

Third, the franchisor provides the franchisee with a range of services which are calculated to ensure, so far as is practicably possible, that the franchisee will enjoy the same or a greater degree of success as the franchisor has achieved; these services will include:

—the application of developed criteria for the selection and identification of trading sites;
—guidance to the franchisee to assist in obtaining occupation rights to the site, complying with zoning laws, preparation of plans for layouts, shopfitting and refurbishment and general assistance in the evaluation of the correct level and mix of stock and in the opening launch of the business;
—the training of the franchisee and staff in the operation of the business format and the provision of an operational manual with detailed operational instructions;
—the training of the franchisee and staff in any methods of manufacture or preparation which may be appropriate; and
—the training of the franchisee in methods of accounting, business controls, marketing and merchandising.

having established the franchisee in business, the franchisor then offers continuing services for which a fee is payable. The fee (often called a royalty or a management service fee) is paid in return for continuing services rendered. These continuing services usually include:

—operational support
—updating of the operational manual
—marketing and promotional support
—advertising on a national or regional basis with funds contributed by franchisees
—standards and performance monitoring
—research and development

—in appropriate cases, the benefits of the bulk purchasing power which the network commands.

In short the franchisee benefits by having support services available which no individual self-employed trader could command and at a price which makes economic sense to him.

Fourth, the franchisee is usually required to make what is for him or her a substantial capital investment from his or her own resources so as to provide both commitment and motivation.

Fifth, the franchisee's ownership and day-to-day involvement in the operation of the business which he or she owns strengthens his or her commitment and motivation and tends to ensure that the business is exploited to the maximum advantage. The value of the consumer as a customer is reflected by the way in which the franchisee's success is enhanced by the personal attention of the owner of the business.

Sixth, the consumer benefits from dealing with what appears to be a multiple network but, as it is in multiple ownership and he or she is in reality dealing with the owner of the business, the uniformity and consistency of quality standards are likely to be better.

As a boost to growth, there are several ways in which franchising provides a powerful alternative to ownership by a business of its own outlets:

—growth is achieved by using the manpower and capital resources of others and can thus be more rapid;
—the commitment and interest of the franchisee, together with the risks the franchisee runs, tend to ensure that standards are maintained and that performance is better;
—the customer invariably receives better services by dealing with an owner instead of a less interested and less committed manager and staff.

The franchisor and franchisee present to the market place a powerful partnership (not in the legal sense) which is calculated to produce profit for both by providing the consumer with:

—a uniform branded product or service at each outlet
—a consistent quality of product and service
—a committed and interested local owner.

The franchisee joins the network and pays the price in order:

—to buy into the success of the franchisor
—to belong to a 'club' and not be a sole trader without the support of the network
—to benefit from the franchisor's knowledge
—to obtain the comfort and assurance of knowing that the initial and continuing services will be available.

The franchisor selects franchisees with certain basic requirements in mind:

—the adequacy of the franchisee's financial resources;
—a judgment that the franchisee has the commitment, the ability to accept the responsibilities and stress of self-employment, and the ability to run the business in accordance with the established format.

The reputable franchisor cannot run the risk for itself or the franchisee that the franchisee will not be able to make a success of the business.

The problem with which a franchisor is confronted when building a network can be simply summed up as follows.

(a) Each outlet must appear to be the same as the others.
(b) Each outlet must carry substantially the same range of products or supply the same services.
(c) The quality of the network must be consistent and in keeping with the standards associated with the branding.
(d) To sell franchises a franchisor has to provide franchisees with sufficient protection from competition from the franchisor and other franchisees. The franchisor also has
  —to recognise the advisory role which he plays when selling a franchise which affords the franchisee the comfort of knowing that the franchisor believes the location or territory is adequate to support the operator;
  —to protect and control the dissemination of his know how which franchisees are licensed and required to use in the operation of the outlet;
  —to ensure that the franchisee's territory is not so large

that the franchisee may overreach his capabilities in
trying to exploit it or may not exploit it at all;
—the preservation of its name and associated goodwill
while entrusted to the franchisee during the term of the
franchise agreement.

In seeking to overcome these problems, the solution of which is
inherent in franchising, there have been a number of traditional
competition law issues which have arisen. Many of these have
been addressed clearly in the Regulation, many less clearly and
some not at all. These issues are:

—the tying of products
—the sourcing of products
—the control of the quality of products and services
—the control of the range of products and services to be offered
—territorial restrictions
—exclusivity
—non-exclusive arrangements, in which the franchisee is limited
to operating within an allocated territory
—location clauses, where the franchisee is restricted to identified premises
—customer restrictions
—control of prices
—non-competition provisions during the term of the agreement
—post termination
—restrictions on use and disclosure of know-how and confidential information.

How the Regulation deals with these issues is the subject of the
chapters which follow and to the extent that problems remain
they are discussed in Chapter 14.

The Commission has extended the Regulation to deal with master
franchise agreements presumably on the strength of their experience in dealing with the notification by Computerland of its
franchise agreement to which exemption was given. However the
provisions of the regulation are not really appropriate for many
types of master franchise arrangement and do not address the
issues which are relevant. A master franchise agreement often has
two elements: the first is the grant of rights to a territory usually
of an exclusive nature with an obligation to develop the area

within an agreed time frame; the second is the right to so develop the territory by opening up sub-franchisor owned outlets or sub-franchised outlets or a combination of both. The outlets by whomever operated are usually subject to a separate agreement. The sub-franchisor essentially becomes the franchisor in the territory.

The fundamental problem which the Commission has created with the Regulation is in the definition of 'master franchise agreements' which 'means an agreement whereby one undertaking, the franchisor, grants the other, the master franchisee, in exchange of direct or indirect financial consideration, the right to exploit a franchise for the purposes of concluding franchise agreements with third parties, the franchisees' (art 1(3)(*c*)). As to what may be exploited, this is contained in the definition of 'franchise': ' "franchise" means a package of industrial or intellectual property rights relating to trade marks, trade names, shop signs, utility models, designs, copyrights, know-how or patents, to be exploited for the resale of goods or the provision of services to end users' (art 1(3)(*a*)). The juxtaposition of the two definitions creates an anomolous situation (*see* Chapter 16).

The Regulation does not deal at all with 'development agreements' which essentially are option arrangements. Under a development agreement a franchise will be granted the exclusive right and have the obligation to open a specified number of outlets within an exclusive defined area on an agreed time scale. Each outlet opened will become subject to an operational franchise agreement which would comply with the Regulation. The position of the development agreement is not dealt with at all notwithstanding that the exclusive grant of territory would bring the arrangement within the scope of art 85(1).

It remains to be considered whether the grant of the 'option' under a development agreement could be regarded in the Regulation's definition of 'franchise agreement' as granting the franchisee 'the right to exploit a franchise for the purposes of marketing specified types of goods and/or services' (art 1(3)(*b*)). If that were the only element of the definition to which regard must be had there may be an argument, although the development agreement is merely an option to take up 'the right to exploit a franchise' and not the actual grant of the right which follows when the franchise agreement is entered into. However very few development agreements would deal with the compulsory minimum obligations which have to be present for there to be a franchise agreement within the meaning of the definition in the Regulation. Development agreements are discussed in more detail in Chapter 16.

Chapter 2

European Community law

A: Obligations under European Community law
B: Economic background to European Community law
C: Creation of an internal market
D: Free movement of goods, services, persons and capital
E: The internal market and the rules on competition

A: Obligations under European Community law

Membership of the European Communities carries with it the obligation to respect the laws contained in, or made by virtue of, the treaties under which the three Communities were established. This book is not concerned with two of the three treaties — the European Coal and Steel Community Treaty or the Euratom Treaty — but only with the treaty establishing the European Economic Community. Throughout the book, this is referred to as the EEC Treaty. It is commonly referred to as the Treaty of Rome; but this is imprecise, as the Euratom Treaty was also the Treaty of Rome. (In the highly unlikely event of a franchise involving coal or steel, or nuclear products, the other treaties could conceivably be relevant.)

From time to time, the EEC Treaty, which was signed in 1957 and came into force in 1958, has been amended, notably by the various Treaties of Accession, the Merger Treaty and the Budgetary Treaty, as well as by the Single European Act, which has the status of a treaty. It is not, however, necessary to refer to these in this book, since they have no separate impact on franchising. Some of the provisions of the Single European Act are certainly important in the present context; but, as they take the form of amendments to the EEC Treaty, it suffices to quote the EEC Treaty in its amended form. Article 100A of the EEC Treaty, for example, was introduced under the terms of art 18 of the Single European Act; but it is the amended article of the EEC Treaty, rather than the amending article of the Single European Act, which is usually cited.

Under the EEC Treaty, there are certain delegated powers to make laws. Most legislative powers are conferred on the EEC Council, which normally legislates on the basis of a proposal put forward by the Commission; a case in point is Council Regulation 19/65. However, some powers are conferred on the Commission, either directly under the EEC Treaty, or under laws made by the Council; a case in point is Commission Regulation 4087/88 (reproduced in full at Appendix II), with which this book is mainly concerned. As a matter of convenience, the rules contained in the treaties are referred to as primary legislation, while the rules contained in measures passed by the Council and Commission are referred to as secondary legislation.

Of the various forms of secondary legislation, there are three which have binding legal effect on the Member States. These are, respectively, regulations, directives and decisions; their scope is defined in art 189 of the EEC Treaty. The book is mainly concerned with regulations and decisions. In the field of franchising, there is no reason why the Council should not, if necessary, issue directives; but this has not so far happened and is not at present contemplated. However, there is currently a proposal for a Council directive in relation to liability for the provision of defective services which would impose joint and several liability on franchisors, master franchisees and franchisees in respect of the provision of defective services. Although decisions by the Commission in franchising cases are akin to judgments in a quasi-judicial proceeding, they are in fact a form of legislative measure and are published in the L Series of the *Official Journal of the European Communities*: they have the force of law, in that they are binding in their entirety on those to whom they are addressed. An example of a formal decision by the Commission is *ServiceMaster*, reproduced in Appendix V.

Decisions of the European Court of Justice are judicial, not legislative, measures; but they also have the force of law, this time under art 187 of the EEC Treaty. An example of a Court Decision is the *Pronuptia* case, reproduced in Appendix IV.

It is a matter for national law to ensure that EC law has effect in each of the Member States. Without enabling laws in the Member States, EC law would be ineffective. The nature of the enabling laws varies from state to state. In the United Kingdom, EC law is given force by virtue of the European Communities Act 1972 and European Communities (Amendment) Act 1986. Section 2(1) of the 1972 Act provides that 'All such rights, powers, liabilities, obligations and restrictions from time to time created or arising by or under the Treaties, and all such remedies and procedures from time to time provided for by or under the Treaties, as in accordance with the Treaties, are without further enactment to be given legal effect or used in the United Kingdom, shall be recognised and available in law, and be enforced, allowed and followed accordingly . . .'.

It follows that the provisions of EC law play their part in national law and in the national courts, and that franchising cases, like many other commercial and even personal cases, may have a European Community dimension. It is essential, in a field such as franchising, where there are already Community rules in force, for those advising franchisors, franchisees, consumers, manufacturers, competing traders, finance houses and any others affected by or interested in the activities of a franchising network, to be aware at all times of the Community dimension of a case, whether actual or potential.

B: Economic background to European Community law

It is not enough, by way of background to the impact of EC law on franchising, for a practitioner to know what the legal impact is and why it is important. He also needs to know the rationale of Community law in economic terms. The EEC Treaty is concerned above all with economics, and the legislation affecting commercial activities generally and franchising in particular has an economic foundation. Cases coming before the Commission and the Court of Justice are often argued on economic and not just on legal grounds. For example, where franchising arrangements are called in question under the provisions of the EEC Treaty, franchisors are obliged, as a later section of this book explains, to provide an assessment of the market conditions in which their franchise agreements have been concluded. As the Court of Justice put it in para 27(1) of *Pronuptia* (*see* Appendix IV): when deciding whether a particular franchise agreement is compatible with the relevant provisions of the EEC Treaty, much depends not only on the clauses contained in the agreement but also on their 'economic context'.

This economic context signifies both the immediate context governing the geographical market and the product or service market conditions concerned and the general context in which the European Community itself is developing. At the time of writing, the Community is devoting much time and effort, as well as great resources, to the completion of the internal market by 31 December 1992. It is seeking to achieve this end and to fulfil the main purposes of the EEC Treaty by ensuring the free movement throughout the Community of goods, services, persons and capital. It is relying heavily, in attempting to fulfil the purposes of the Treaty, on the provisions of the Treaty concerned with the rules on competition. These are not abstract points. If a controversial case arises, whether in franchising or in any other commercial sector, it is as well to be in a position to argue the case by reference to these larger economic objectives. The paragraphs which follow give some illustrations of how this may be done.

C: Creation of an internal market

Under art 2 of the EEC Treaty, the European Economic Community has as its task, by establishing a common market and progressively 'approximating' the economic policies of Member States, to promote throughout the Community a harmonious development of economic activities, a continuous and balanced expansion, an increase in stability, an accelerated raising of the standard of living and closer relations between the states belonging to it.

Beyond this, the term 'common market' has not been defined, though it is referred to in various other articles of the Treaty. Essentially, it is a market in which it is as easy for traders to operate, for professional people to practise, for employees to take jobs and for citizens generally to live and to buy products and

services, as if there were no restrictive national boundaries. The
ideal result is that a traveller, whether on business or not, passes
from Manchester to Milan or from Berlin to Barcelona, as readily
as from Manchester to London or from Berlin to Bonn.

To achieve this result, difficulties arising from the conflicts
between different national laws are having to be overcome. All
rules or practices which directly or indirectly restrict imports and
exports between the Member States have to be eliminated. All
obstacles to the free movement of persons, services or capital
have to be abolished. Common policies in the agricultural and
transport sectors have to be adopted. A system has to be instituted, ensuring that competition is not distorted. Procedures have
to be applied by which the economic policies of Member States
can be coordinated. The laws of Member States have to be har-
monised to the extent necessary for the proper functioning of the
common market. These and other requirements for the creation
of a common market were laid down in art 3 of the EEC Treaty.

By 31 December 1969, or at the latest by 31 December 1972, the
process of establishing a common market was intended, under art
8 of the Treaty, to be completed. The Community failed in this
objective. There had been a lack of political will, particularly
in France under President de Gaulle, to complete the process.
Legislative procedures had become absurdly protracted. The
Commission, instead of being a dynamo for the Community,
became obsessed with the idea of harmonisation. There was a
lack of public interest in the common market; commercial firms
were largely indifferent to it, the larger corporations having more
or less mastered the complexities of inter-state trade, and the
smaller firms having resigned themselves to the fact that for most
of them inter-state trade was fraught with too many problems.
Above all, perhaps, there was the overriding problem that, if
national barriers were to come down, the Member States would
have to change their cherished policies on the taxation of goods
and services.

By the early 1980s, it was evident that the Community would have
to produce new plans for completing the common market, if the
whole concept of an economic community were to survive at all.
A White Paper was prepared by the Commission on the com-

pletion of the internal market — it was no longer fashionable to refer to the 'common' market — proposing a list of legislative measures needed to ensure the creation of the internal market by 31 December 1992. In 1986, Member States concluded a further treaty, the Single European Act, to facilitate the legislation, and the whole concept of 1992 sprang to the attention of the public.

One of the strengths of the 1992 programme of legislation was that it concentrated on the three barriers to inter-state trade: the physical barriers (the customs checks and immigration controls, among others), the technical barriers (mostly, those laid down by the different laws of the Member States, ranging from intellectual property laws to standards for motor vehicles and food safety) and the fiscal barriers (that is, primarily, value added tax and excise duties). By showing that the removal of these barriers could create vast new opportunities for competitive trade, the national and Community authorities stimulated a far wider public interest in the aims of the EEC than there had ever previously been.

Moreover, the very conditions which had stultified earlier efforts to complete the internal market were rapidly reversed. Ratification of the Single European Act reflected a new political will, and legislative procedures introduced under the Act were speedier. Instead of comprehensive harmonisation, officials began to think in terms of 'mutual recognition' — in other words, instead of trying to ensure that all the Member States' laws in a given sector should be the same, they were content to provide that what was legal in one Member State should in general be recognised as legal in other Member States, a principle suggested by the *Cassis de Dijon* case (120/78) in 1979.) Public interest was aroused by the possibility of much easier travel, commercial interest by the promises of greater opportunities and by the threat of harsher competition. There was and, at the time of writing, still is a problem over taxation; but the ideas canvassed during the five years following the Commission's White Paper have shown a resourcefulness and determination altogether lacking in previous years.

Whether the efforts to complete the internal market by the end of 1992 will succeed is not a matter for this book. What is important, for the purposes of a full understanding of how EC law operates in practice, is to be able to relate individual problems in business generally and in franchising in particular to the larger aims of the European Community. A practice which may seem reasonable from the point of view of the individual trader may, even in a small way, be operating against the general objectives of the Community. If, for example, the Community authorities are struggling to abolish direct or indirect restrictions on trade between the Member States, a distribution or franchise network operating on the basis of banning parallel imports may well find itself in trouble. Before explaining this in detail, it is worth looking more closely at the 'four freedoms', on which the creation of an internal market is based, and at the thinking behind them.

D: Free movement of goods, services, persons and capital

If the removal of barriers to trade between Member States is regarded as the negative way of expressing the action needed to create an internal market, the positive way is to speak of the free movement of goods, the free movement of persons (which includes the free movement of employees and the right of establishment of the self-employed and companies), freedom to provide services and the free movement of capital. Although there is far more to the EEC Treaty than the provisions governing the four freedoms, they are at the very heart of the Treaty and its objectives. All of them have a bearing on the activities of franchisors and franchisees.

Articles 9–37 of the EEC Treaty govern the free movement of goods. The earlier articles in this Title of the Treaty are largely directed towards the principle that, once goods have been lawfully imported into the Community from a non-member state, those goods are in 'free circulation': wherever they may have entered the Community, they may pass from one Member State to another without hindrance. The later articles in the Title are directed towards the removal of 'quantitative restrictions' on imports (art 30) or exports (art 34) between Member States and 'all measures having equivalent effect'. (This formidable phrase is taken from international trade law and is enshrined in the General Agreement on Tariffs and Trade; a reasonable paraphrase is all direct or indirect restrictions on imports or exports.)

Exceptions to the principle of free movement of goods are strictly limited. Article 36 of the Treaty (which the Court of Justice has said on several occasions must be 'strictly interpreted') allows prohibitions or restrictions on imports, exports or goods in transit justified on grounds of:

(a) public morality,
(b) public policy,
(c) public security,
(d) the protection of health and life of humans, animals or plants,
(e) the protection of national treasures possessing artistic, historic or archaeological value, or
(f) the protection of industrial and commercial property (that is, patents, trade marks, copyright and the like).

Such prohibitions must not constitute a means of arbitrary discrimination or a disguised restriction on trade between Member States. There is much case law in this area. Few restrictions on inter-state trade, whether in the form of national laws or by way of trade association rules, can easily be justified under EC law. From the point of view of franchise networks, the principle of free movement of goods is in the long run of paramount importance, especially for networks seeking to extend beyond the confines of an individual Member State; and the temptation to restrict sources of supply and thereby restrict imports may be expected to diminish.

It is also becoming increasingly difficult to prevent the free movement of services within the Community, though many cases of attempts either by national authorities or by professional associations to block nationals from other Member States continue to arise. The free movement of services is intended to be guaranteed under two groups of provisions in the Treaty. The first, comprising arts 52–58, provides for a right of establishment. The aim is to enable persons and incorporated companies to establish themselves in any part of the Community; in principle any measures which frustrate this aim are contrary to EC law. In practice, there is still much work to be done, for example to ensure that companies can operate throughout the Community — this is one area in which the Community clings to the idea of harmonisation, rather than mutual recognition. In general, the franchisor's right to extend a network across national borders within the Community does not present undue legal difficulties, and such problems as may arise may be determined by reference to Community law.

As to the second set of provisions of the Treaty, designed to promote free movement of services, these are contained in arts 59–66, governing the freedom to provide services within the Community and the progressive abolition of any restrictions on this freedom. In this context, services include activities of an industrial character, of a commercial character, of craftsmen and of the professions. Some of these activities are the subject of specific directives, dating mainly from the period when the Community authorities thought in terms of harmonising the rules applying to such activities in the Member States; but, as far as most professional activities are concerned, a relatively recent directive on the mutual recognition of national qualifications applies. Some service franchises make use of professionally qualified persons, in the broad sense in which this term is used in the Treaty; it is as well to ensure compliance with any specific rules under EC law governing those activities. If, for example, the franchise depends on the services of persons whose qualifications are covered by the directive, it may be easier to use them in more than one Member State than if they are not.

In one sense, the free movement of persons is an altogether simpler proposition; in another, it presents some difficulties. It is simpler, in that the rights of employed persons (the Treaty refers to 'workers' in the relevant arts 48–51, but uses the term to describe all kinds of paid employees) are clearly laid down in the Treaty itself, with an exception only in respect of employment in the public service of each of the Member States. It is more difficult in that there are many cases, some of which go to the Court of Justice, involving social security rights in the respective countries of the employees' nationality and employment.

Nevertheless, it is important for franchisors and franchisees to know that, subject to limitations justified on grounds of public policy, public security or public health, nationals of the Member States have the right

(a)   to accept offers of employment actually made,

(b) to move freely within the territory of the Member States for the purpose of employment,

(c) to stay in a Member State for the purpose of employment (subject to national rules), and

(d) to remain in the territory of a Member State after having been employed in that state (subject to conditions laid down in EC regulations).

National rules must not be discriminatory; indeed, all Member States are subject to the general rule contained in art 7 of the Treaty, that within the scope of the Treaty, and without prejudice to any special provisions contained in it, any discrimination on grounds of nationality is prohibited.

It is important for all businessmen, including franchisors and franchisees, who (for example) either operate across national borders within the Community or seek financial support outside the Member State in which they operate, to know something of the provisions of the Treaty concerned with the free movement of capital. These provisions are contained in arts 67–73 and are largely operative. Member States continue to use emergency powers in relation to exchange control, but, in general, capital movements have already been substantially liberalised and, from the end of 1992, controls will not be imposed at national borders and will in any case be strictly monitored at Community level. Taken together with the measures designed to liberalise banking, insurance and other financial services, and the measures (not all of them within the scope of the EEC Treaty itself) to create a European Monetary System, the financial scene affecting small and large businessmen alike is rapidly being transformed.

E: The internal market and the rules on competition

According to the White Paper on completing the internal market, 'any action taken to ensure the free movement of factors of production must necessarily be accompanied by increased surveillance by the Commission in the field of competition rules to ensure that firms and Member States adhere to those rules'. A more competitive European industry is at the heart of the proposals for improving the Member States' economic prosperity: 'A strong competition policy will play a fundamental role in maintaining and strengthening the internal market. It will contribute to an improved allocation of resources and to reinforcement of the efficiency and competitiveness of European companies.' More specifically, 'as the Community moves to complete the internal market, it will be necessary to ensure that anti-competitive practices do not engender local forms of protectionism, which would only lead to a re-partitioning of the market'. The significance of this principle to franchisors and franchisees will be spelt out in the chapters which follow. Franchise networks often have national boundaries, and EC law allows a certain amount of 'partitioning' of the market in the interests of making the business viable. But there is a fine line between allowing territorial exclusivity and disallowing the creation of commercial boundaries at a time when political boundaries are being eased.

At all events, while the various rules of EC law touched on in this chapter all affect franchising activities in one way or another, it so happens that the principal impact of EC law on franchising is in the field of competition rules. (The reasons for this are explained in Chapter 4.) It is under the EEC Treaty provisions on competition, considered in more detail in Chapter 3, that the Regulation has been made effectively governing the contents of franchising agreements and the operations of franchising networks; as this book is at pains to point out, the rules on competition may affect franchising even beyond the extent to which it is affected by the Regulation. Of all the provisions of the EEC Treaty, the provisions on competition are in some respects the most effective, the most far-reaching and the most drastic, and they need to be treated with caution and respect.

At the same time, the rules on competition should always be seen in their proper context, like the other rules briefly described in this chapter, as an instrument designed to make a reality of the internal market. This in turn has three objectives, endorsed by the Heads of State and Governments of the Member States. These objectives are as follows:

   (a)   the welding together of the twelve individual markets of the Member States into one single market of 320 million people;

(b) ensuring that this single market is also an expanding market — not static, but growing; and

(c) to this end, ensuring that the market is flexible, so that resources, both of people and materials and of capital and investment, flow into the areas of greatest economic advantage.

Chapter 3

Rules on competition in the European Community

A: Introduction to the rules on competition
B: Restrictive agreements
C: Negative clearance and exemption
D: Procedure: investigation, Decision and appeal
E: Penalties for infringement; civil liabilities
F: Block exemption

A: Introduction to the rules on competition

As already noted in the previous chapter, the activities of the Community include the institution of the system ensuring that competition in the common market is not distorted (art 3 of the EEC Treaty). The relevant provisions of the Treaty on competition are contained in arts 85–94 inclusive. These Articles are in Part 3 of the Treaty (Policy of the Community), Title one (Common Rules), Chapter one (Rules on Competition), Section one of which contains the rules applying to undertakings, Section two the rules on dumping between the Member States and Section three aids granted by states — that is, state subsidies and the like.

For the most part, the rules on dumping are no longer relevant within the common market. Article 91, which covers the subject, is important these days only in relation to Spain and Portugal, having been extended under the Treaty of Accession of those two countries. Dumping is defined in art VI of the General Agreement on Tariffs and Trade as 'the introduction of a product into the commerce of another country if the price of the product exported is less than its normal value, the latter normally being the price of the like product in the domestic market of the exporting country'. This is still an important aspect of commercial life in relation to imports into, and exports from, the Community; these aspects are governed by the provisions of the Treaty dealing with external policy (particularly art 113) and not the internal rules on competition. At some stage, it is possible that franchisors and franchisees may encounter the problem of dumping, for example, if the goods which they distribute are imported from outside the Community and are the subject of anti-dumping proceedings. This is a problem which has to be treated in the context of the Community's general commercial policy and is not described further in this book.

Similarly, state aids, whether by way of Government subsidies or by way of indirect support for traders, through tax concessions, special interest rates and other devices, though technically part of the rules on competition under the EEC Treaty, are the subject of a separate and specialised literature. Franchisors and franchisees may at some stage find themselves in competition with traders who receive direct or indirect support from the state, in which case they are well advised to seek advice on how to deal with what is manifestly unfair competition. Here again however, the present book does not, beyond mentioning the problem, propose to deal with it in detail.

It follows that the rules on competition, applying most directly to the interests of franchisors and franchisees, are contained in the provisions relating to undertakings. These provisions are set out in arts 85–90. Article 85 will be dealt with in considerable detail in the course of this book; it relates to restrictive agreements or cartels, and it may come as a surprise to some franchisors and franchisees to know that many of the arrangements which they make fall under this heading. This does not necessarily mean that the arrangements are illegal, but it does mean that those who are parties to the arrangements have to be particularly vigilant about their rights and obligations.

Article 86 of the EEC Treaty is concerned with the abuse by one or more undertakings of a dominant undertaking within the common market or in a substantial part of it. It is perfectly possible that at some stage in the development of franchise networks throughout the EEC, a situation may arise in which one of these networks acquires a dominant position on the market. So far, this has not happened; for this reason art 86 is given only brief treatment here. (The fact that a franchise system satisfies the requirements of art 85 of the Treaty does not mean that it necessarily satisfies the requirements of art 86. The two sets of requirements are separate and cumulative, according to the Court of Justice in the *Tipp-Ex* case (279/87).)

Whether a franchise network has a dominant position on the market depends on at least two important considerations. The first is the product market concerned which, if narrowly defined, may show that the network has a more powerful position in the relevant market than if the product market is widely defined. For example, a network handling cameras would be likely to have a relatively small share of a highly competitive market; however, a network specialising in reflex cameras may well have a larger share of the market in this more specialised field, and a network handling special reflex cameras might even find itself with a dominant position on the market (see the *Hasselblad* case 86/82). Secondly, much depends on the geographical market. Article 86 refers to the common market or a substantial part of it: what constitutes a substantial part has been the subject of much case law. A whole Member State might well be regarded as a substantial part of the common market, even if the Member State is as small as Luxembourg. In that case, a network might well find itself in a dominant position within a substantial part of the common market, even though its activities in the European Community as a whole are more limited.

It is one thing to have a dominant position within the common market or in a substantial part of it, but quite another to abuse that position. The mere possession of a dominant position is not in itself an infringement of the EEC rules on competition (though mergers and acquisitions are subject to control, as indicated below). For an infringement to take place there must be an abuse. These abuses are not exhaustively defined in art 86, but an indication of the kinds of abuse which the Treaty sets out to prohibit is contained in the four examples listed in this Article. These are, respectively:

(a) directly or indirectly proposing unfair purchase or selling prices or other unfair trading conditions;
(b) limiting production, markets or technical development to the prejudice of consumers;
(c) applying dissimilar conditions to equivalent transactions with other trading parties, thereby placing them at a competitive disadvantage; and
(d) making the conclusion of contracts subject to acceptance by the other parties of supplementary obligations which, by their nature or according to commercial usage, have no connection with the subject of such contracts.

Companies may acquire a dominant position by merging with or taking over other companies: in principle, this can happen to franchise networks, just as it can to other business undertakings. It will be seen from a reading of the provisions of the EEC Treaty that no specific arrangements are made to prevent companies acquiring a dominant position. However, an important and far reaching piece of secondary legislation, known briefly as the Mergers Regulation and more formally as Council Regulation 4064/89 on the control of concentrations between undertakings, has provided a form of control since 21 September 1990. Although the majority of franchise systems are unlikely to reach the threshold bringing them within the scope of this Regulation, there are some large corporations which run franchise networks as part of a much wider commercial operation. These corporations need to bear the provisions of the Mergers Regulation in mind before contemplating any further 'concentration' of their activities.

Secondary legislation implementing the rules on competition is authorised by virtue of art 87 of the EEC Treaty, which gives the Council power to adopt any appropriate regulations or directives to give effect to the principles set out in arts 85 and 86. (As the Mergers Regulation did not fall squarely within the terms of arts 85 and 86, it has a double legal basis. In addition to art 87, it is based on art 235 of the EEC Treaty, which is a kind of 'catch-all' provision to cover cases which are not squarely within the terms of specific articles of the Treaty.) Several of the Regulations discussed later in this book are based on art 87. However, the Regulation with which this book is mainly concerned is a Commission Regulation, made under delegated powers conferred by a Regulation made in turn under art 87. The legal parentage of the franchising block exemption regulation will be discussed later.

Although art 88 of the EEC Treaty is not technically a transitional provision, it is nevertheless largely superseded and does not merit further mention in the present context. Article 89, on the other hand, lays down the important rule that it is the Commission that is charged with the application of the principles laid down in arts 85 and 86. On application by a Member State or on its own initiative, and in co-operation with the competent authorities in the Member States, which are required to give the Commission their assistance, the Commission is under a duty to investigate cases of suspected infringement of those principles. If the Commission finds that there has been an infringement, it must propose appropriate measures to bring it to an end. If the infringement is not brought to an end, the Commission must record the infringement of the principles in a reasoned decision. The Commission may (not 'must') publish its decision and authorise Member States to take the measures (the conditions and details of which it has to determine) needed to remedy the situation.

Several of the provisions of art 89 are refined and amplified in secondary legislation. For example, while it is still true that cases to be investigated may begin with an application by a Member State or with action taken by the Commission on its own initiative, EEC Council Regulation 17 of 1962, described later in this chapter, includes among those entitled to make application 'natural or legal persons who claim a legitimate interest' (art 3(2)(*b*) of Regulation 17). Franchisors and franchisees may well find themselves in a position in which they wish to make an application (or, more bluntly, a complaint) about the activities of traders who they believe are competing unfairly.

It is the object of art 90 of the EEC Treaty to make clear that public undertakings (including nationalised industries) and undertakings to which Member States grant special or exclusive rights are covered by the EEC rules on competition. There are some exceptions to this principle; it is unlikely, though not impossible, that a franchise network itself may fall within this category. The important point for all franchise networks, however, is to know that their competitors cannot take unfair advantage of their being in some respect public bodies. Even a local authority has been held by the Court of Justice to be subject to the ordinary rules on competition under the EEC Treaty, where that authority has been carrying out 'services of general economic interest': funeral services carried out under the aegis of a local authority were the subject of one of the leading cases in the Court of Justice on this matter, *Bodson v Pompes Funebres* (30/87).

B: Restrictive agreements

From the point of view of franchising, by far the most important of the provisions of the EEC Treaty is the one relating to restrictive agreements; that is, art 85 (reproduced in Appendix I). Strictly speaking, the article applies to more than agreements as such: it covers 'all agreements between undertakings, decisions by associations of undertakings and concerted practices'. A single person, acting in a business or professional capacity, may count as an undertaking; therefore an agreement between a franchisor and a franchisee is an agreement between undertakings within the meaning of art 85. Decisions by associations of undertakings refer to the decisions of trade associations (to which franchisors and franchisees may also belong), including the trade associations rules (there is a good deal of case law on the activities of trade associations, which is outside the scope of this book).

Concerted practices, however, may involve franchisors and more particularly franchisees rather more directly. The Court of Justice decided many years ago in *ICI* (48/69) that a concerted practice was established if it was shown that 'there was a form of co-operation between undertakings which, without having reached the stage where an agreement properly so called has been concluded, knowingly substitutes practical co-operation for the risks of competition'. As a later case in the Court of Justice expressed it (*Suiker Unie* (40/75)), 'such co-operation amounts to a concerted practice, particularly if it enables the persons concerned to consolidate established positions to the detriment of effective freedom of movement of the products in the common market and of the freedom of consumers to choose their suppliers'.

Still more important, as para 25 of *Pronuptia* makes clear (*see*

Appendix IV), it is in the matter of pricing that problems are likely to arise. Franchisors may communicate indicative prices to franchisees, always on conditions that, as between the franchisor and the franchisees or between franchisees there is no concerted practice with a view to the effective application of those prices. It can be hard to prove the existence of a concerted practice, and there is a fine line between deliberate action by undertakings and action spontaneously taken by a number of undertakings operating independently (*see* Appendix VI).

Under art 85(1), all agreements between undertakings, decisions by associations of undertakings and concerted practices are prohibited as incompatible with the common market if:

(a)   they may affect trade between Member States, and

(b)   they have as their object or effect the prevention, restriction or distortion of competition within the common market.

In Chapter 5, further consideration is given to the question whether a franchise agreement is likely to affect trade between Member States. What needs to be emphasised here is that art 85 speaks of agreements which 'may' affect trade between Member States; it is not necessary therefore for the Commission to show that the agreements do affect trade between Member States.

As to the question of the second condition, it will be seen that the prohibited agreements are those which have a certain object or a certain effect. An effect does not have to be proved, if there is evidence that the object is to restrict competition. By the same token, a prohibited agreement may have an acceptable object but a restrictive effect. Both types of agreement are prohibited. Franchise agreements do not normally have as their object the restriction of competition: indeed, the opportunity to take part in a franchise network does as a rule encourage increased competition in the sector in which new outlets are created. Nevertheless, as later chapters of the book will show, there are many clauses in franchise agreements which, however innocent their object, can have as their effect a technical or substantial restriction of competition within the meaning of art 85.

It should just be added at this point that art 85 gives illustrations, which are not intended to be exhaustive, of the types of 'prevention, restriction or distortion of competition' which are specifically prohibited. Five illustrations are given of agreements, decisions or practices which infringe the rules, namely those which:

(a) directly or indirectly fix purchase or selling prices or any other trading conditions;
(b) limit or control production, markets, technical developments or investment;
(c) share markets or sources of supply;
(d) apply dissimilar conditions to equivalent transactions with other trading parties, thereby placing them at a competitive disadvantage; and
(e) make the conclusion of contracts subject to acceptance by the other parties of supplementary obligations which, by their nature or according to commercial usage, have no connection with the subject of such contracts.

All five of these practices can, in one form or another, find themselves all too easily in the operations of a franchise network.

C: Negative clearance and exemption

If the parties to an agreement are uncertain whether the agreement is restrictive of competition within the meaning of art 85, or if they believe that the agreement is only technically restrictive, they may apply to the Commission for 'negative clearance'; that is, for a certificate from the Commission that, on the basis of the facts in its possession, there are no grounds under art 85(1) of the EEC Treaty for action on its part in respect of the agreement in question. If, on the other hand, the parties to an agreement are aware that the agreement is restrictive of competition, but believe that the restrictions are justified in terms of the general objects of the agreement, the economic context of the agreement and so on, they may apply to the Commission for exemption of the agreement; that is, a declaration by the Commission that art 85(1) is inapplicable to the agreement in question. If the parties to an agreement are uncertain whether to apply for negative clearance or for exemption, they may make an application to the Commission for both, as alternatives.

So far as franchise agreements are concerned, the great majority will fall within the terms of the exemption regulation, and, unless the conditions described in Chapter 12 of this book apply to the individual franchise agreement, there is no need for notification to the Commission. It is rather unlikely that any ordinary franchise agreement would be so worded that it could qualify for negative clearance, though it is theoretically possible.

There is no reference in the Treaty itself to the concept of negative clearance: it is a creation of Council Regulation 17 of 1962, and more specifically of art 2 of that Regulation. Applications for negative clearance have to be made on the prescribed Form A/B (Commission Regulation 4261/88). Thirteen copies (one for the Commission and one for each Member State) have to be supplied. According to the Commission, the purpose of the negative clearance procedure is to allow a business to ascertain whether the Commission considers that any of its arrangements or behaviour are prohibited under art 85(1) of the EEC Treaty. (Negative clearance may also be sought in respect of art 86; but see the remarks earlier in Section A of this chapter on the abuse of a dominant position (re *Hasselblad*).) The Commission emphasises that the certificate is provided only on the basis of the facts in its possession: if the facts are incomplete, the Commission can withdraw negative clearance. Any party may apply for negative clearance, even without the consent, but not without the knowledge, of other parties to the arrangements. The Commission is not obliged to give negative clearance, and it does not usually issue negative clearance decisions in cases which, in its opinion, so clearly do not fall within the scope of the prohibition of art 85(1) that there is no reasonable doubt for its resolve by such a decision.

Negative clearance is valuable, in that it certifies that the Commission has no grounds for taking further action in the matter. This is not in itself a guarantee that the parties concerned are free from civil action in respect of the agreement, decision or practice in question. However, the Commission's certificate is likely to have persuasive force in national courts in many of the Member States.

Exemption, unlike negative clearance, is specifically provided for under the Treaty: art 85(3) governs the conditions. It will be seen from this paragraph of art 85 that exemption may be granted not only for any individual agreement but also for categories of agreements. For convenience, these two forms of exemption are known as individual exemption and block exemption. This book is primarily concerned with the block exemption of categories of franchise agreements. Since not all franchise agreements fall within the block exemption regulation it is useful to comment briefly on the practice of individual exemption, while noting that there is provision under the block exemption regulation for a special procedure for certain types of franchise agreement to be subject to individual exemption. Both individual and block exemption are subject to the same general principles described below.

Four conditions govern the grant of exemption. Two of them are positive, two negative. The agreements for which exemption is sought must:

(a)   contribute to improving the production or distribution of goods or to promoting technical or economic progress;
(b)   allow consumers a fair share of the resulting benefit;
(c)   not impose on the undertakings concerned restrictions which are not indispensable to the attainment of these objectives; and
(d)   not afford such undertakings the possibility of eliminating competition in respect of a substantial part of the products in question.

Whenever the Commission publishes a Decision on individual exemption cases, whether the exemption is granted or not, it will be found that the Decision applies each of these four important criteria to the facts of the case. Even a block exemption (described in Section F below) is subject to the overall application of the four criteria, and if, in any individual case, it comes to the Commission's attention that any one of the four criteria has been infringed, the Commission may withdraw the benefit of block exemption in that particular case. (*See*, generally, Chapter 14 on withdrawal of benefit.)

Applications for exemption, like applications for negative clearance, are made on Form A/B. The detailed rules governing the treatment of applications for exemption are contained in Regulation 17 of 1962, particularly in arts 4, 6, 8 and 9. Article 4 contains the important provision that agreements, in respect of which the parties seek exemption, must be notified to the Commission and that, until they have been notified, no exemption decision may be taken. It makes no difference how deserving a case may be of exemption: it will not be granted exemption without due notification made to the Commission on Form A/B.

Whenever the Commission grants exemption, it must, under art 6 of Regulation 17, specify in the Decision the date from which it takes effect. The date must not be earlier than the date of notification, but it may be later. The date from which the exemption runs can be of great importance, both as regards fines for infringement and liability in civil cases. If the agreement antedates notification and, but for exemption, is illegal, it follows that between the date of the agreement and the date of the notification there has been an infringement of art 85(1). Similarly, if the agreement and the date of notification are the same, but the agreement has to be amended to qualify for exemption, there may be a period between the date of notification and the date of amendment of the agreement, during which the agreement was illegal. Later in this chapter the penalties and civil liabilities likely to arise when there is an infringement of art 85(1) are discussed.

Where the Commission decides to grant exemption, the Decision must, under art 8 of Regulation 17, be issued for a specified period and may contain conditions and obligations. When the specified period comes to an end, the Decision may be renewed on application, provided the exemption requirements continue to be satisfied. An exemption decision may be revoked by the Commission or amended, or specified acts by the parties may be prohibited where:

(a)   there has been a change in any of the facts which were basic to the making of the decision;
(b)   the parties commit a breach of any obligation attached to the decision;
(c)   the decision is based on incorrect information or was induced by deceit; or
(d)   the parties abused the exemption.

In any of these cases revocation of the decision may have retro-active effect.

It is only the Commission, under art 9 of Regulation 17, which has the power to grant exemption under art 85(3) of the Treaty. In other words, exemption cannot be granted by any other administrative or judicial authority. Even the European Court of Justice does not have specific power to grant exemption: if a party challenges in the Court of Justice a decision by the Commission not to grant exemption, and the Court upholds the parties' application, the matter is sent back to the Commission for reconsideration. The Court does not grant exemption but may rule that the Commission is wrong in law for having withheld it.

D: Procedure: investigation, Decision and appeal

To some extent, the procedure followed when the Commission looks into restrictive agreements depends on how the case arises in the first place. Generally speaking, cases arise in the following circumstances:

(a) when the Commission on its own initiative (this may be from its own reading of public information or from the results of a survey it has carried out in a specific industrial sector) finds that there is an infringement of the rules on competition;

(b) where the Commission receives a notification, containing either a request for negative clearance or an application for exemption;

(c) where a Member State draws the Commission's attention to an infringement; and

(d) where 'natural or legal persons who claim a legitimate interest' make an application to the Commission (in other words, a complaint).

There are two aspects of the question of complaints which it is wise for franchisors and franchisees to take fully into account. The first is that they may be the subject of a complaint themselves, either from other traders or possibly from consumers. The second is that they may wish to make a complaint about the activities of other traders, where these are trading unfairly or restricting competition in the market as a whole. It follows that franchisors and franchisees may, like other traders, be both at the receiving end and at the delivery end of this procedure.

Whatever the manner in which a particular case comes to the notice of the Commission, it has extensive powers of investigation. In practice, however, these are normally applied at their most draconian when the Commission investigates a matter either on its own initiative or on an application by a Member State or on a complaint. In all cases it has the power, through its officials'

(a) to examine the books and other business records of the undertaking (or association of undertakings);
(b) to take copies of or extracts from the books and business records;
(c) to ask for oral explanations on the spot; and
(d) to enter any premises, land and means of transport of undertakings.

The so-called 'dawn raids' carried out by Commission officials are alarming enough; but, in the first place, large firms — this suggests franchisors, rather than franchisees — are well advised to have compliance programmes, so that dawn raids either do not take place or do not present the same alarming features as if the firms concerned are caught entirely unawares; and, in the second place, there are indeed limits to the officials' powers, as recent case law (in particular *Hoechst* (46/87) and *Dow* (227/88)) has demonstrated.

Before taking any decision on negative clearance, exemption or penalties of the kind referred to in the next part of this chapter, the Commission is required under art 19 of Regulation 17 to give the undertakings concerned the opportunity of being heard on matters to which the Commission has taken objection. The detailed arrangements for hearings are contained in Commission Regulation 99 of 1963. There is a hearing officer to carry out the hearings in question. Where the Commission intends to give negative clearance or to grant exemption, it must publish a summary of the relevant application or notification and invite all interested third parties to submit their observations within a time limit of not less than one month; the publication is normally in the C Series of the *Official Journal*. There is an obligation on the Commission to respect professional secrecy. At the same time, this still leaves ample room for the Commission to publish a number of significant details of the application.

Although the EEC Treaty itself, as already noted, does not require the Commission to publish its Decisions, Regulation 17 of 1962 requires the Commission to publish all Decisions on negative clearance, infringements and exemptions. These are published in the L Series of the *Official Journal*.

When the Commission has delivered its Decision to the parties, which is usually some time before publication in the *Official Journal*, the parties may apply to the Court of Justice for the total or partial annulment of the Decision. The basis of these proceedings is art 173 of the Treaty. Under this, the Court of Justice reviews the legality of acts of the Council and Commission other than recommendations and opinions. Decisions may be challenged on the grounds of lack of competence, infringement of an essential procedural requirement, infringement of the Treaty or of any rule of law relating to its application or misuse of powers. Any natural or legal person (that is, person or company) may institute proceedings against a decision addressed to that person or against a decision which, although in the form of a regulation or decision addressed to another person, is of direct and individual concern to the former. These proceedings have to be instituted within two months of the publication of the measure or of its notification to the plaintiff. Since 1989, it is the Court of First Instance in Luxembourg which normally hears competitiveness.

E: Penalties for infringement; civil liabilities

Two kinds of penalties may be imposed by the Commission: fines and periodic penalty payments. Each may be imposed either for an infringement of the substantive rules or for an infringement of the procedural rules. The fine for an intentional or negligent infringement of art 85(1) or art 86 or breach of any obligation imposed in pursuance of art 85 is anything from one thousand to one million ECU, or even more, subject to a limit of ten per cent of the turnover for the preceding year of each of the participating undertakings. The gravity and duration of the infringement have to be taken into account. The fine for intentionally or negligently supplying incorrect or misleading information in a notification or application for exemption, or incorrect information in response to an enquiry by the Commission, or incomplete business records, or failing or refusing to supply required information, is from one hundred to five thousand ECU. (A French firm, Secretama, was fined the full amount under this heading in 1990 (*Official Journal* No L 35, 7.2.91).) Fines are not imposed during the period between a valid notification or application and a Decision by the Commission. They are not in any case 'of a criminal law nature'.

Periodic penalty payments are similar to fines, except that they are imposed for continuing infringements and are limited to an amount of between fifty and one thousand ECU per day.

There is no specific provision under the EEC rules on competition for civil remedies for infringements of the rules: this is a matter for national law. By the same token, there is no provision, as in the United States, for 'triple damages'. Nevertheless, some of the fines imposed by the Commission in recent years have amounted to many millions of ECU; and there are some respects in which the consequences of civil actions can be even more severe for the offending parties, particularly if the agreements in question are declared void under art 85(2) of the EEC Treaty. (*See* (*Pronuptia*) Appendix IV and the discussion of the case in Chapter 4.)

F: Block exemption

Under art 85(3) of the EEC Treaty, there is provision for declaring art 85(1) inapplicable either to individual agreements or to 'categories of agreements'; and, under art 87, Council Regulations have been made conferring power on the Commission to make what are commonly described as 'block exemption regulations'. Council Regulation 19/65 gives the Commission power by regulation to declare art 85(1) inapplicable to two broad categories of agreement. The first is dealership agreements, including franchising and distribution; the second, licensing agreements involving industrial property rights.

More particularly, Regulation 19/65 gives powers in respect of agreements to which only two undertakings are party and

(a) whereby one party agrees with the other to supply only to that other certain goods for resale within a defined area of the common market; or

(b) whereby one party agrees with the other to purchase only from that other certain goods for resale; or

(c) whereby the two undertakings have entered into obligations, as in (a) and (b), with each other in respect of exclusive supply and purchase for resale.

(The significance of the words 'to which only two undertakings are party' is discussed in Chapter 7.)

In addition, the Regulation provides that Commission regulations must define the categories of agreements to which they apply and must specify in particular the restrictions or clauses which must not be contained in agreements, and the clauses which must be contained in the agreements or the other conditions which must be satisfied. The Regulation mentions 'agreements'; it also applies to 'concerted practices' (to which only two undertakings are party).

Two other points in Regulation 19/65 are worth noting here. The first is that the Commission is entitled to exercise its powers (to make block exemption regulations) only after 'sufficient experience has been gained in the light of individual decisions'. Thus, the Commission was not in a position to introduce a block exemption regulation for franchising directly after the Court's decision in *Pronuptia*: four out of the five Commission decisions reproduced in Appendix V had been issued before the draft regulation was adopted.

Secondly, the Regulation points to the practical justification of the individual block exemption regulations when it speaks of 'the large number of notifications submitted in pursuance of Regulation 17' and of 'the need to facilitate the task of the Commission'. The preamble to the Regulation, in which these observations are made, might also have noted the incalculable saving of time to commercial and professional firms. The automatic exemption, conferred by a block exemption regulation, is a great relief to those who would otherwise have to complete the details required in Form A/B, submit thirteen copies, wait an uncertain period of time, see the company's plans published, wonder if third parties were going to lodge objections and finally wait for a Commission decision, which might or might not be favourable. As Chapter 6 explains, the block exemption regulation for franchise agreements removes much of the anxiety and reduces much of the expense of establishing franchise networks within the EEC.

Chapter 4

Rules on competition applied to franchising

A: Franchising and distribution
B: The Court's decision in the *Pronuptia* case
C: Commission decisions on franchising

A: Franchising and distribution

For some years before the *Pronuptia* case in the European Court of Justice (discussed in the next section of this chapter), franchising was regarded simply as another form of distribution. It is therefore surprising that, while the Court and Commission dealt with an abundance of cases from the field of distribution, properly so called, it never dealt with a case concerned with franchising. Part of the reason for this may have been the confusion, which may have arisen from the practice in civil law countries, over the different categories of distribution, such as the 'concession' system in France. As late as 1978, a Commission study found no special problems, from the point of view of competition law, in the system of franchising.

Later, the Commission appears to have become aware of a potential problem arising from the impact of franchising on the EEC rules on competition. Together with the French Government, it had organised an international seminar in Strasbourg in 1983 to look at the legal and economic aspects of exclusive and selective dealing and franchising. 'The conclusion,' according to the Commission's Thirteenth Report on Competition Policy, 'was that these various forms of distribution and the relationships they involve posed fewer problems in a large, integrated and highly competitive market like that of the United States than in a large market that had not yet attained a very high degree of integration of its commerce like the European Community'. It was, however, left to the *Pronuptia* case to distinguish franchising from other forms of distribution and to identify the impact of the rules on competition.

B: The Court's decision in the *Pronuptia* case

In 1984, the first case involving a franchise agreement was referred to the Court of Justice for consideration, with particular reference to the question whether the agreement was prohibited under art 85(1) of the EEC Treaty. The reference to the Court arose in the context of litigation between the firm Pronuptia de Paris GmbH from Frankfurt am Main, the franchisor and a subsidiary of the French company of the same name, and Madam Schillgallis from Hamburg, who carried on business under the name Pronuptia de Paris in her role as a franchisee. The litigation concerned the franchisee's obligation to pay the franchisor arrears of fees based on her turnover during the years 1978 to 1980.

Most of the terms of the franchise agreements were familiar enough to the franchisors and franchisees throughout the world: in many respects it was a typical franchise agreement. However, after being ordered by the German Court of First Instance to pay the arrears of fees, the franchisee lodged an appeal, arguing, in order to escape payment of these arrears, that the contract in question violated art 85(1) of the EEC Treaty. The provincial Court of Appeal in Frankfurt upheld this judgment. The franchisor appealed to the Federal Court, which referred the matter to the Court of Justice for a preliminary ruling on the question whether art 85(1) of the EEC Treaty applied to franchise agreements such as the contracts between the parties, which had as their object the establishment of a special distribution system, whereby the franchisor provided to the franchisee, in addition to goods, certain trade names, trade marks, merchandising material and services. In January 1986, the Court of Justice delivered its decision, reproduced in Appendix IV.

In response to the main questions put to it by the German Federal Court, the Court of Justice stated the law as follows:

(a) the compatibility of distribution franchise contracts with art 85(1) depends on the clauses contained in those contracts and on the economic context in which they have been included;

(b) clauses which are indispensable for the purpose of preventing the know-how provided and the help given by the franchisor from benefiting competitors do not constitute restrictions of competition within the meaning of art 85(1);

(c) clauses which institute controls indispensable for the preservation of the identity and reputation of the network symbolised by the sign do not constitute restrictions of competition within the meaning of art 85(1);

(d) clauses which result in a sharing of markets between franchisor and franchisees or between franchisees constitute restrictions of competition within the meaning of art 85(1).

(e) the fact that the franchisor may communicate to the franchisee indicative prices does not constitute a restriction of competition, provided that, as between the franchisor and the franchisees or between the franchisees, there is no concerted practice with a view to the effective application of these prices.

(f) distribution franchise contracts which contain clauses leading to market sharing between franchisor and franchisee or between franchisees are liable to affect trade between Member States.

In two respects, the effects of the *Pronuptia* judgment are perfectly clear. In the first place, clauses which limit the franchisee's freedom to determine his prices are restrictive of competition and are therefore prohibited under art 85(1) of the EEC Treaty (*see* para 25, Appendix IV). Price fixing has always been anathema to the anti-trust authorities both of Member States and of the Commission of the European Communities in particular. Minimum or standard prices are therefore contrary to the EEC rules.

In the second place, clauses in a franchise agreement which result in a sharing of markets between franchisor and franchisees or between franchisees are restrictive of competition, prohibited under art 85(1) and most unlikely to qualify for exemption (*see* para 23, Appendix IV). Here again, market-sharing is rightly and strongly disliked by the anti-trust authorities, whether in the context of general business activities, of general distribution or of franchising. The idea that independent firms — and, for this purpose, franchisee *A*, franchisee *B* and franchisor *Z* are all independent firms — can, by agreements between themselves, stitch up a given market is precisely the kind of arrangement to which anti-trust authorities take exception. Franchisors and franchisees may not see things in the same way: the closeness of their association, more nearly resembling the internal arrangements between branch managers and a regional director of the same firm, is mainly directed towards competing with other firms or networks in the same field of products or services. However, they are in law separate enterprises, and the law takes a harsh view of multilateral attempts to share markets between the members of a single network, however closely that network may be integrated.

Similar thinking is applied by the Court to the general relationship between franchisees in the same network. In the *Pronuptia* case the Court accepts that a clause in the franchise agreement, providing that the franchisee should sell only those goods originating with the franchisor or with suppliers chosen by the franchisor, may in certain conditions be considered necessary by way of protection for the reputation of the network. But this 'should not lead to a situation in which the franchisee is prevented from acquiring those goods from other franchisees' (*see* para 21, Appendix V). It may well be thought that this is in any case rare. However, it could happen, particularly in cases of unexpected shortage, and, given the Court's clear and express view on the subject, it would be most unwise to introduce into any franchise agreement a provision which effectively prevented franchisees from dealing with one another.

All the foregoing points are straightforward enough. They indicate certain areas in which it is quite wrong for the franchise agreement to attempt to oppose the rules on competition. Some of the other points in the judgment of the Court in the *Pronuptia* case are less unequivocal. There is no doubt that the Court realised the importance of protecting the franchisor's know-how and of preserving the reputation of the network. The franchisor has to be able to communicate to franchisees his know-how and to provide them with the necessary help in implementing his methods, without running the risk that this know-how and this help benefit, however indirectly, his competitors (*see* para 16, Appendix IV). In addition, the franchisor must be able to take appropriate measures to preserve the identity and the reputation of the network symbolised by the sign used by himself and the franchisees (*see* para 17, Appendix IV). However, the Court draws back from giving franchisors and franchisees a blank cheque, so far as these two considerations are concerned. While recognising the importance of the two factors, it still maintains an instinctive dislike of clauses in contracts which restrict the freedom of independent operators to take their own commercial decisions. Consequently, the Court qualifies all its comments on the types of clause in a franchise agreement which restrict the franchisee's room for manoeuvre by saying that they must be 'indispensable' for the purpose. By this standard, clauses which are indispensable for the purpose of preventing the know-how provided and the help given by the franchisor from benefiting competitors, and clauses which institute controls indispensable for the preservation of the identity and reputation of the network symbolised by the sign, do not constitute restrictions of competition under the EEC Treaty (*see* para 27, Appendix IV). The onus is therefore on the parties to the agreement to show that the clauses in the agreement concerned with these matters are indeed indispensable for the purpose; this may not always be self-evident to the anti-trust authorities.

Moreover, it is perfectly possible that the question whether the clauses concerned are indispensable may be governed by another consideration which the Court introduced into its judgment in *Pronuptia*. According to the Court, the compatibility of distribution franchise contracts with the EEC rules on competition depends not only on the clauses contained in those contracts but also on the economic context in which they have been included (*see* para 27, Appendix IV). Unfortunately, the Court does not develop this point. To some extent it may be thought obvious from other EEC competition law cases what this signifies in practice; it has also to be inferred from the terms in which Form A/B (on which firms notify applications for negative clearance or exemption) is expressed. To put it in layman's language, the Commission wants to know more about conditions in the market in which the franchise agreement is expected to operate, before it will pass judgment on the question as to whether certain clauses in the agreement are indispensable, and hence whether there has been an infringement of the rules on competition. The more competitive the market, the more indulgent the Commission is likely to be in deciding whether the clauses should be allowed to stand.

On several other points the judgment is either hard to follow or completely silent. For example, in one of the more complex parts of this judgment, the Court considers the question of the location clause. On the face of it, the Court accepts the need for a clause which obliges the franchisee to sell the contract goods only from the location specified in the contract. However, what the Court does not appear to like is the situation which arises when a location clause is related to the commitment entered into by the franchisor to ensure that the franchisee has within a certain territory the exclusive use of the licensed sign (*see* para 24, Appendix IV). The Court pays lip service to the justification for this type of arrangement being included in a franchise agreement: the franchisee would be unwilling 'to pay a substantial annual fee, if he could not, thanks to a certain protection against competition by the franchisor and by other franchisees, have some hope that his business could be profitable'. The Court concludes that arrangements with this object or effect have to be examined in the light of the provisions of the EEC Treaty governing promotion of economic progress while reserving to users an equitable share in the profit resulting therefrom and do not impose on the enterprises concerned any restrictions which are not indispensable to the attainment of those objectives nor enable the enterprises to eliminate competition in respect of a substantial proportion of the goods concerned.

A further point on which the judgment is not entirely clear is that, while price fixing is prohibited, the same is not true of the fact that the franchisor may communicate indicative prices to franchisees. This is on the condition that, as between the franchisor and franchisees or between franchisees, there is no concerted practice with a view to the effective application of these prices (*see* para 25, Appendix IV). (This raises a problem, discussed in

Chapter 16, about the reference in advertising to the prices charged by members of the same franchise network.)

Lastly, by drawing a distinction between distribution franchises, service franchises and manufacturing franchises, and addressing its comments in *Pronuptia* only to the first of these categories, the Court left open the question (decided in practice by the Commission in *ServiceMaster* — *see* Appendix V — and the block exemption regulation), whether its strictures generally applied to the other two categories (para 13 of *Pronuptia*). To some extent the categories are artificial — or, more accurately, they overlap. There may well be mixed service and distribution franchises; and there may well be service franchises, in which the question of restrictive practices applying to the goods used by the franchise network — for example, the equipment used by fast food restaurants — raises questions of competition policy.

As a footnote to the detailed discussion of franchising as such, the Court of Justice addressed the question, whether franchising agreements like the Pronuptia agreement fell within the terms of the block exemption regulation on exclusive distribution. It will be seen from the judgment (para 33, Appendix IV) that the Court took into consideration four factors and concluded, in the light of those factors, that the block exemption regulation did not apply to distribution franchise contracts such as those examined in the *Pronuptia* proceedings. The third and fourth factors are perhaps the most persuasive. The third was that the block exemption regulation listed the restrictions and obligations which might be imposed on the exclusive concessionaire, without making reference to those which might be stipulated by the other party to the contract; while in the case of the distribution franchise contract, the obligations assumed by the franchisor, and particularly those governing the provision of know-how and help to the franchisee, acquired a special importance. As to the fourth consideration, the list of obligations on the part of the concessionaire, covered by the distribution block exemption regulation, allowed for the inclusion of neither the obligation to pay fees nor clauses which set up controls indispensable for preserving the identity and reputation of the network. These are essential differences between distribution franchise contracts and other forms of distribution agreement. They were simply not contemplated in the block exemption regulation on exclusive distribution.

C: Commission Decisions on franchising

Since the date of the *Pronuptia* by the Court of Justice (28 January 1986), there have been five Decisions by the Commission on franchising cases, as follows:

(a)   *Pronuptia*,
(b)   *Yves Rocher*,
(c)   *Computerland*,
(d)   *ServiceMaster*,
(e)   *Charles Jourdan*.

Full texts of the Commission's Decisions in these cases will be found in Appendix V. The *Pronuptia* Decision was separate from the Court case and, like the other four cases referred to above, arose from an application for negative clearance or exemption.

Following closely the terms of the Court's Decision, the Commission distinguished the clauses in the Pronuptia agreement which came within the terms of art 85(1) and those which did not. As the Court had held in its judgment (paras 23 and 24) that 'clauses that involve market sharing between franchisor and franchisee or between franchisees do constitute restrictions of competition within the meaning of art 85(1)', the Commission identified two clauses in the Pronuptia agreement which were covered by this dictum. The first was the exclusivity granted to the franchisee to operate under the franchisor's name in a given sales area; and the second was the obligation on the franchisee to carry on the franchise business exclusively from the premises approved for that purpose. According to the Commission, the combined effect of these clauses was to protect each franchisee against competition from other franchisees. The Commission pointed out that there was an effect on trade between Member States and that Pronuptia held a significant share of the French market for the relevant products and that its network covered several EEC countries. Consequently the clauses referred to were restrictions of competition likely to affect trade between Member States and therefore prohibited under art 85(1).

However, the Commission applied the criteria for exemption (described in the last chapter) and concluded that the restrictions on competition might be expected to benefit consumers; contributed to an improvement in the distribution of the products; did not contain restrictions that were not indispensable to the attainment of the benefits to distribution and consumers; and did not give the firms concerned the possibility of eliminating competition for a substantial part of the products in question. The reference to the benefit to consumers is worth quoting in full.

> Consumers may be expected to benefit, first of all, from a coherent distribution network offering uniform product quality and a comprehensive range of the articles and accessories available in the trade. Consumers will also benefit from the efficient and attentive service the franchisee will be encouraged to provide as a self-employed businessman who has a personal and direct interest in the success of his business, since he alone bears the financial risks. Consumers will further directly benefit from the continuity of supplies of products which satisfy their wants and reflect changes in tastes and fashion emerging in the market. Finally, the competitiveness of the market, and the freedom consumers have to purchase the products elsewhere in the network, will tend to force franchisees to pass a reasonable part of the benefits of the rationalisation of production and distribution on to consumers. Post-finally [sic], consumers can tell that they are dealing with independent traders, who can be held responsible.

It is clear from this Decision that the Commission was at pains to point out the economic advantages of a franchising system, even if it did contain clauses which were restrictive of competition.

In the *Yves Rocher* case, the Commission discussed in detail the clauses in the franchise agreements which were not restrictive of competition. Its conclusions (as in *ServiceMaster*) are to a large extent reflected in the terms of the block exemption regulation, discussed later in this book. As to the clauses restrictive of competition, the Commission pointed out that Yves Rocher's selection of only one franchisee for a given territory within which the franchisee had an exclusive right to use the franchisor's identifying marks and know-how for the sale of Yves Rocher products in a Beauty Centre, the franchisor undertaking not to establish a shop itself in the territory of each of its franchisees, combined with the prohibition on the opening by franchisees of a second shop stemming from the prohibition on using Yves Rocher's identifying mark in a location other than that specified in the contract, resulted in a degree of sharing of markets between the franchisor and the franchisee or between franchisees, thereby restricting competition within the distribution network. By virtue of such clauses, Yves Rocher's franchise contracts prevented franchisees from setting up in business in another Member State and might thus affect trade between Member States to an appreciable extent in view of the size of the Yves Rocher Group, its market share — greater than five per cent of the Member States concerned — the reputation of its products, the expansion of the Yves Rocher chain of shops throughout a substantial part of the common market and the existence alongside that chain of a highly developed mail order business. The notified contracts therefore fell within the terms of art 85(1).

Again, however, as in *Pronuptia*, the Commission regarded the conditions for exemption as having been satisfied. At the same time, it is clear that Yves Rocher was obliged to make some adjustments in the system before the Commission could agree to exemption: the Commission says that the loosening up of the system, adjusted by Yves Rocher at the Commission's request, has brought about a degree of price competition within the network in that franchisees can now freely obtain supplies from any other franchisee and profit from any difference between selling prices which Yves Rocher fixes in each Member State at a level somewhere between those charged by its major local competitors. (This is an example of the Commission's liking for intra-brand competition.) The Commission adds that Yves Rocher will be unable to prevent or hinder, on pain of revocation of the exemption, recourse by franchisees to the transnational cross supplies which the price differences between certain Member States are likely to encourage, especially in the case of franchisees operating near national frontiers.

Several special features characterised the *Computerland* case. In addition to the conjunction of the location clause and the exclusivity clause, there were provisions in the contract, on the franchisee's obligation to sell only to end users or to other Computerland franchisees unless otherwise authorised, which were also restrictive of competition. In certain franchise systems, as the Commission points out, for example where franchisees sell products bearing the franchise name or trade mark (or both), the prohibition on resale by franchisees to resellers who do not belong to that franchise network is based on the legitimate concern that the name, trade mark or business format could be damaged if the contract products were sold by resellers who did not have access to the franchisor's know-how and were not bound by the obligations aimed at preserving the reputation and unity of the network and its identifying marks. The case highlighted, however, that the Computerland name and trade mark covered the business format as such, but not the micro-computer products being sold, which bore the name and trade mark of each individual manufacturer. The prohibition on Computerland franchisees to sell the products to otherwise qualified resellers was thus restrictive.

On the other hand, the Commission recognised that this restriction was mitigated by a feature peculiar to sales in the micro-computer field, namely the fact that retailers could be part of the franchise network such as Computerland and at the same time be appointed an authorised dealer in a selective distribution system established by a manufacturer to ensure that his products were handled only by qualified resellers. A Computerland franchisee who thus operated simultaneously in two or more different networks must be in a position to fulfil the obligations and exercise the rights which flowed from each. Accordingly, the Commission granted exemption though, as in *Yves Rocher*, but for different reasons, the agreements had to be modified in one or two ways. In particular, the clauses relating to the non-competition obligation both during the term of the agreement and after termination thereof were considered to be unreasonably broad. The clauses in question were redrafted and exemption backdated to the date on which the franchisees were informed by Computerland of the amended version of the agreement.

Of the five Decisions by the Commission, the *ServiceMaster* Decision is the only one concerned with a service franchise: the notified standard form concerned the supply of housekeeping, cleaning and maintenance services to commercial and domestic customers according to the instructions of ServiceMaster and, on an ancillary basis, the supply of goods directly linked to the provision of those services. Apart from the fact that this was a service franchise, there are some important features of this case. One feature is the special importance which the Commission attached to know-how in the context of a service franchise. Another is the Commission's discussion of inter-brand and intra-brand competition at para 27 of the Decision:

> The inter-brand competition in the market concerned is both very strong and open: the market for cleaning, housekeeping and maintenance services is highly competitive, with a large number of firms supplying similar or identical services. It is also a market with no barriers to entry, with the result that new suppliers can at any time challenge any attempt by ServiceMaster or its franchisees to increase their prices.
>
> Intra-brand competition within the ServiceMaster network itself is also preserved: the limited territorial protection does not grant the franchisees any marketing or customer exclusivity. Franchisees are free to provide services to non-solicited customers resident outside their own territory. This brings about a certain degree of price competition between franchisees, who are free to determine those sales prices.

This is a state of affairs of which the Commission clearly approves. Originally, the notified provisions excluded intra-brand competition between franchisees; but, following observations made by the Commission, ServiceMaster agreed to make a number of amendments to the agreement, for example in the matter of unsolicited customers. The agreement had been notified on 3 June 1987; the amended agreement was communicated to the Commission on 10 May 1988: 'therefore the date on which the exemption can take effect is the date of communication of the amended agreement'. The Commission added that it was appropriate in this case, in view of the highly competitive nature of the market concerned and the absence of any barriers to entry to that market, to grant the exemption for a period of ten years. (This may be compared with the Commission's observation in *Yves Rocher* that in view of 'the novel character of the notified standard form contracts and the speed at which the structure and methods of cosmetics distribution are liable to change', the period of validity of exemption should be limited to five years.)

The *Charles Jourdan* Decision is somewhat longer than the others. This is partly due to the fact that Charles Jourdan has a more complicated system of distribution through four types of shop:

(a)   branches, owned and managed by the Charles Jourdan Group;

(b)   franchised shops, independent of the Group but subject to franchise agreements;

(c)   franchise corner retailers, who are independent traders, subject to a distribution agreement with the Charles Jourdan Group allowing them to represent the Charles Jourdan trade marks within a specified territory in a separate part of the shop premises, the articles in question being in competition with those of other brands; and

(d)   traditional retailers, who have no legal link with the group apart from agreements to sell articles bearing the trade mark.

The notification by Charles Jourdan related only to the network of standard form franchise and franchise corner distribution agreements.

As in most of the other cases, Charles Jourdan had to alter the agreements after notification to meet some of the Commission's requirements. In particular, as the result of amendments, the Charles Jourdan Group draws up price lists every season. These price lists are intended for guidance purposes and retailers are not required to abide by them. The freedom for retailers to determine their selling prices was expressly specified in the agreements at the Commission's request.

Chapter 5

Prior considerations on block exemption

A: Trade between Member States
B: *De minimis* rules

A: Trade between Member States

Before considering whether a given franchise agreement is likely to qualify for block exemption (or, for that matter, individual exemption), two questions have to be asked. The first is whether the agreement needs to be exempted: that is, whether the criteria laid down in art 85(1) of the EEC Treaty, and fully described in the last two chapters, are satisfied. If they are, there is a restrictive agreement which, unless exempted, will constitute an infringement of the rules on competition. However, it is not always necessary to go through the criteria in detail, since there is one test which, if not satisfied, rules out the application of art 85(1) *in limine*. This test is whether the agreement concerned 'affects trade between Member States'.

Many franchise agreements are local in character. They may relate to operations in a region of a Member State (like East Anglia or Wales) or to several regions falling short of the Member State as a whole (ie to mainland Britain without Northern Ireland). They may extend throughout a Member State, but stop short at its borders, with no transnational operations either in being or contemplated. In these cases, it is often difficult to imagine how trade between Member States can possibly be affected by the agreements in question. It therefore seems to be a reasonable assumption that these cases cannot possibly infringe art 85(1) and that there is no further need even to consider the matter of exemption.

However, the assumption may not be justified. Several cases in the European Court of Justice have held that an operation may be limited to a single Member State but may nevertheless affect trade between Member States. The *Belasco* decision (246/86) was a case in point: the fact that the operations were confined to Belgium did not prevent those operations from affecting inter-state trade. Whether inter-state trade is affected depends on a variety of factors, of which the geographical area of operations is only one.

Applied to franchising, the test extends to such questions as the sources of supply. The franchise network may be confined to a whole or to only a part of a single Member State, but if the products handled by the network come from another Member State, or could reasonably do so, then it follows that the activities of the network may affect inter-state trade. If, for example, a franchise agreement specifies that franchisees must obtain their supplies from a particular source, and if there is more than one source of equally good supplies in another Member State, then trade between Member States is, at least potentially, affected.

Several provisions of the block exemption regulation underline the importance of leaving franchisees free to obtain supplies from other sources, provided that the supplies are of an equivalent quality. This is fundamental to the competition policy of the EC Commission. It follows that if there were a regional franchise, in which traders from another Member State were arbitrarily denied the opportunity to supply goods of an equivalent quality, trade between Member States could have been affected. The franchise agreement, therefore, would not only come within the purview of the EEC rules on competition, but also constitute a *prima facie* infringement, and might not qualify for either individual or block exemption.

As the result of a curiously-worded passage at para 26 of the *Pronuptia* judgment, there is almost a presumption that certain types of franchise agreement affect trade between Member States:

> distribution franchise contracts which contain clauses leading to a sharing of markets between the franchisor and franchisees or between franchisees are in any event liable to affect trade between member

states, even if they are concluded between firms established within the same member state, to the extent that they prevent franchisees from setting up in another member state.

By contrast, the legislative provisions governing notification refer only to agreements, decisions and practices relating 'either to imports or to exports between Member States' (Regulation 17/62, art 4(2)(*i*)), which gives the impression that only imports or exports as such may be taken into account in determining whether trade between Member States is affected. However, although still on the statute book, the passage in question has to some extent been superseded; in any event, a judgment of the Court prevails over any Council or Commission Regulation.

There may be other ways in which a franchise agreement may, perhaps to the surprise of the parties, directly or indirectly affect trade between Member States, and parties and their advisers are cautioned against too ready an assumption that their particular agreement does not do so. At the same time, if the franchise arrangements are free of any element which can possibly be said to affect trade between Member States, or if the effect on trade is not 'appreciable', in the sense in which that word has been used by the Court of Justice in a series of cases (one of the more recent is *Erauw-Jacquery* (27/87)), then it is unnecessary to proceed further with an examination of the agreement in the light of the EEC rules on competition.

B: *De minimis* rules

As to the second factor which should be considered before any further action is taken in relation to the EEC rules on competition, the agreement should be looked at in the light of the *de minimis* rules issued by the EC Commission (reproduced in Appendix III). Even if the agreement affects trade between Member States, and has features which make it technically uncompetitive, it does not have to be notified and does not need to be exempted where the *de minimis* principles apply. Nor will the Commission normally open proceedings in cases to which the *de minimis* rules apply; even where it does, for exceptional reasons, it will not impose fines. Where firms wrongly believe that the *de minimis* rules apply, the Commission will not consider imposing fines unless the mistake was due to negligence.

At the same time, it has to be emphasised that the *de minimis* rules, in their present form, do not have the force of law. They are contained in an administrative notice published by the Commission and are not enshrined in any formal legal measure. The Commission itself is at pains to say that the notice is without prejudice to the jurisdiction of the national courts in applying art 85(1), though it adds that the notice constitutes a factor which the national courts may take into account; national jurisdictions generally respect the *de minimis* principle in some form or another. The Commission points out that the notice is without prejudice to any interpretation which may be given by the Court of Justice. It is conceivable that a civil action in the national courts, and *a fortiori* one which is referred to the Court of Justice, may result in a decision overruling the terms of the Commission's notice. If parties to a franchise agreement are aware of the existence of any hostile third party, eager for some reason to challenge the legal validity of the agreement, there should be some caution about the application of the *de minimis* rules followed by the Commission. Despite these qualifications, the *de minimis* rules are an important factor in assessing whether an agreement is ruled out *in limine* from the application of art 85. The Commission says that it regards the notice as a step in helping to facilitate co-operation between small and medium-sized enterprises, of which franchise networks are an obvious and deserving example. Moreover, the Commission's promulgation and own acceptance of the *de minimis* rules is nine-tenths of the law, since its role as guardian of the EEC Treaty gives it a decisive and influential position in the application of the EEC rules on competition.

What the Commission has sought to do in its notice is to give some sort of definition of the word 'appreciable' in the context of the many cases in which it has held that a given agreement or practice has or has not had an appreciable effect on competition. The definition is quantitative, being related to the parties' share of the market and to their annual turnover. It is not, however, absolute: 'in individual cases, even agreements between undertakings which exceed these limits may still have only a negligible effect on trade between Member States or on competition'.

It should be noted that the market share and turnover requirements are cumulative: both must be satisfied if the agreement is
to be covered by the *de minimis* rules. Also, both are more
complex than they seem at first sight. The market share is five
per cent of the total market for the goods or services in question
in the area of the common market affected by the agreement; the
turnover threshold — that is, the aggregate annual turnover of
the participating firms — is 200 million ECU.

This seems simple enough. However, the market share has to be
assessed in relation to both the relevant product market and the
relevant geographical market, described in detail in the notice,
and the participating undertakings are defined in terms which are
sometimes difficult to interpret in practice. In particular, a realistic
view must be taken of what constitutes the relevant market since
there is a risk that it could be more narrowly defined than one
might wish. Moreover, the Commission feels entitled to treat the
figures as dynamic and not just as a static analysis of the position.
As it said at para 23 of the *ServiceMaster* Decision (reproduced
in Appendix V), which concerned a franchise network:

> At the present time, ServiceMaster is only developing this network.
> However, when assessing the appreciable effect on trade between
> Member States the Commission must also take into account the likely
> future development of such a network. In this respect it must be
> considered that ServiceMaster is an important competitor in the market
> which is capable of setting up a great number of outlets throughout
> the EEC as it has done before in the United States and Canada where
> ServiceMaster has over 2 900 franchisees. ServiceMaster already has
> a 6% market share in the United Kingdom and reckons that its EEC
> market share will exceed 5% in the near future. Given this context,
> the Commission considers that there exists a sufficient probability that
> the restrictions contained in the notified standard form agreement are,
> at the least, such as to affect intra-Community trade appreciably. The
> notified standard form franchise agreement therefore falls within art
> 85(1).

The applicants were granted the exemption they had sought, after
it had been slightly amended.

All the paragraphs of the Commission's notice, setting out the *de
minimis* rules, and particularly those defining the elements making

up the market share test and the turnover test, are important for franchisors and franchisees and should be studied carefully in assessing the position in any given franchise operation, although two paragraphs merit special consideration. One of these provides that aggregate turnover includes the turnover in all goods and services, excluding tax, achieved during the last financial year by the participating undertakings; in cases where an undertaking has concluded similar agreements with various other undertakings in the relevant market, the turnover of all participating undertakings must be taken together. It is the whole franchise network which must be taken into account, not the purely bilateral relationship between the franchisor and the individual franchisee, and where the franchise network is part of a larger distribution network, as in *Jourdan* (*see* Appendix V), the whole operation is relevant. Although there is an exception here in favour of dealings between participating undertakings, the net is clearly cast far more widely than may first appear on a reading of the notice.

In the second place, the notice does not apply where in a relevant market competition is restricted by the cumulative effects of parallel networks of similar agreements established by several manufacturers or dealers. (In the franchise block exemption regulation, there is a corresponding provision, which is considered more closely in Chapter 14.) Like the turnover provision mentioned above, this could prove to be a trap for franchisors and franchisees.

Chapter 6

The origins of the block exemption regulation

A: The consequences of *Pronuptia*
B: The loose ends after *Pronuptia*
C: The numbers of expected cases

A: The consequences of *Pronuptia*

In the mid-1980s it became apparent from the *Pronuptia* case before the European Court of Justice that franchise agreements, hitherto thought to be untouched by the EEC rules on competition, were on the contrary all too often restrictive of competition, either technically or substantially. Indeed, in the *Pronuptia* case itself (reproduced in Appendix IV) it will be seen that the franchisee sought to have the franchise agreement declared void under art 85(2) of the EEC Treaty, because it infringed art 85(1). (The franchisee's interest in having the agreement declared void was a defence to the claim by the franchisor for arrears of fees payable under the agreement.) The case caused some consternation to franchise interests, since there was nothing unusual about the franchise agreement: it contained many of the provisions common to franchise agreements generally. It followed that, if the franchisee in *Pronuptia* were successful, the legality of a vast number of franchise agreements throughout the Community could be in question.

As it happened, the Court of Justice gave a reassuring judgment on 28 January 1986. It recognised the purposes of the franchising system, distinguished it from other forms of distribution or sales concession and made clear that 'such a system, which allows the franchisor to share his success, does not in itself jeopardise competition'. The Court went further and emphasised that a franchise system depended on two important conditions. The first was that the franchisor had to be able to communicate to franchisees his know-how and to provide them with the necessary help in implementing his methods without running the risk that this know-how and this help would benefit, however indirectly, his competitors. The second was that the franchisor had to be able to take appropriate measures to preserve the identity and the reputation of the network symbolised by the franchise name or trade mark. Therefore, clauses in a franchise agreement which were indispensable to avoid the risk and to institute the requisite controls did not constitute restrictions of competition within the meaning of art 85(1).

On the other hand, the Court made it clear in *Pronuptia* that there were many clauses in franchise agreements which were not indispensable for the purposes mentioned above and that these clauses restricted competition between the members of a franchise network. In this connection, the Court singled out clauses which led to a sharing of markets between franchisor and franchisees or among franchisees and clauses which prevented franchisees from competing among themselves on prices. In passing, it should be added that, while franchisees and their advisers may have thought it inappropriate for members of the same network to compete with one another, there is on the contrary a strong belief in the Commission and to some extent in the Court that intra-brand competition should be encouraged and not only inter-brand competition. As the Commission and Court see it, franchisees are separate economic entities which should, other things being equal, be free to compete with one another (particularly, but not exclusively, on prices).

An example of the sharing of markets between the franchisor and the franchisees, or among franchisees, arises where clauses in the franchise agreement include the undertaking by the franchisor not to become established himself in the franchisees' territory and to require from other franchisees an undertaking not to open another shop beyond their own. This is, according to the Court, a restriction of competition: the Court cited *Consten and Grundig v the Commission* (56, 58/64). On the other hand, to the extent that the arrangement was necessary for the operation of the franchise, it might be subject to exemption under art 85(3).

Two further points in the Court's judgment in *Pronuptia* merit special comment. The first is that a franchisor may communicate 'indicative' prices to franchisees, provided that, as between the franchisor and franchisees, or among franchisees, there was no concerted practice with a view to the effective application of those prices. (There is a body of case law on concerted practices, which is considered in detail in Appendix VI, with particular reference to the possible application of the case law to franchise agreements.)

The second is the Court's observation, already noted in the previous chapter, that distribution franchise agreements which contained clauses leading to a sharing of markets between the franchisor and franchisees, or among franchisees, were in any event 'liable to affect trade between member states', even if they were concluded between firms established within the same Member State, to the extent that they prevented franchisees from setting up in another Member State. It is in practice the location clause which effectively ties down the franchisee to a particular place of operations in the absence of territorial allocations or restrictions.

B: The loose ends after *Pronuptia*

If the rules of law laid down in the *Pronuptia* case and in the cases decided thereafter by the Commission (*see* the Decisions at Appendix V) are taken together, they will be found to constitute a fairly substantial code of law to which franchisors and their advisers may refer. However, in the nature of things, cases are decided on what are to some extent fortuitous sets of circumstances; one Court case and five Commission cases do not in themselves provide a complete or entirely coherent code.

It is partly for this reason that franchise interests urged the Commission to formulate a code of rules. The Commission is not, however, empowered to produce a code of rules for block exemption unless it has experience of individual cases of the kind which the code is intended to cover. This is because the parent measure (Council Regulation 19/65) gives the Commission power to make a block exemption regulation only on the basis of experience, enabling it to define the categories of agreements in question. By the time the first three cases had been decided, the Commission felt that it had the necessary experience, but even after five cases it still has no experience of industrial franchise agreements. As the preamble to the block exemption regulation explains, the Regulation 'does not cover wholesale franchise agreements because the Commission has no experience in that field'.

C: The numbers of expected cases

One of the objects of a block exemption regulation is to save the time and the trouble, both for parties and for the Commission, involved in making and dealing with individual applications for exemption. It is certain that the numbers of applications which should have been made before the regulation came into force, as well as the number which should have been made thereafter if the regulation had not come into force, would have been great. The fact that no case had arisen before *Pronuptia* is not an indication of the small number of franchise agreements technically infringing the rules on competition, but more probably a reflection of the widespread uncertainty about the possible relationship between the rules on competition and the organisation of franchise systems, and the consequent failure to notify franchise agreements.

After *Pronuptia*, there was a serious threat that the Commission might be inundated with applications from franchisors suddenly aware of their responsibility for notifying agreements which might infringe the rules on competition; this did not happen. To some extent, the realisation that franchise agreements were not immune from the rules on competition may have been offset by relief at the wisdom of the Court's judgment. However that may be, the Commission decided to go ahead with the drafting of the block exemption regulation; after consultations with interested parties and experts in the field, it adopted the Regulation, as it was empowered to do without further reference to the Council or to the European Parliament. Adoption of the Regulation took place on 30 November 1988, only just over two and a half years after the judgment in *Pronuptia*.

Chapter 7

The rationale of the Regulation

A: Legal importance of the preamble
B: Comments on the preamble

A: Legal importance of the preamble

Under art 190 of the EEC Treaty, Commission regulations, among other instruments, must state the reasons on which they are based. In practice, this means that the Articles of a regulation are preceded by a series of recitals, sometimes numbered, sometimes not, which together form the 'preamble', in which the Commission discharges its legal duty to state the reasons on which the regulation is based. In many regulations, each recital begins with the word 'whereas'. As a result the recitals are often referred to as the 'whereas clauses', but this is both inelegant and incorrect. The regulation governing franchising has the word 'whereas' only once, at the beginning of the recitals, which are numbered; there are 17 in all.

Since the statement of the reasons on which a regulation is based is a strict legal requirement, there are two legal consequences. In the first place, the statement is open to legal challenge. If a challenge in the European Court of Justice is successful, the whole regulation may be held to be *ultra vires*; but, at the least, a part of the regulation may be struck out by the Court. In the second place, the preamble forms part of the regulation as a whole and may be taken into account in interpreting the specific provisions of the regulation.

Often the language of the preamble differs from the language used in the Articles. In one sense, this is logical enough, since the recitals are intended to explain, and not merely to repeat, the

Articles themselves; but where the wording differs between recitals and articles there can be some confusion. In general, this does not arise in the franchise regulation, which is on the whole well drafted. The fact that the definition of franchise agreements in recitals 2, 4 and 5 is not identical with the definition in art 1(2), (3)(*a*)(*b*) is explained by the difference between the purposes of the two texts.

B: Comments on the preamble

Recital 1

> Regulation No 19/65/EEC empowers the Commission to apply Article 85(3) of the Treaty ... to certain categories of bilateral exclusive agreements falling within the scope of Article 85(1) which either have as their object the exclusive distribution or exclusive purchase of goods, or include restrictions imposed in relation to the assignment or use of industrial property rights.

As explained in Chapter 3, it is art 85(1) which prohibits restrictive agreements and art 85(3) which provides for exemption from the prohibition. The recital correctly speaks of 'industrial property' rights, the parent regulation being restricted to this branch of intellectual property, but the next recital and art 1 of the regulation speak of 'industrial or intellectual property' rights.

Recital 2

> Franchise agreements consist essentially of licences of industrial or intellectual property rights relating to trade marks or signs and know-how, which can be combined with restrictions relating to supply or purchase of goods.

Thus franchise agreements have the two elements which bring them within the scope of the parent regulation and enable the Commission to make a block exemption regulation for this category of agreements. To some extent, the essential character of franchise agreements is distorted for the purpose of conforming with the parent regulation: there are, for example, many elements of the business format, as described in Chapter 1, which do not constitute industrial property rights properly so called.

Recital 3

> Several types of franchise can be distinguished according to their object: industrial franchise concerns the manufacturing of goods, distribution franchise concerns the sale of goods, and service franchise concerns the supply of services.

This reflects the distinction made by the Court of Justice in para 13 of *Pronuptia* (*see* Appendix IV). So far, the Commission has had no applications for exemption for industrial, manufacturing or production franchises, and does not therefore have the experience necessary for including them within the scope of the block exemption regulation.

Recital 4

> It is possible on the basis of the experience of the Commission to define categories of franchise agreements which fall under Article 85(1) but can normally be regarded as satisfying the conditions laid down in Article 85(3). This is the case for franchise agreements whereby one of the parties supplies goods or provides services to end users. On the other hand, industrial franchise agreements should not be covered by this Regulation. Such agreements, which usually govern relationships between producers, present different characteristics from the other types of franchise. They consist of manufacturing licences based on patents and/or technical know-how, combined with trade-mark licences. Some of them may benefit from other block exemptions if they fulfil the necessary conditions.

As already noted in Chapter 3, the Commission must have experience of individual cases before introducing a block exemption regulation, and its experience so far has been limited to five cases (*see* Appendix V). Four of these cases relate to goods, the other — *ServiceMaster* — to services. Industrial franchises may, in some cases, be covered by the block exemption regulations on patent licensing or know-how licensing.

Recital 5

> This Regulation covers franchise agreements between two undertakings, the franchisor and the franchisee, for the retailing of goods or the provision of services to end users, or a combination of these activities, such as the processing or adaptation of goods to fit specific needs of their customers. It also covers cases where the relationship

between franchisor and franchisees is made through a third undertaking, the master franchisee. It does not cover wholesale franchise agreements because of the lack of experience of the Commission in that field.

There are four points to note in this recital. First, the fact that a franchise network is a multilateral grouping does not alter the fact that individual agreements between franchisors and franchisees are bilateral agreements, covered by the Regulation. If franchisors have standard contracts with franchisees, one exemption may be taken to cover all the agreements. Second, there is no definition of 'end user' in the Regulation. Third, the question of master franchising is not altogether satisfactorily dealt with in the Regulation (*see* Chapter 16). Fourth, until the Commission has more experience of wholesale franchises, these agreements must be notified, and exemption sought, on an individual basis (*see* Chapter 15, Section E).

Recital 6

Franchise agreements as defined in this Regulation can fall under Article 85(1). They may in particular affect intra-Community trade where they are concluded between undertakings from different Member States or where they form the basis of a network which extends beyond the boundaries of a single Member State.

Franchise agreements are defined in art 1(3) of the Regulation (*see* Chapter 8, Section C). If they fulfil one or more of the conditions specified in art 2, they must fall under art 85(1) of the Treaty, unless the restriction of competition is not 'appreciable'. This recital refers to two ways in which franchise agreements may affect trade between Member States, without prejudice to any of the other ways — including that referred to specifically by the Court of Justice in *Pronuptia* (*see* Chapter 5, Section A).

Recital 7

Franchise agreements as defined in this Regulation normally improve the distribution of goods and/or the provision of services as they give franchisors the possibility of establishing a uniform network with limited investments, which may assist the entry of new competitors on the market, particularly in the case of small and medium-sized undertakings, thus increasing interbrand competition. They also allow independent traders to set up outlets more rapidly and with higher chance of success than if they had to do so without the franchisor's experience and assistance. They have therefore the possibility of competing more efficiently with large distribution undertakings.

The opening words of this recital correspond to the first requirement of art 85(3) of the Treaty, laying down the general conditions on which exemption may be granted. Emphasis is placed on the importance of market access, that is, opportunities for entry into the market, although the possibility that franchise systems may not always encourage market access, where the economic context is unfavourable, is recognised in art 8(*a*) of the Regulation (*see* Chapter 14). For the rest, the recital is a fair statement of the rationale of franchising, especially in relation to inter-brand competition. None of the recitals refers explicitly to intra-brand competition, though recitals 8, 12 and 13 may be regarded as containing indirect references.

Recital 8

As a rule, franchise agreements also allow consumers and other end users a fair share of the resulting benefit, as they combine the advantage of a uniform network with the existence of traders personally interested in the efficient operation of their business. The homogeneity of the network and the constant cooperation between the franchisor and the franchisees ensures a constant quality of the products and services. The favourable effect of franchising on interbrand competition and the fact that consumers are free to deal with any franchisee in the network guarantees that a reasonable part of the resulting benefits will be passed on to the consumers.

The opening and closing words of this recital reflect the second requirement of art 85(3) of the Treaty on the criteria for exemption. The reference to the consumers' freedom to deal with any franchisee, taken in conjunction with the reference to parallel imports in recital 12 and the reference to the franchisees' freedom to fix their own prices in recital 13, reflect the Commission's wish to ensure that there is some degree of competition between the franchisees themselves ('intra-brand' competition).

Recital 9

This Regulation must define the obligations restrictive of competition which may be included in franchise agreements. This is the case in particular for the granting of an exclusive territory to the franchisees combined with the prohibition on actively seeking customers outside that territory, which allows them to concentrate their efforts on their allotted territory. The same applies to the granting of an exclusive territory to a master franchisee combined with the obligation not to conclude franchise agreements with third parties outside that territory. Where the franchisees sell or use in the process of providing services, goods manufactured by the franchisor or according to its instructions and/or bearing its trade mark, an obligation on the franchisees not to sell, or use in the process of the provision of services, competing goods, makes it possible to establish a coherent network which is identified with the franchised goods. However, this obligation should only be accepted with respect to the goods which form the essential subject-matter of the franchise. It should notably not relate to accessories or spare parts for these goods.

Exclusivity of territory or supply implies a degree of restriction on competition. Territorial exclusivity is acceptable in a franchise network for the reasons given in this recital, which largely reflects the reasoning of the Court of Justice in para 24 of *Pronuptia* (*see* Appendix IV). Exclusivity in the matter of supply is qualified by the reference to accessories and spare parts. There are two problems here. One is that the recital, unlike the text of the Regulation, speaks of the 'essential' subject-matter of the franchise. The other is that it may be difficult in practice to apply the term 'accessories' to certain types of franchise goods. These points are discussed further in the chapters which follow. Another point to be noted is that, while the prohibition on soliciting customers outside the territory is treated as a reasonable restriction, a different attitude is adopted towards the treatment of unsolicited customers (*see* the comments on art 5(*g*) in Chapter 11). In the *ServiceMaster* decision (*see* Appendix V) however, the franchisee is only given a non-exclusive right within his territory. The Commission (*see* para 22) found that despite non-exclusivity the prohibition against the franchisee setting up further outlets and actively seeking customers outside his territory fell within art 85(1).

Recital 10

> The obligations referred to above thus do not impose restrictions which
> are not necessary for the attainment of the abovementioned objectives.
> In particular, the limited territorial protection granted to the fran-
> chisees is indispensable to protect their investment.

This recital reflects the wording of art 85(3) of the Treaty, in its
third condition for the granting of exemption. In speaking of the
'limited' territorial protection, the Commission probably has in
mind the point made in the comments on recital 9, that franchisees
are not to be prevented from dealing with unsolicited customers
from outside their territory.

Recital 11

> It is desirable to list in the Regulation a number of obligations that
> are commonly found in franchise agreements and are normally not
> restrictive of competition and to provide that if, because of the particu-
> lar economic or legal circumstances, they fall under Article 85(1), they
> are also covered by the exemption. This list, which is not exhaustive,
> includes in particular clauses which are essential either to preserve the
> common identity and reputation of the network or to prevent the
> know-how made available and the assistance given by the franchisor
> from benefiting competitors.

The list referred to is set out in art 3 of the Regulation (*see*
Chapter 9, Sections B and C). There may be other clauses in
existence which are essential for the two purposes mentioned in
the recital but which are not covered by Article. Clauses which
are restrictive would appear to be covered by art 6 (*see* Chapter
12).

Recital 12

> The Regulation must specify the conditions which must be satisfied for
> the exemption to apply. To guarantee that competition is not elimi-
> nated for a substantial part of the goods which are the subject of
> the franchise, it is necessary that parallel imports remain possible.
> Therefore, cross deliveries between franchisees should always be poss-
> ible. Furthermore, where a franchise network is combined with another
> distribution system, franchisees should be free to obtain supplies from
> authorised distributors. To better inform customers, thereby helping
> to ensure that they receive a fair share of the resulting benefits, it must

be provided that the franchisee shall be obliged to indicate its status as an independent undertaking, by any appropriate means which does not jeopardise the common identity of the franchised network. Furthermore, where the franchisees have to honour guarantees for the franchisor's goods, this obligation should also apply to goods supplied by the franchisor, other franchisees or other agreed [sic: sc 'appointed'] dealers.

In speaking of the elimination of competition for a substantial part of the goods, the recital is repeating the words used in the concluding part of art 85(3). The conditions referred to are set out in art 4 of the Regulation (*see* Chapter 10). As to the reference to parallel imports, this is a part of the case law and goes wider than the example given in the recital or the condition set out in art 4. In its broader context, the term 'parallel imports' refers to imports of products through channels other than those authorised under the manufacturers' normal distribution arrangements; they operate in parallel to the authorised channels. They often originate from sources which have a surplus of products to dispose of. The attraction of parallel imports to speculative — or simply competitive — traders is greatest when there is a difference of price in the exporting and importing countries.

Recital 13

The Regulation must also specify restrictions which may not be included in franchise agreements if these are to benefit from the exemption granted by the Regulation, by virtue of the fact that such provisions are restrictions falling under Article 85(1) for which there is no general presumption that they will lead to the positive effects required by Article 85(3). This applies in particular to market sharing between competing manufacturers, to clauses unduly limiting the franchisee's choice of suppliers or customers, and to cases where the franchisee is restricted in determining its prices. However, the franchisor should be free to recommend prices to the franchisees, where it is not prohibited by national laws and to the extent that it does not lead to concerted practices for the effective application of those prices.

The restrictions on competition are listed in art 5 of the Regulation (*see* Chapter 11). While there is no general presumption that such clauses may qualify for exemption, individual cases may arise in which a franchise agreement qualifies for exemption, even though it contains one or more of the clauses in question; in that case, individual exemption must be applied for (as described in Chapter 15, Section E). However, it will be hard to justify restrictions of the kind set out in the list. Above all, any kind of price fixing will be almost impossible to keep in any franchise agreement: it is difficult enough in any kind of agreement, as the case law shows (for example in *BNIC* (123/83) and *Belasco* (246/86)). Recommended or indicative prices are permissible on the conditions indicated in this recital, which closely follows the wording of the Court of Justice in para 25 of *Pronuptia* (*see* Appendix IV). As the recital suggests, recommended prices may not always be permitted under national laws. Paragraph 61 of the *Yves Rocher* decision (*see* Appendix IV) is puzzling since it appears to approve the Yves Rocher pricing policy. The para deals with the requirement of art 85(3) that consumers should be allowed a fair share of the benefits 'resulting from the improvement in distribution'. The Commission state 'Lastly Yves Rocher's policy of charging prices mid-way between those of specialist and non-specialist retailers helps to widen the circle of cosmetics users'.

Recital 14

Agreements which are not automatically covered by the exemption because they contain provisions that are not expressly exempted by the Regulation and not expressly excluded from exemption may nonetheless be generally presumed to be eligible for application of Article 85(3). It will be possible for the Commission rapidly to establish whether this is the case for a particular agreement. Such agreements should therefore be deemed to be covered by the exemption provided for in this Regulation where they are notified to the Commission and the Commission does not oppose the application of the exemption within a specified period of time.

This recital refers to the so-called 'opposition procedure', which is a feature of some, though by no means all, of the other existing block exemptions (such as the patent licensing and know-how licensing regulations). The procedure is set out in art 6 (*see* Chapters 12 and 15, Section D). The specified period is approximately six months.

Recital 15

If individual agreements exempted by this Regulation nevertheless have effects which are incompatible with Article 85(3), in particular as interpreted by the administrative practice of the Commission and the case law of the Court of Justice, the Commission may withdraw the benefit of the block exemption. This applies in particular where competition is significantly restricted because of the structure of the relevant market.

How, in procedural terms, the Commission withdraws the benefit of the Regulation in any given case is set out in art 8 (*see* Chapter 14). The circumstances in which the Commission resorts to this procedure may be external to the franchise or internal, but seldom result from a process by which the clauses in an otherwise acceptable agreement are somehow vitiated *ex post facto*. External circumstances may arise where, through no fault of the franchisor or franchisees, the market becomes uncompetitive. Internal circumstances may arise where the franchisor or franchisees misuse their position.

Recital 16

Agreements which are automatically exempted pursuant to this Regulation need not be notified. Undertakings may nevertheless in a particular case request a decision pursuant to Council Regulation No 17 as last amended by the Act of Accession of Spain and Portugal.

Although it is implicit in the block exemption procedure that notification of individual agreements is unnecessary, this is not stated in any of the Articles of the Regulation, nor even in the parent regulation, except by implication in the third recital (*see* Regulation 19/65). It is therefore a salutary reminder of the main purpose of block exemptions, which is to save both the Commission and the parties the time and trouble of dealing with individual notifications and applications for exemption. At the same time, parties may submit an individual application if they wish: this may possibly be helpful to the parties in marginal cases.

Recital 17

Agreements may benefit from the provisions either of this Regulation or of another Regulation, according to their particular nature and provided that they fulfil the necessary conditions of application. They may not benefit from a combination of the provisions of this Regulation with those of another block exemption Regulation.

This is another point of law which has not been spelt out in any of the Articles. If a franchise agreement contains clauses which are outside the scope of the franchise block exemption regulation, but are covered by the provisions of, say, the patent licensing regulation, an individual application for exemption has to be made to the Commission (*see* Chapter 15).

In addition to being an introduction to the main text of the Regulation, the recitals serve as a point of reference back from the individual Articles, where the purpose of the Articles is not self-evident. Thus, the rationale of the Regulation, as well as of its specific provisions, can often be illuminated by checking the relevant recitals.

Chapter 8

The scope of the Regulation (art 1)

A: Declaration of exemption
B: Definition of 'franchise'
C: Definition of 'franchise agreement'
D: Goods and premises
E: 'Know-how' definitions

A: Declaration of exemption

Under art 85(3) of the EEC Treaty, the provisions of art 85(1),
prohibiting certain restrictive agreements, may be declared inapplicable in the case, *inter alia*, of any category of agreements
between undertakings. A declaration of this sort is generally
known as exemption. The Regulation applying art 85(3) of the
Treaty to categories of franchise agreements is set out, with comments, in this chapter and in Chapters 9–14.

Article 1(1)

Pursuant to Article 85(3) of the Treaty and subject to the provisions
of this Regulation, it is hereby declared that Article 85(1) . . . shall
not apply to franchise agreements to which two undertakings are party,
which include one or more of the restrictions listed in Article 2.

Thus, if an agreement complies with the provisions of the Regulation, it receives automatic exemption; it need not be notified,
and, even if technically or substantially restrictive of competition,
it does not constitute an infringement nor attract a fine. The
limited exceptions to this principle are considered in Chapters 12
and 14.

At first sight, a franchise network comprises multiple agreements;
but, in practice, the agreements are generally bilateral, that is,

between the franchisor and each of the individual franchisees. The first condition noted in the foregoing paragraph is therefore normally satisfied where franchise agreements are concerned. Under Community law, a trader, whether an individual person or a multinational corporation, is an undertaking (see, for example, the observations of the Court of Justice in *Hydrotherm* (173/83)), and it follows that, even if a franchisor or franchisee is an individual person, he or she is referred to as such. Throughout the Regulation the franchisor or franchisee is referred to as 'it'.

So far as the other condition is concerned, that the agreement must include one or more of the restrictions listed in art 2 of the Regulation, this is a way of defining the type of agreement to be covered by the Regulation. If the agreement does not contain any of the restrictions listed in art 2, it is not an agreement to which the Regulation applies. The fact that art 2, as Chapter 9 explains, provides for the exemption of agreements containing specific restrictions should not mislead the reader into thinking that the Article merely contributes to the list of permissible clauses: it does far more. The list in art 2 is also a list of qualifying clauses: that is, of clauses 'restrictive of competition' which, if included in the agreement, make it *prima facie* eligible for exemption under the Regulation when otherwise the clause would be void.

Article 1(2)

The exemption provided for in paragraph 1 shall also apply to master franchise agreements to which two undertakings are party. Where applicable, the provisions of this Regulation concerning the relationship between the franchisor and the franchisee shall apply *mutatis mutandis* to the relationship between franchisor and master franchisee and between master franchisee and franchisee.

A 'master franchise agreement' is defined in art 1(3)(*c*).

B: Definition of 'franchise'

Article 1(3)(*a*)

'franchise' means a package of industrial or intellectual property rights relating to trade marks, trade names, shop signs, utility models,

designs, copyrights, know-how or patents, to be exploited for the resale
of goods or the provision of services to end users;

This is not a wholly satisfactory definition, but is probably so
worded as to bring it within the ambit of Regulation 19/65. As
the Court of Justice recognised in *Pronuptia*, a franchise is a
method of 'exploiting financially . . . a collection of skills'. Some
of these skills are business methods: they may amount to some
form of 'know-how', but may well fall short of intellectual property in the strict sense of the term. (It is wrong, by the way, for
the Regulation to speak of industrial or intellectual property
rights, since industrial property is a branch of intellectual property. It would also be wrong to include know-how as though it
were an accepted category of intellectual property, which is not
yet the case. The definition oddly refers to such intellectual property rights as relate to 'shop signs, . . . know-how', as well as to
recognised intellectual property rights, such as trade marks and
patents.) In practice, it can probably be argued that some at least
of the franchisor's business methods, as communicated to the
franchisee in the operation of the franchise, are capable of being
protected by intellectual property laws, even where they are not
the subject of registered rights. Franchise manuals, for example,
are almost certainly protected either *de lege* by copyright, subject
to the usual copyright rules, or under the terms of the contract
itself. The definition in the Regulation may not, therefore, be a
cause of any serious practical problems.

C: Definition of 'franchise agreement'

Article 1(3)(*b*)

'franchise agreement' means an agreement whereby one undertaking,
the franchisor, grants the other, the franchisee, in exchange for direct
or indirect financial consideration, the right to exploit a franchise for
the purposes of marketing specified types of goods and/or services; it
includes at least obligations relating to:

—the use of a common name or shop sign and a uniform presentation
of contract premises and/or means of transport,

—the communication by the franchisor to the franchisee of know-
how,

—the continuing provision by the franchisor to the franchisee of commercial or technical assistance during the life of the agreement;

There is a slight overlapping of words in this rather more satisfactory definition and the previous definition, but the general intention is plain.

Three essential characteristics of a franchise agreement are referred to in the definition, of which the most important is the communication by the franchisor to the franchisee of know-how; this will be considered shortly. What it amounts to, briefly, is that a franchisor may not find his agreement falling squarely within the terms of the Regulation if the business methods which he communicates to the franchisee as part of the deal are no more than a rather insubstantial body of materials. A dissatisfied franchisee may well be tempted to challenge the legality of a franchise agreement under the rules on competition, if he can prove to the Commission that the know-how which he receives from the franchisor is insubstantial and that the franchise agreement does not therefore meet the requirements of the definition in the Regulation.

By the same token, it is essential for the franchisor to be able to show that he makes continuing provision to the franchisee of commercial or technical assistance during the life of the agreement. (Vague promises of help at the discretion of the franchisor, of the type sometimes contained in clauses in franchise agreements, will not suffice.) Otherwise, the third condition in the above definition will not have been satisfied, and the franchisor may find himself in legal difficulties. The agreement will in such cases have to be restructured to qualify for exemption. The date of the agreement, and the extent to which the franchise is based on a developing system, are relevant factors in this process.

There is probably little difficulty over the other condition for the definition of a franchise agreement. If an agreement does not make provision for the use of a common name or shop sign and a uniform — perhaps, 'consistent and recognisable' would have been a less drastic term — presentation of contract premises and/or means of transport, it can hardly be described as a franchise agreement, since the adoption of common business methods strongly implies a readily recognisable outlet or vehicle.

Article 1(3)(*c*)

'master franchise agreement' means an agreement whereby one undertaking, the franchisor, grants the other, the master franchisee, in exchange of direct or indirect financial consideration, the right to exploit a franchise for the purposes of concluding franchise agreements with third parties, the franchisees;

Although it is helpful that the Regulation covers the types of master franchise agreement included within this definition, it does not cover all types, as Chapter 16 explains. Franchisors therefore need to ensure that agreements referred to as master franchise agreements do in fact fall squarely within the definition if the agreement is to be covered by the Regulation.

D: Goods and premises

Article 1(3)(d)

'franchisor's goods' means goods produced by the franchisor or according to its instructions, and/or bearing the franchisor's name or trade mark;

There are some important substantive provisions in the Regulation relating to the franchisor's goods, particularly in arts 2(*a*)(*e*) and 4(*b*). But, in art 5(*c*), the words 'goods manufactured by the franchisor or third parties designated by the franchisor' are used. These are slightly but significantly different from the words used in this definition. Two further points in the definition call for comment. One is the reference to the franchisor's 'instructions', an odd word in this context ('specifications' would perhaps be the more familiar concept). The other is the reference to the trade name or trade mark, which is either a cumulative or an alternative characteristic of the franchisor's goods. One might also question whether goods not manufactured by the franchisor or according to his instructions could legitimately bear his trademark.

Article 1(3)(*e*)

'contract premises' means the premises used for the exploitation of the franchise or, when the franchise is exploited outside those premises, the base from which the franchisee operates the means of transport used for the exploitation of the franchise (contract means of transport);

This second definition is important when taken in conjunction with the provisions of the Regulation on the 'contract territory', a term used and indirectly defined in art 2(*a*).

The subsidiary definition, of the 'contract means of transport', is also important in the context of mobile franchises. These are often service franchises, in which the public recognition of the network depends more, or exclusively, on seeing the franchisees' vehicles than their premises, though the base, which may be a garage or warehouse, from which the franchisees operate may also be important.

E: 'Know-how' definitions

Article 1(3)(*f*)

'know-how' means a package of non-patented, practical information, resulting from experience and testing by the franchisor, which is secret, substantial and identified;

Since it is essential, for the purposes of the Regulation, that the franchise agreement should include the communication by the franchisor to the franchisee of know-how, it is no less essential that the know-how communicated by the franchisor should meet the definition which the Regulation provides. Except, perhaps, for the last four words, which are considered below, the definition presents few if any problems. It is reasonable enough that the reference to experience and testing should be included: this is the essence of a franchise system and is often the subject of a pilot scheme by the franchisor. If the franchisee finds either that the information is not based on experience or that it has not been tested, he may be in a position to challenge the legal validity of the agreement, in terms of the EEC rules on competition; and, if he is successful, the agreement will not benefit from exemption under the Regulation.

Article 1(3)(*g*)

'secret' means that the know-how, as a body or in the precise configuration and assembly of its components, is not generally known or easily accessible, it is not limited in the narrow sense that each individual component of the know-how should be totally unknown or unobtainable outside the franchisor's business;

This definition corresponds, in all but two particulars, to the definition in the know-how licensing regulation; it is not an entirely satisfactory transposition. One difference, which is minor, is the substitution of the word 'franchisor' for the word 'licensor'. The other is the omission of the words 'so that part of its value consists in the lead time gained when the communication is passed to him'. In the context of franchising, as distinct from the context of patent and know-how licensing, the lead time is less important than the exclusivity of the information made available by the franchisor.

Article 1(3)(*h*)

'substantial' means that the know-how includes information which is of importance for the sale of goods or the provision of services to end users, and in particular for the presentation of goods for sale, the processing of goods in connection with the provision of services, methods of dealing with customers, and administration and financial management; the know-how must be useful for the franchisee by being capable, at the date of conclusion of the agreement, of improving the competitive position of the franchisee, in particular by improving the franchisee's performance or helping it to enter a new market;

If a franchise agreement fails to pass the test implied in this definition, and the know-how conveyed to the franchisee is in practice found to be insubstantial or less than useful from a commercial and competitive point of view, the franchise agreement will not be covered by the Regulation. There is little case law on the extent to which the Court and Commission may be prepared to find that know-how is insubstantial. In the Commission's decision in *Rich* (*Official Journal*, L 69, 15.3.88), the Commission looks at the nature of the know-how involved in a case involving the preparation of food; otherwise, official guidance is slender. Probably the best guide is to be found indirectly in the Commission's assessment of the know-how provided by the franchisors in the five franchising cases on which it has reached a formal decision (*see* Appendix V). The Commission's views on know-how in para 6 of *ServiceMaster* are interesting:

Know-how is often more important in the supply of services than in the supply of goods because each service requires the execution of particular work and creates a close personal relationship between the provider of the service and the receiver of the service.

It should be noted that the test of substantiality is to be applied at the date of conclusion of the agreement by reference to the usefulness of the know-how in improving the franchisee's performance or helping it to enter a new market. In the case of a new entrant to the franchise system this will invariably be so even where the franchisee is running an existing business which is being converted to the franchise.

The application of this test as at the date of the conclusion of the agreement creates a 'hidden' trap for franchisors when renewal of the franchise agreement takes place. The invariable practice in franchising is for the franchisor to grant to the franchisee the right to renew the agreement at the expiration of the term. Upon the exercise of that right the franchisor and the franchisee normally execute the then current version of franchise agreement being used by the franchisor. That would fix the date of the conclusion of the agreement at that time and not when the first agreement was entered into. It will be necessary for the franchisor to be certain at the date of conclusion of such agreement that the requirements of the definition of 'substantial' are satisfied. It would be argued that the ability for the franchisee to continue to benefit from the franchisor's know-how will improve the franchisee's competitive position and will continue to improve the franchisee's performance.

Article 1(3)(*i*)

'identified' means that the know-how must be described in a sufficiently comprehensive manner so as to make it possible to verify that it fulfils the criteria of secrecy and substantiality; the description of the know-how can be set out either in the franchise agreement or in a separate document or recorded in any other appropriate form.

This requirement can easily be overlooked, but it is important for the eligibility of the agreement for exemption under the Regulation. It is probably advisable to have a clause in the agreement referring to the document in which the know-how is identified, and it will be usual for the description itself to be included in the operating manual.

To summarise the contents of the definitions in art 1(3)(*f*)–(*i*), the definition of know-how is essential to the whole concept of franchising in the Regulation, and the definitions of 'secret', 'substantial' and 'identified' create strict requirements. The general intention is clear. First, the know-how as a package must not simply be common knowledge: that is, information in the public domain and readily available in that form from other sources. Second, the know-how must be substantial: that is, it must be important and useful at the time the contract is made. Third, the description of the know-how must be recorded in the franchise agreement or elsewhere so that the secrecy and 'substantiality' of the know-how can be verified.

Chapter 9

Generally acceptable clauses in franchise agreements (arts 2 and 3)

A: Qualifying clauses (art 2)
B: Conditionally acceptable clauses (art 3(1))
C: Other generally acceptable clauses (art 3(2))

A: Qualifying clauses (art 2)

Article 2 lists a number of restrictions of competition. The list serves three purposes. In the first place it identifies those clauses which the Commision regards as falling within art 85(1). In the second place, it refers to clauses which, if included in a franchise agreement, qualify the agreement for exemption under the Regulation, provided that the other requirements of the Regulation are met; this stems from art 1, discussed in Chapter 8 above. In other words, if the agreement contains none of the restrictions listed in art 2, it is not covered by the Regulation. It may not be restrictive of competition at all, in which case no problem arises under the EEC rules on competition, and no notification or application for exemption is needed; or it may be restrictive of competition in some way other than those listed in art 2, in which case an individual notification to the Commission and an application for exemption should be made. The procedure for making an application in these circumstances is described elsewhere (*see* Chapters 12 and 14). Only one of the restrictions listed in art 2 is needed to qualify for exemption under the Regulation; however, if more than one of the restrictions listed in art 2 are found in the same agreement, as they sometimes are, the agreement still qualifies for exemption.

In the third place, the list of restrictions in art 2 serves as the first category of generally acceptable clauses in franchise agreements under the terms of the Regulation. These clauses are described here as 'generally' acceptable because, while they are acceptable in themselves, they are subject to certain extraneous conditions listed in art 4 of the Regulation (discussed more fully in Chapter 10).

Article 2(*a*)

The exemption provided for in Article 1 shall apply to the following restrictions of competition:

(*a*) an obligation on the franchisor, in a defined area of the common market, the contract territory, not to:
— grant the right to exploit all or part of the franchise to third parties,
— itself exploit the franchise, or itself market the goods or services which are the subject-matter of the franchise under a similar formula,
— itself supply the franchisor's goods to third parties;

Of the restrictions referred to in art 2, the first and most important concerns the contract territory. As the Court of Justice recognised in *Pronuptia* (para 24 — *see* Appendix IV), the question of territorial restriction is likely to be at the heart of many franchise agreements. The need for an exclusive territory is justified by the Commission in its decision in *Yves Rocher* (para 60 — *see* Appendix V) in the following terms:

The grant to franchisees of an exclusive territory, combined with the prohibition on setting up outside this territory, enables them to pursue a more intensive policy of selling Yves Rocher products by concentrating on their allotted territory, helped in this by the fact that the Yves Rocher retailing formula is based on a single brand. Territorial exclusivity also simplifies planning and ensures the continuity of supplies.

Three further restrictions listed in art 2 also concern the contract territory or the contract premises.

Article 2(*b*)

an obligation on the master franchisee not to conclude franchise agreement with third parties outside its contract territory;

This applies a similar principle *mutatis mutandis* to master franchises as to direct franchises.

Article 2(*c*)

an obligation on the franchisee to exploit the franchise only from the contract premises;

This is usually known as the 'location clause'. Even where there is no territorial clause, it amounts to a sharing of the market since the franchisee cannot trade at any other location and gives rise to the presumption that trade between Member States is affected (*see* Chapter 5).

Article 2(*d*)

an obligation on the franchisee to refrain, outside the contract territory, from seeking customers for the goods or the services which are the subject-matter of the franchise;

However, a clause prohibiting the franchisee from supplying unsolicited customers would be unacceptable (*see* Chapter 11).

Article 2(*e*)

an obligation on the franchisee not to manufacture, sell or use in the course of the provision of services, goods competing with the franchisor's goods which are the subject-matter of the franchise; where the subject-matter of the franchise is the sale or use in the course of the provision of services both certain types of goods and spare parts or accessories therefore, that obligation may not be imposed in respect of these spare parts or accessories.

It is fundamental to the Commission's policy on competition that franchisees, dealers and others should be in a position to choose for themselves all spare parts, accessories and other products which are not contract goods. The expression used in arts 2(*d*) and (*e*) 'the goods or services which are the subject-matter of the franchise' is unclear in its meaning. The preamble (*see* Chapter

7, recital 9) refers to 'goods which form the *essential* (author's emphasis) subject-matter of the franchise', which expression clearly indicates that the Commission feels that one can isolate what can be regarded as the essential goods or services. Most franchisors would probably take the view, as is the case with the 'know-how' definition, that it is the total package of goods and services and their blend which is essential, and that any tampering with any individual product or service detracts from the totality of the common identity and reputation of the franchise network. It would not be possible to say with confidence what the essential goods and services are in a fast food operation where individual menu items are selected by the consumer to produce the final meal. Such a final choice might include hamburgers, pizza, French fries, dessert and a beverage. All these goods and the service which produces them are the subject-matter of the franchise. It is the ability to select the items which appeal to the consumer and to be served quickly with products which appeal which causes the consumer to patronise any particular fast food operation. It appears that the Commission takes the view that a hamburger fast food restaurant has hamburgers as the goods which are the subject-matter of the franchise. Thus beverages, for example, are not within that category. How far a franchisor can go in specifying, for example, the brands of beverages which may be served in a fast food outlet has not been tested in law: this is one of a number of problems left unresolved by the Regulation (*see* Chapter 16).

In the meantime, franchisors may wish to give franchisees the maximum freedom in this respect consistent with their brand image and business methods. It should be added that clauses covering the sale or use of goods, and the sources of supply available to the franchisee, need to be examined in the light not only of art 2(*e*), but also of arts 3(1)(*a*)(*b*) and 5(*b*). The cumulative effect of these provisions is discussed in Chapter 11 below.

B: Conditionally acceptable clauses (art 3(1))

Under the first paragraph of art 3, there is a list of seven obligations of a kind often imposed on franchisees, which are acceptable from the point of view of obtaining automatic exemption under the Regulation. However, they are subject to an overriding condition and if, in any individual case, that condition is not met, the franchise agreement cannot benefit from the Regulation.

Article 3(1)

Article 1 shall apply notwithstanding the presence of any of the following obligations on the franchisee, in so far as they are necessary to protect the franchisor's industrial or intellectual property rights or to maintain the common identity and reputation of the franchised network:

Any obligation on the franchisee which goes beyond what is necessary for these purposes will take the agreement outside the scope of the Regulation. Whether the obligation is indeed necessary depends on the facts of the individual case, the wording of the clauses in question and the economic context (as the Court of Justice put it in *Pronuptia*) in which the clauses have been included. Subject to this general condition, the clauses considered acceptable are those concerned with the following obligations imposed on the franchisee.

Article 3(1)(*a*)

to sell, or use in the course of the provision of services, exclusively goods matching minimum objective quality specifications laid down by the franchisor;

As already noted, this provision is one of several provisions governing the nature of the goods sold by the franchisor or used by the franchisor in the provision of services; the cumulative effect of the provisions is discussed in Chapter 11 below.

Article 3(1)(*b*)

to sell, or use in the course of the provision of services, goods which are manufactured only by the franchisor or by third parties designed [sic: sc 'designated'] by it, where it is impracticable, owing to the nature of the goods which are the subject-matter of the franchise, to apply objective quality specifications.

The Court of Justice recognised in *Pronuptia* (para 21 — *see* Appendix IV) that it might be 'impracticable in certain cases, as in the field of fashion goods, to formulate objective quality specifications. Ensuring respect for these specifications may also, in view of the large number of franchisees, involve too great a cost'; a similar conclusion in relation to fashion goods was reached by the Commission in its decision in the *Charles Jourdan* case (para 28, fourth indent — *see* Appendix V).

The question of whether the cost of monitoring compliance with the franchisor's specifications is becoming too great may indicate that the opposition procedure should be employed so that the issue is put beyond doubt and cannot be raised by a franchisee in any proceedings (*see* Chapter 12).

Article 3(1)(*c*)

> not to engage, directly or indirectly, in any similar business in a terri-
> tory where it would compete with a member of the franchised network,
> including the franchisor; the franchisee may be held to this obligation
> after termination of the agreement, for a reasonable period which
> may not exceed one year, in the territory where it has exploited the
> franchise;

Clauses providing for two-year post-term limitations are unacceptable, and even the periods of up to a year have to be 'reasonable'. The Commission's observations in para 25(i) of *Pronuptia* (*see* Appendix V) are pertinent:

> The ban on competition during the period of the contract is necessary
> to protect the know-how and other assistance supplied. These benefits
> lend themselves to use with other products which would benefit com-
> petitors, if only indirectly. Other ways of preventing this risk might
> not be as effective

> The period of one year after the ending of the contract during which
> the franchisee continues to be bound by the non-competition covenant
> can in the present case be regarded as reasonable, within the meaning
> of the Court's judgment (ground 16), both for the purpose stated above
> and to allow Pronuptia to establish a new outlet in the territory of the
> former franchisee, which it is unable to do during the term of the
> contract because of the franchisee's exclusivity.

This is perhaps an overstatement, and the very fact that the Commission refers specifically to the circumstances of this particular suggest that in other cases the test of what is reasonable may be different. In para 22(iii) of *Computerland* (*see* Appendix V) the Commission adds that the franchisee has, after all, had the opportunity during the term of the contract to acquire custom outside his territory: 'he can thus continue to reap the benefits of the efforts he has made as a franchisee, only being prevented from competing during [the post-term] period in the vicinity of his former outlet'. It is a fair assumption that there are no greater restrictions on the franchisee's right to deal with unsolicited customers from other territories during the post-term period than during the term of the agreement itself.

On the other hand, in para 11 of *ServiceMaster* (*see* Appendix V) the Commission took the view that it was not an appreciable restriction of competition to restrain the franchisee, post termination, from being engaged 'for a period of one year' in a competing business within any territory within which he has provided services prior to the termination of the agreement. This perhaps explains the reference in the Article to 'the territory where it has exploited the franchise' which authorises the franchisor to extend the area of the post-termination restraint to include territories, outside that allocated to the franchisee by contracts, from which the franchisee has drawn non-solicited customers. This provision may well only be relevant where franchisees visit customers in the course of the conduct of business.

Article 3(1)(*d*)

> not to acquire financial interests in the capital of a competing undertaking, which would give the franchisee the power to influence the economic conduct of such undertaking;

The interests of the franchisor and of the Commission are different here. The franchisor includes the clause, so that the franchise in the territory in question is not subordinated to the interests of a competing company. The franchisor will also be concerned that if the franchisee has an interest in a competing business there will be a risk of know-how leakage motivated by the franchisee's desire to protect his investment. The Commission's interest is in ensuring that the franchisee is not in a position to tie up the market in any given area either at the expense of the franchise network or at the expense of the competing firm. At para 10 of *ServiceMaster* (*see* Appendix V) the Commission took the view that a clause prohibiting franchisees, during the term of the agreement, from being engaged in a competing business, except through the acquisition of a financial interest not exceeding five per cent in the capital of a publicly owned company, was not an 'appreciable' restriction of competition (*see* Chapter 16).

Article 3(1)(*e*)

> to sell the goods which are the subject-matter of the franchise only to end users, to other franchisees and to resellers within other channels of distribution supplied by the manufacturer of these goods or with its consent;

Under the Regulation, it is considered reasonable, subject always to the overriding condition mentioned above, to restrict the range of traders, as distinct from ordinary customers, to whom the franchisee may resell the goods. One of the reasons for this kind of clause, according to the *Charles Jourdan* Decision (para 28, third indent — *see* Appendix V), is to maintain the unity of the network and the link, in the consumer's mind, between the Charles Jourdan Group's product and the place where it is sold. The limit on supply to 'end users', which is the expression used in the definition of 'franchise' and the exempting provision of the Regulation, is to make it plain that franchising at wholesale level, of which the Commission has no experience (recital 5), is not within the scope of the Regulation. The expression 'end user' would appear to mean the person who uses the product or service for himself either as a consumer or as part of his own activities within which the product as a service is used. However, any restriction going beyond that permitted under this Article may mean that the benefit of automatic exemption under the Regulation is not available (although *see* Chapter 12 below).

Article 3(1)(*f*)

> to use its best endeavours to sell the goods or provide the services that are the subject-matter of the franchise; to offer for sale a minimum range of goods, achieve a minimum turnover, plan its orders in advance, keep minimum stocks and provide customer and warranty services;

This obligation, subject to variations in particular circumstances, goes some way beyond the terms of the corresponding clauses usually found in franchise agreements ('best endeavours' suggest a heavier obligation under English law than the draftsmen of the Regulation may have intended).

Article 3(1)(*g*)

> to pay to the franchisor a specified proportion of its revenue for advertising and itself carry out advertising for the nature of which it shall obtain the franchisor's approval.

This clause has its origins in para 22 of *Pronuptia* (*see* Appendix IV):

> Finally, as advertising contributes towards forming the image which the public has of the sign symbolising the network, the clause which subjects all advertising by the franchisee to the franchisor's consent is also indispensable for the preservation of the network's identity, provided that it concerns only the nature of the advertising.

This is a common and reasonable clause, in one form or another; but, taken in conjunction with the prohibition on price-fixing, referred to in Chapter 11 below, it can result in some anomalies. These are discussed in Chapter 16 below. The expression 'specified proportion' is presumably a reference to the common practice of requiring franchisees to make a contribution to advertising on behalf of the return by the franchisor of X per cent of gross revenue. Some franchise systems have fixed amount contributions either to the franchisor for network advertising or to be spent by the franchisee on local advertising. On the face of it, these different approaches do not in themselves amount to a restriction of competition, particularly if the requirement can be justified as being necessary to protect the franchisor's industrial and intellectual property rights to maintain the common identity and reputation of the franchise network.

C: Other generally acceptable clauses (art 3(2))

No overriding condition, of the kind described in connection with art 3(1), applies to the list of obligations contained in art 3(2). Under the latter provisions, the following clauses in a franchise agreement, imposing obligations on the franchisee, are considered to be generally acceptable. This list is not exhaustive.

Article 3(2)(*a*)

> not to disclose to third parties the know-how provided by the franchisor; the franchisee may be held to this obligation after termination of the agreement;

Franchisors should note that the franchisee must not (under art 5(*d*)) be prevented from continuing to use the licensed know-how after termination of the agreement where the know-how has become generally known or easily accessible (provided that the franchisee himself has not made it generally known or easily accessible contrary to the terms of his contract). There appears to be no constraint on a clause requiring the franchisee to extend to his staff the duty to maintain the confidential nature of the business system.

Article 3(2)(*b*)

> to communicate to the franchisor any experience gained in exploiting the franchise and to grant [to the franchisor and to] other franchisees, a non-exclusive licence for the know-how resulting from that experience;

This provision differs from the corresponding provision in the know-how licensing regulation, which envisages a sharing of new technology on the basis of compensation from other licensees. The reason for the difference is twofold. In the first place, the know-how developed by franchisees has less of the technical character; in the second place, franchisees are part of a single network which ought, given the nature of franchising, to benefit collectively from commercial techniques developed by its members. There is a reflection of this thinking in para 14 of *ServiceMaster* (*see* Appendix V).

Article 3(2)(*c*)

> to inform the franchisor of infringements of licensed industrial or intellectual property rights, to take legal action against infringers or to assist the franchisor in any legal actions against infringers;

All the members of a franchise network have an interest in protecting the patents, the trade marks, the designs and the copyright comprised in the franchise. At the same time, the franchisee must not, under art 5(*f*) (*see* Chapter 11), be prohibited from challenging the intellectual property rights which form part of the franchise. There is no contradiction here. Either the intellectual property rights are genuine and substantial and belong or are licensed to the franchisor or are registered in his name, in which case, the franchise is genuine, valuable and worth defending, or the rights are flimsy or questionable, in which case the franchisee should be free to challenge them.

Article 3(2)(*d*)

not to use know-how licensed by the franchisor for purposes other than the exploitation of the franchise; the franchisee may be held to this obligation after termination of the agreement;

As the Commission said in para 8 of *ServiceMaster* (Appendix V): 'This field-of-use restriction is necessary to protect the franchisor's know-how because it lends itself to use with competitive services provided by either the franchisee or other competitors'. On the other hand, there are limits to the restrictions which may be imposed on the franchisee after the term of the agreement (art 5(*d*) − *see* Chapter 11).

Article 3(2)(*e*)

to attend or have its staff attend training courses arranged by the franchisor;

This provision is justified by the need to keep up common standards within the franchise network.

Article 3(2)(*f*)

to apply the commercial methods devised by the franchisor, including any subsequent modification thereof, and to use the licensed industrial or intellectual property rights;

In this passage, it will be noted that the Commission prefers to use the expression 'commercial methods' to know-how, which is both a narrower and a wider term. This recognises the invariable practice in franchising for franchisors to develop new ideas through research, development and market testing and to introduce those which are successful to the network. This is commonly done by changes to the operational manual from time to time, supplemented by training at the franchisor's training facility or at the franchisee's premises.

Article 3(2)(*g*)

to comply with the franchisor's standards for the equipment and presentation of the contract premises and/or means of transport;

As to this latter obligation, there is an illustration of the rationale in para 43 of *Yves Rocher* (Appendix V).

The obligation on the part of the franchisee to sell Yves Rocher products only in a Beauty Centre fitted out and decorated in accordance with plans and specifications which Yves Rocher causes to be drawn up at its own expense is also intended to ensure compliance with the original distribution formula communicated by the franchisor. The exterior appearance and interior lay-out of a Beauty Centre and the presentation of products are not factors which can be divorced from the methods and procedures transmitted by Yves Rocher or from the network's brand image.

In practice, there are at least four methods of requiring or allowing a franchisee to equip his premises. First, there is a turnkey operation, in which the franchisor is responsible for fitting out the premises (including equipment) which are then taken over in their entirety by the franchisee. Second, there is an arrangement by which the franchisee carries out the task, but does so with equipment supplied by the franchisor. Third, there is an arrangement by which the franchisee carries out the task, using equipment from suppliers nominated by the franchisor, with or without alternatives. Fourth, there is an arrangement by which the franchisee carries out the task, using equipment from any supplier he wishes, provided it complies with the franchisor's specifications.

Article 3(2)(*h*)

to allow the franchisor to carry out checks of the contract premises and/or means of transport, including the goods sold and the services provided, and the inventory and accounts of the franchisee;

This is reasonable enough, but if the franchisor uses his rights under a clause imposing this obligation for reasons other than protecting his intellectual property rights, maintaining the common identity and reputation of the franchised network or verifying that the franchisee abides by his obligations under the agreement, the benefit of exemption under the Regulation may be withdrawn (*see* Chapter 14 below). A similar qualification applies to obligations (*i*) and (*j*) imposed on the franchisee.

Article 3(2)(*i*)

not without the franchisor's consent to change the location of the contract premises;

If the franchisor refuses his agreement for reasons other than those referred to in the foregoing paragraph, the benefit of exemption under the Regulation may be withdrawn. In para 27 of *Charles Jourdan* (*see* Appendix V), the Commission observed that:

the clauses prohibiting the franchisee from transferring its franchise contract, subletting its shop, setting up a sub-franchise, placing its business under management by a third party or appointing a salaried shop manager without the express approval of the Charles Jourdan Group enabled the Group to ensure that the franchisee possesses the professional qualities necessary for the exercise of its functions . . .

Article 3(2)(*j*)

not without the franchisor's consent to assign the rights and obligations under the franchise agreement.

The same remarks by the Commission in *Charles Jourdan* apply to this provision as to the previous provision.

Article 3(3)

In the event that, because of particular circumstances, obligations referred to in paragraph 2 fall within the scope of Article 85(1), they shall also be exempted even if they are not accompanied by any of the obligations exempted by Article 1.

This is likely to be rather uncommon but emphasises that the provisions contained in paragraph 2 do not have anti-competitive objectives or effect.

Chapter 10

Conditions on which clauses in franchise agreements are acceptable (art 4)

A: General effect of conditions
B: Specific conditions

A: General effect of conditions

If all the clauses in a franchise agreement satisy the tests laid down in arts 1–3 of the Regulation (described in Chapters 8 and 9 above), and if the franchise agreement contains no clauses of the kind listed in arts 5 and 6 (described in Chapters 11 and 12 below), the agreement as a whole is automatically exempted by virtue of art 1. But there are three conditions which must be satisfied, if exemption is to be automatic. Breaches of these conditions may not necessarily be in the form of unacceptable clauses in the franchise agreement. They may arise from collateral arrangements, from a 'gentlemen's agreement', from a concerted practice or from an implied threat of sanctions by one or more parties in a franchise network. At all events, whether breaches of the conditions are *de facto* or *de jure*, and whether they are enshrined in the franchise agreement or not, agreement cannot qualify for automatic exemption under the Regulation.

B: Specific conditions

Article 4(*a*)

The exemption provided for in Article 1 shall apply on condition that:

    (*a*)   the franchisee is free to obtain the goods that are the subject-matter of the franchise from other franchisees; where such

goods are also distributed through another network of authorised distributors, the franchisee must be free to obtain the
goods from the latter;

Any restriction of sources of supply is potentially a restriction of
imports and *ipso facto* contrary to EEC rules. As recital 12 puts
it: 'To guarantee that competition is not eliminated for a substantial part of the goods which are the subject of the franchise, it is
necessary that parallel imports remain possible. Therefore, cross
deliveries between franchisees should always be possible'. On the
other hand, there seems to be a slight difference between the
recital and the article, inasmuch as the recital refers to cases in
which 'the franchise network is combined with another distribution system', which is not an element in the Article. However
that may be, compliance with the condition may be ensured either
by inserting a clause specifically recognising the franchisee's rights
in the matter of sources of supply or by taking care to see that
no clause is inserted and no practice allowed which may challenge
the condition.

In practice it is extremely rare to find a provision in a franchise
agreement which prohibits franchisees from selling to each other.
There is one practical issue which would arise if this practice were
to become widespread which is the possibility of double franchisee
(royalty) payments on the sale by franchisee A to franchisee B
and on the sale by franchisee B to the consumer. This issue was
addressed in para 26 of *Pronuptia* (*see* Appendix V):

it should be noted that no royalties are payable on goods that the
franchisee sells to other franchisees in the Pronuptia network.

This sort of provision is unlikely to be used widely in view of the
small number of cases in which it will be applicable and the
possibilities which it would present to franchisees for manipulating
their gross revenues.

Article 4(b)

where the franchisor obliges the franchisee to honour guarantees
for the franchisor's goods, that obligation shall apply in respect of
such goods supplied by any member of the franchised network or

other distributors which give a similar guarantee, in the common market;

This provision stems, at least in part, from the many cases under the EEC rules applying to distribution arrangements (the *ETA* case (31/85) is an example), in which the Commission has condemned the partitioning of the market as regards the honouring of guarantees. In a common market, the purchaser of a product covered by guarantee should not find that there are parts of the common market in which the guarantee will not be honoured. This would be completely contrary to the principle, described in Chapter 2, of a Community-wide market for traders and consumers. The condition is therefore reasonable. As it stands, however, it appears that the franchisor should reach a decision on whether to include the obligation as to guarantees in the franchise agreement, in which case the clause in the agreement should spell out the consequential obligations on the franchisee's part, or to omit such a clause altogether. Either way, the condition laid down in art 4(*b*) will have been met. It should also be noted that the condition as to guarantees applies only to goods and not to services.

Article 4(*c*)

the franchisee is obliged to indicate [the status of his outlet] as an independent undertaking; this indication shall however not interfere with the common identity of the franchised network resulting in particular from the common name or shop sign and uniform appearance of the contract premises and/or means of transport.

As the Commission said, in para 35 of *Pronuptia* (Appendix V), 'consumers can tell that they are dealing with independent traders, who can be held responsible' (for example, for guarantees, product safety and the like). To be on the safe side, franchisors are probably well advised not only to include a specific clause in the agreement, ensuring that there is manifest compliance with the condition, but also to ensure compliance in practice. Although not the subject of this book it is relevant to mention that at the time of writing there is a proposal for a Council directive on the supply of defective services which would impose (as the proposal stands) joint and several liability on franchisors, master franchisors and franchisees for the supply of defective services. This proposal is intended to deal with the same issue as that which is dealt with by this condition but abandons the Commission's view that notice to the consumer will suffice.

Chapter 11

Unacceptable clauses in franchise agreements (art 5)

A: Circumstances preventing grant of exemption
B: Clauses preventing grant of exemption

A: Circumstances preventing grant of exemption

In art 5 of the Regulation there is a list of seven cases, (a)–(g), in which agreements cannot benefit from exemption under the Regulation. The first of these cases arises independently of the existence of any particular clause in a franchise agreement. The other six are related to specific clauses which may appear in a franchise agreement.

Article 5(a)

The exemption granted by Article 1 shall not apply where:

(a) undertakings producing goods or providing services which are identical or are considered by users as equivalent in view of their characteristics, price and intended use, enter into franchise agreements in respect of such goods or services;

It is evident that this condition does not arise from the content of the franchise agreement, but from the fact that a franchise agreement is entered into at all. According to recital 13 (*see* Chapter 7), the purpose of this provision is to prevent market sharing between competing manufacturers. Franchises must not, in other words, be used as a device with which to defeat the rules on competition.

It is noted that the provision does not in any way limit the undertakings to each other; it seems only to apply if the undertakings choose to use the franchise method of marketing.

This provision contrasts with similar provisions in the block exemption regulations for exclusive distribution (1983/83) and exclusive purchasing (1984/83) relating to manufacturers, which respectively refer to 'reciprocal exclusive distribution agreements between themselves' and 'reciprocal exclusive purchasing agreements between themselves'.

B: Clauses preventing grant of exemption

Article 5(*b*)

> without prejudice to Article 2(*e*) and Article 3(1)(*b*), the franchisee is prevented from obtaining supplies of goods of a quality equivalent to those offered by the franchisor;

Thus the inclusion in a franchise agreement of a clause which restricts the franchisee's sources of supply takes the agreement outside the scope of the Regulation, except where:

- —the goods are competing with the franchisor's goods which are the subject-matter of the franchise, and the rules on accessories and spare parts do not apply (*see* Chapter 9, Section A); or
- —it is impracticable, owing to the nature of the goods which are the subject-matter of the franchise, to apply objective quality specifications for the purpose of making it possible to obtain equivalent goods from other suppliers (*see* Chapter 9, Section B); or
- —ensuring respect for [these specifications] may also, in view of the large number of franchisees, involve too great a cost (para 21, *Pronuptia* — *see* Appendix IV).

In its Decisions in both *Yves Rocher* and *ServiceMaster*, the Commission provided a rationale for the foregoing rules. In para 45 of *Yves Rocher* (Appendix V), the Commission said that:

> The obligation on the franchisee to sell only products bearing the Yves Rocher trademark — except in the case of accessories previously approved by the franchisor — is inherent in the very nature of the

Yves Rocher distribution formula, the purpose of which is to enable independent traders to sell the complete range of Yves Rocher products using a sign, a trademark and symbols, as well as trading methods which have proved effective. The retailing of products bearing trademarks other than that of the franchisor exposes Yves Rocher to the risk of the use of their know-how for the benefit of competing producers and would detract from the identity of the network, which is symbolised by the Yves Rocher sign.

Slightly different considerations applied in *ServiceMaster* (para 17 — *see* Appendix V). As the Commission said:

The franchisee's obligation to purchase certain cleaning equipment and certain chemicals used in the operation of the business from Service-Master or other suppliers nominated or approved by ServiceMaster ... is essential for the efficient working of the business and acts as a form of quality control. The obligation does not prevent franchisees from obtaining supplies of equipment and goods of equivalent quality from third-party suppliers. ServiceMaster will not withhold its approval of suppliers proposed by franchisees [whose products meet] the requirements of safety, non-toxicity, biodegradability and effectiveness.

The Commission recognised the special importance of quality control in service franchise systems.

Article 5(*c*)

without prejudice to Article 2(*e*), the franchisee is obliged to sell, or use in the process of providing services, goods manufactured by the franchisor or third parties designated by the franchisor and the franchisor refuses, for reasons other than protecting the franchisor's industrial or intellectual property rights, or maintaining the common identity and reputation of the franchised network, to designate as authorised manufacturers third parties proposed by the franchisee;

By itself, the clause may be permissible in certain circumstances, for example, in those envisaged under art 2(*e*). The franchisor's refusal may also be permissible, where he can show that intellectual property rights or the common identity and reputation of the network are at issue. But there is a danger for franchisors where the combination of circumstances operates in the manner indicated above. Subject to the expressed reasons the franchisee must not be unnecessarily restricted in his sources of supply, within or outside the terms of the franchise agreement.

Article 5(*d*)

the franchisee is prevented from continuing to use the licensed know-how after termination of the agreement where the know-how has become generally known or easily accessible, other than by breach of an obligation by the franchisee;

Here again, the condition implicit in this provision depends not only on the existence of a specific clause in the agreement, in this case an otherwise legitimate restriction on the disclosure of confidential know-how (art 3(2)(*a*) — *see* Chapter 9, Section C), but also on circumstances extraneous to the agreement itself. The circumstances are the entry of the know-how into the public domain, other than by the action of the franchisee himself in breach of a disclosure clause. (What the position is when the know-how has been disclosed by another franchisee is not entirely clear.) It is arguable that this provision is redundant, since information which is generally known or easily accessible is not know-how as defined in art 1(3)(*f*) of the Regulation (*see* Chapter 1). Franchisors are well advised to be cautious about the wording of any post-term restrictions in the light of art 5(*c*). The wording of the provision which refers to the franchisee being 'prevented' suggests that one can prohibit the franchisee from using the know-how post-termination without qualification. The Article would be infringed if the franchisor sought to enforce the contractual provision when the know-how had become generally known or easily accessible.

Article 5(*e*)

the franchisee is restricted by the franchisor, directly or indirectly, in the determination of sale prices for the goods or services which are the subject-matter of the franchise, without prejudice to the possibility for the franchisor of recommending sale prices;

This provision is one of the strictest in the Commission's whole body of anti-trust rules, whether in relation to franchising or to any other commercial sector. Price-fixing is anathema to the authorities responsible for competition policy. The use of the expression 'directly or indirectly' suggests that the restriction may be expressed in the form of a clause in the agreement or may arise in some other way. Whichever form the restriction takes, it precludes automatic exemption of the agreement under art 1 of the Regulation, but leaves open the possibility that the franchisor may recommend sale prices. All this is in line with para 25 of *Pronuptia* (*see* Appendix IV) to the effect that 'the franchisor may communicate indicative prices to franchisees, always on condition that, as between the franchisor and franchisees or between franchisees, there is no concerted practice with a view to the effective application of these prices'. (As to concerted practices, *see* Appendix VI.) At all events, a clause in a franchise agreement restricting the franchisee's freedom to determine prices takes the agreement out of the scope of the Regulation and makes it most unlikely that the agreement will qualify even for individual exemption. There have been extremely few cases in which price-fixing in any form has been accepted by the Commission or Court of Justice under the EEC rules on competition. It is up to the franchisor and his advisors to decide whether he should include in the franchise agreement a clause specifically preserving the franchisee's rights in this regard; there may be some advantage in putting the matter beyond doubt. A great deal of care is needed, however, when drafting a clause covering recommended prices, which can be defeated if the franchisor behaves in a manner which leads one to the conclusion that in practice price recommendations are being enforced. A franchisor who is giving business and financial advice to franchisees will inevitably comment on prices being charged if the franchisee is not achieving the projected margins. Such a franchisor must take care to ensure that such advice cannot amount to the fixing and enforcement of prices. The fixing of maximum prices by the franchisor is not acceptable in the context of this Regulation: it may not be restrictive of competition in the context of some types of business, but can have the indirect effect of setting standard prices.

Article 5(*f*)

the franchisor prohibits the franchisee from challenging the validity of the industrial or intellectual property rights which form part of the franchise, without prejudice to the possibility for the franchisor of terminating the agreement in such a case;

No-challenge clauses, as they are sometimes called, are unacceptable in agreements seeking to qualify for exemption under the Regulation. It suffices, from the Commission's point of view, if the franchisor reserves the sanction of terminating the contract in the event of a challenge to his intellectual property rights. The Article does not tackle the question whether acknowledgment or disclaimer clauses can be caught. A clause commonly found in franchise agreements, under which the franchisee is required to acknowledge the validity of the franchisor's intellectual property rights or something similar is almost certain to be regarded as a no-challenge clause in (rather thin) disguise. It would be foolish to include in a franchise agreement a clause likely to prejudice the legality of the agreement under the EEC rules on competition for the sake of a relatively narrow safeguard. The franchisor's best safeguard is to ensure, before entering into franchise agreements, that his intellectual property rights are soundly based and well protected.

Article 5(*g*)

> franchisees are obliged not to supply within the common market the goods or services which are the subject-matter of the franchise to end users because of their place of residence.

This is a classic instance of what recital 13 calls a restriction on competition for which there is no general presumption that it will lead to the positive effects required by the provisions of art 85(3) of the EEC Treaty on exemption. As the Commission said in para 37 of *Pronuptia* (Appendix V), franchisees 'compete with one another, because they can sell to any customer, whether resident in the allotted territory or coming from outside it . . .'. The issue was most relevant in *ServiceMaster* (paras 22 and 27 — *see* Appendix V) where franchisees visit customers to provide services. The Commission concluded that the following provisions fell within art 85(1):

> The combined effect of the clause which prohibits the franchisee from setting up further outlets outside his own territory, and the territorial protection clause which prevents the franchisee from actively seeking customers outside his territory, results in a certain degree of market-sharing between the franchisees, thus restricting competition within the ServiceMaster network.

> This territorial protection is, however, limited by two elements: the franchisee holds a non-exclusive right only within his territory with regard to ServiceMaster itself and each franchisee is entitled to provide services to non-solicited customers outside his territory[;]

and in justifying the application of art 85(3) of the EEC Treaty:

> the limited territorial protection does not grant the franchisees any marketing or customer exclusivity. Franchisees are free to provide services to non-solicited customers resident outside their own territory. This brings about a certain degree of price competition between franchisees who are free to determine their sales prices.

Chapter 12

The treatment of clauses not covered by the regulation (art 6)

A: Clauses not covered by the Regulation
B: Procedure for dealing with agreements containing clauses not covered by the Regulation

A: Clauses not covered by the Regulation

Some franchise agreements fall nearly, but not quite, within the scope of the provisions of arts 1–5 of the block exemption regulation; art 6 provides a special procedure for dealing with them.

A franchise agreement, which

—meets the conditions set out in art 4 (*see* Chapter 10) and
—contains none of the clauses set out in art 5 (*see* Chapter 11),

may nevertheless contain clauses which restrict competition and are not covered by art 2 (Chapter 9) or art 3(3) (Chapter 10). If so, the agreement does not qualify for automatic exemption under art 1, although there is a special procedure for obtaining exemption. This procedure is not available if any of the conditions set out in art 4 are not met, nor if any of the circumstances set out in art 5 apply to the agreement: in such cases, the agreement must either be amended or submitted to the Commission for individual exemption.

The special procedure is a compromise between automatic exemption and individual notification. Essentially, it involves individual notification, but results in automatic exemption if the Commission does not oppose it within a period of approximately six months. It is a familiar procedure in some other block exemption regulations — such as the patent licensing and know-how licensing regulations — and is sometimes referred to as the 'opposition procedure'. A description of the special procedure is in the following paragraphs.

B: Procedure for dealing with agreements containing clauses not covered by the Regulation

Article 6(1)

The exemption provided for in Article 1 shall also apply to franchise agreements which fulfil the conditions laid down in Article 4 and include obligations restrictive of competition which are not covered by Articles 2 and 3(3) and do not fall within the scope of Article 5, on condition that the agreements in question are notified to the Commission in accordance with the provisions of Commission Regulation No 27 and that the Commission does not oppose such exemption within a period of six months.

To notify the agreement, the normal notification procedure described in Chapter 3 above should be followed, subject to the provisions of art 6(3)(*a*). The onus is then on the Commission to oppose the application for exemption: if it does not do so, the agreement is automatically exempted.

Article 6(2)

The period of six months shall run from the date on which the notification is received by the Commission. Where, however, the notification is made by registered post, the period shall run from the date shown on the postmark of the place of posting.

Notifications may also be delivered by hand, in which case the Commission normally gives a receipt, confirming the date of delivery.

Article 6(3)(*a*)(*b*)

Paragraph 1 shall apply only if:

    (*a*) express reference is made to this Article in the notification or in a communication accompanying it;

Form A/B (see Chapter 3) does in fact include the question 'Do you claim that this application may benefit from an opposition procedure?'

(b) the information furnished with the notification is complete and in accordance with the facts.

This is a general requirement applying to all notifications under Regulations 17/62 and 27/62.

Article 6(4)

The benefit of paragraph 1 can be claimed for agreements notified before the entry into force of this Regulation by submitting a communication to the Commission referring expressly to this Article 6 and to the notification. Paragraphs 2 and 3(*b*) shall apply *mutatis mutandis*.

The date on which the Regulation came into force was 1 February 1989 (art 9).

Article 6(5)

The Commission may oppose exemption. It shall oppose exemption if it receives a request to do so from a Member State within three months of the forwarding to the Member State of the notification referred to in paragraph 1 or the communication referred to in paragraph 4. The request must be justified on the basis of considerations relating to the competition rules of the Treaty.

In the absence of a request by a Member State, the Commission acts at its own discretion. The Commission may not be totally opposed to exemption in any given case, but may formally oppose exemption to give time for considering possible amendments to the agreement, in which case the provisions of art 6(8) below apply.

Article 6(6)

The Commission may withdraw its opposition to the exemption at any time. However, where that opposition was raised at the request of a Member State, it may be withdrawn only after consultation [sic: sc 'with'] of the advisory Committee on Restrictive Practices and Dominant Positions.

The Committee referred to in this paragraph was established under art 10 ('Liaison with the Authorities of Member States') of Regulation 17/62. It comprises officials appointed by the Member States.

Article 6(7)

If the opposition is withdrawn because the undertakings concerned have shown that the conditions of Article 85(3) are fulfilled, the exemption shall apply from the date of the notification.

The importance of the date from which the exemption takes effect has already been noted (*see* Chapter 3, Section C).

Article 6(8)

If the opposition is withdrawn because the undertakings concerned have amended the agreement so that the conditions of Article 85(3) are fulfilled, the exemption shall apply from the date on which the amendments take effect.

In general, it will be the Commission's aim to secure the parties' agreement, if possible, to amendments to any offending clauses; this may be a matter of direct negotiation with Commission officials.

Article 6(9)

If the Commission opposes exemption and its opposition is not withdrawn, the effects of the notification shall be governed by the provisions of Regulation No 17.

In particular, arts 6, 8 and 9 of Regulation 17/62, governing the nature, duration and consequences of Commission decisions, are applicable. This assumes that an opposition is indeed a decision. The matter is not entirely clear; it is not covered specifically by the terms of the parent regulation. Whether the opposition procedure, under the present Regulation or any of the other block exemption regulations, is *intra vires* the parent measure is a matter which only the Court of Justice can determine, if a Member State or an interested party with a *locus standi* ever decides to challenge it.

Chapter 13

Confidentiality of information (art 7)

A: Provisions of the Regulation
B: Other rules governing confidentiality

A: Provisions of the Regulation

Under art 7 of the Regulation, the Commission lays down rules which bind itself and other authorities. In other words, the Article imposes no legal duties on parties to franchise agreements, but does in effect confer rights on them, in respect of the confidential nature of the information acquired in the course of the procedure envisaged under art 6 (described in Chapter 12 above).

Article 7(1)–(3)

1. Information acquired pursuant to Article 6 shall be used only for the purposes of this Regulation.
2. The Commission and the authorities of the Member States,

their officials and other servants, shall not disclose information acquired by them pursuant to this Regulation of a kind that is covered by the obligation of professional secrecy.

A breach of this prohibition could, in principle, be the subject of an action under the second paragraph of art 215 of the EEC Treaty.

3. Paragraphs 1 and 2 shall not prevent publication of general information or surveys which do not contain information relating to particular undertakings or associations of undertakings.

The Commission prepares, or invites experts to prepare, surveys of special sectors affected by the EEC rules on competition.

Particulars of these surveys are usually carried in the Commission's annual reports on competition policy.

B: Other rules governing confidentiality

To a large extent, the provisions of art 7 of the Regulation are already laid down in the Treaty itself, art 214 of which extends the prohibition to officials 'even after their duties have ceased'. Under this Article professional secrecy includes in particular information about undertakings, their business relations or their cost components. Regulation 17/62 has a provision (art 20) corresponding closely to the provisions of art 7 of the franchise regulation.

Chapter 14

Withdrawal of the benefit of the regulation (art 8)

A: Principle of withdrawal of the benefit of the Regulation
B: Circumstances in which the benefit is withdrawn

A: Principle of withdrawal of the benefit of the Regulation

There is provision in the Regulation for the Commission to withdraw the benefit of automatic exemption (that is, under art 1) or of the partly automatic exemption (that is, under art 6) where it finds in a particular case that an agreement exempted by the Regulation nevertheless has certain undesirable effects. The Commission may learn of these effects from a discontented franchisee, from a competing trader, from a dissatisfied customer, from a public authority in the Member States or from its own sources of information. The result of withdrawing the benefit of exemption is to create an infringement of the rules on competition and expose the parties to the penalties for infringement, unless the cause of the problem is removed. In addition there will be the consequences of trying to operate with an agreement of which the validity can effectively be challenged, rendering the restriction unenforceable.

For the most part, the circumstances envisaged in the following provisions of the Regulation cannot be put right simply by an amendment of the agreement, since they are largely extraneous; in any case, the provisions presuppose that at an earlier stage the clauses in the agreement complied with the terms of the Regulation. The list of five cases in which the benefit of exemption under the Regulation may be withdrawn is not exhaustive.

B: Circumstances in which the benefit is withdrawn

Article 8(*a*)

The Commission may withdraw the benefit of this Regulation, pursuant to Article 7 of Regulation No 19/65/EEC, where it finds in a particular case that an agreement exempted by this Regulation nevertheless has certain effects which are incompatible with the conditions laid down in Article 85(3) of the EEC Treaty, and in particular where territorial protection is awarded to the franchisee and:

(*a*)   access to the relevant market or competition therein is significantly restricted by the cumulative effect of parallel networks of similar agreements established by competing manufacturers or distributors;

This is one aspect of the 'economic context' (or the 'structure of the relevant market' as recital 15 puts it), against which the Court of Justice said in the *Pronuptia* case that franchise agreements had to be examined. The relevant market is the market for a certain category of goods or services in a given geographical area. There is much room for argument in any given case about the extent to which competition is in fact restricted in the circumstances described here, since the normal circumstances in which franchise networks operate are highly competitive; although it is possible for a market to be saturated by competitive franchising activities, it is somewhat rare. As is the case with the provisions of art 5(*a*) (*see* Chapter 11), there is nothing in the provision to link the particular franchisor to any one or more of the parallel networks or those who establish them.

Article 8(*b*)

the goods or services which are the subject-matter of the franchise do not face, in a substantial part of the common market, effective competition from goods or services which are identical or considered by users as equivalent in view of their characteristics, price and intended use;

In practice, most franchise networks operate in competitive markets and are themselves competitive. However, it is conceivable that a franchisor may see a franchise network as an instrument of monopoly, and this provision is designed to prevent that from happening. On the other hand, this provision could, if literally interpreted, lead to the absurd result that a franchise network with a genuinely original, perhaps even unique, product or service to offer might be inhibited from operating simply because there was nothing comparable, in consumers' eyes, to compete with it. Since the provision is discretionary, it may be expected that the Commission would not invoke it in these circumstances. Alternatively the franchisor would be faced with the expense of making a notification seeking exemption, perhaps under the opposition procedure. This added cost to the establishment of a new business could be a fatal deterrent if capital resources were limited. The elimination or restriction of new entrants in business is in principle incompatible with the objectives of competition law.

Article 8(c)

> the parties, or one of them, [to the agreement] prevent end users, because of their place of residence, from obtaining, directly or through intermediaries, the goods or services which are the subject-matter of the franchise within the common market, or use differences in specifications concerning those goods or services in different Member States, to isolate markets;

Whether or not these practices are common in the field of franchising, they are both implicitly caught by the wording of art 85(1) of the EEC Treaty, which prohibits among other things agreements or practices which limit markets or apply dissimilar conditions to equivalent transactions to other trading parties. In several areas of Community law — the directives on public contracts are a case in point — the Commission has tried to prevent barriers to 'inter-state' trade trading from being created by means of specifications specially designed either to favour the products of a particular Member State or to exclude the products originating from other Member States. If a franchisor draws up specifications with this object, the Commission may not unreasonably invoke art 8. The first part of the Article ties in with the provision relating to end users in art 5(g) (*see* Chapter 11), which prohibits refusals to supply to end users because of their place of residence.

Article 8(d)

> franchisees engage in concerted practices relating to the sale prices of the goods or services which are the subject-matter of the franchise;

In other words, these concerted practices are not only an infringement of the rules on competition in themselves, as a direct result of the provisions of art 85(1) of the EEC Treaty; they also run the risk that offending provisions are void. (For the meaning of 'concerted practices', *see* Appendix VI.) To save the agreement, the concerted practices must be stopped: probably a threat by the Commission to invoke art 8 will suffice. Franchisors, however, need to be in a position to do something about franchisees who engage in such practices, advisedly by specifically prohibiting them from doing so in the franchise agreement.

Article 8(*e*)

> the franchisor uses its right to check the contract premises and means of transport, or refuses its agreement to requests by the franchisee to move the contract premises or assign its rights and obligations under the franchise agreement, for reasons other than protecting the franchisor's industrial or intellectual property rights, maintaining the common identity and reputation of the franchised network or verifying that the franchisee abides by its obligations under the agreement.

Like several of the preceding provisions, this arises, not from the presence in the agreement of unacceptable clauses, but from the misuse of powers conferred on the franchisor under an otherwise legitimate agreement. It is right that the franchisor should carry out the requisite checks, if the efficiency and consistency of the network are to be maintained. However, it is quite wrong if, for example, these checks are used to apply pressure on a franchisee to keep his prices in line with those of other franchisees. The normal sort of controls which one finds in franchise agreements should not cause any difficulties. Controls on new entrants to the network by sale of business by the franchisee can be justified by the need to protect the franchisor's industrial or intellectual property rights and to maintain the common identity and reputation of the franchise network. The same principle would apply in the case of a provision or practice relating to a change of premises. It must be emphasised that the franchisor must in practice be able to justify its actions as being necessary to protect such rights, identity and reputation.

Chapter 15

Procedure for obtaining exemption

A: Questions to be asked
B: Modification of agreement or arrangements
C: Automatic exemption without notification
D: Automatic exemption after notification
E: Individual exemption after notification

A: Questions to be asked

When a franchise network is being planned, and an agreement between the franchisor and the respective franchisees is being drafted, a series of questions can usefully be asked to establish whether the arrangements which are contemplated are going to be consistent with the EEC rules on competition.

(1)   Is the agreement unlikely to affect trade between the Member States of the European Community? (*See* Chapter 5.)

(2)   Does the agreement fall within the scope of the *de minimis* rules? (*See* Chapter 5.)

(3)   Do the arrangements covered by the agreement really constitute a franchise, as defined in the Regulation? (*See* Chapter 8.)

(4)   Is the agreement in question really a franchise agreement, as defined in the Regulation? (*See* Chapter 8.)

(5)   Does the package of information and guidance provided by the franchisor meet the definition of know-how in the Regulation? (*See* Chapter 8.)

(6)   Does the agreement contain one or more of the clauses (or sets of clauses) which qualify the agreement for exemption under the Regulation? (*See* Chapter 9, Section A.)

(7)   If the agreement contains any of the clauses, which are

allowed under the Regulation on condition that they are necessary to protect the franchisor's intellectual property rights or to maintain the common identity and reputation of the franchised network, is that condition fulfilled? (*See* Chapter 9, Section B.)

(8) Does the agreement meet the three specific conditions on which exemption under the Regulation applies? (*See* Chapter 10.)

(9) Does the agreement contain any clauses, or operate in any circumstances, which make it impossible for exemption under the Regulation to apply? (*See* Chapter 11.)

(10) Does the agreement, while meeting the three conditions referred to in Question 8 above, contain any clauses which:
  (a) include obligations restricting competition, and
  (b) are not covered by the provisions of the Regulation listing acceptable clauses, and
  (c) are not covered by the provisions of the Regulation listing unacceptable clauses or circumstances
    (*See* Chapter 12.)

(11) Is there:
  (a) ready access to, and
  (b) effective competition in
    the product and geographical markets in which the franchise network is planning to operate? (*See* Chapter 14.)

B: Modification of agreement or arrangements

If the answer to (1) or (2) above is affirmative, there is probably no need to consider further whether the agreement is compatible with the EEC rules on competition.

If the answer to any of the questions (3)–(8) inclusive is negative, it is a matter for consideration whether the agreement cannot be amended in some way to bring it in line with the requirements of the Regulation. This is partly a legal and partly a commercial decision. From the point of view of the legal adviser, the franchise arrangements will have a far smoother passage, in terms of compliance with EC law, if the agreement matches the Regulation; but, from the commercial point of view, it would be foolish to put the franchise arrangements into a legal straitjacket, if there is at least a reasonable chance that the agreement will comply with the requirements of EC law outside the terms of the Regulation. In other words, if the franchisor's commercial requirements make it highly undesirable to amend the agreement, it is open to the franchisor to notify the agreement and have it considered under the procedures referred to in Section D or E below.

If the answer to (9) is affirmative, it is essential either that the agreement should be amended, or that the circumstances in question should be changed, since the agreement will not otherwise qualify for exemption under the Regulation and will be unlikely to qualify for individual exemption (described in Section E below).

On the other hand, if the answer to (10) is affirmative, the same considerations apply as to the negative answers to questions (3)–(8): that is to say, it is open to the franchisor to amend the agreement, so that it complies with the Regulation, or to notify the agreement and take his chance on Commission approval or non-opposition.

Finally, if the answer to (11) is negative, there may be little the franchisor can do to put right the agreement: he may have to recast the franchise arrangements in some way, so that they operate in a more competitive product or service market.

C: Automatic exemption without notification

If the franchisor and his advisers are satisfied that the franchise agreement, whether in its original form or after being amended in the light of the considerations set out above, complies with the Regulation, it may be entered into without any need to notify it. (This does not prevent a party to the agreement in a particular case from seeking a formal decision by the Commission: then the procedure referred to in Section D below applies. The advantage of this course of action is to be on the safe side, if there is any doubt about the agreement being eligible for automatic exemption. The disadvantages are that there may be delay, as well as a degree of uncertainty in the meantime.) Although the foregoing statement of the law may be inferred from the procedural rules, it is in fact based on recital 16 of the Regulation. This would also not prevent the franchisee from challenging whether the agreement does benefit from the Regulation.

D: Automatic exemption after notification

This is the procedure which may be followed when the franchise agreement contains clauses of the kind indicated in (10) in Section A above. The procedure is explained in Chapter 12. The agreement must be notified, but, if the Commission does not oppose it within a period of six months, it is automatically exempted.

E: Individual exemption after notification

This is the procedure which may be followed when the franchise agreement contains clauses which are not covered by the Regulation and do not meet all the conditions implicit in (10) above. It is the standard procedure for seeking a Commission decision in an individual case and is described in Chapter 3. The agreement has to be notified; the Commission publishes in the *Official Journal* a notice about the application for exemption; observations are invited from third parties, within a stated time-limit; and in due course, which may be between six and twenty-four months or longer, the Commission may issue a Decision. Publicity, delay and an uncertain outcome are the main drawbacks of this procedure.

Chapter 16

Review of the Regulation

A: Merits of the Regulation
B: Problems which remain

A: Merits of the Regulation

By contrast with many Community regulations, the franchising
block exemption regulation is well drafted and achieves its main
objectives. There are some infelicities of translation; there are
some slight inconsistencies in the wording; and, in the English
version published in the *Official Journal*, there are many typo-
graphical errors. (A disconcerting error is the use of the word
'designed', when the word 'designated' is clearly intended; this
occurs in art 3(1)(*b*), though not in art 5(*c*), where similar wording
is used.) Nevertheless, the Regulation has greatly clarified the
legal position, to the great benefit of franchisors, franchisees, their
advisers and other parties; the very fact that there is a regulation
in force at all means that an incalculable number of individual
applications will be saved. The Regulation takes to its logical
conclusion most of the points made by the Court of Justice in
Pronuptia and presents in systematic or codified form the reasoning employed by the Commission in the individual franchise cases
with which it dealt in the five years after *Pronuptia*.

B: Problems which remain

Perhaps not surprisingly, the Regulation does not cover com-
prehensively all the problems associated with reconciling the
objectives of franchising and the objectives of the EEC rules on
competition.

Post-term restraints

For example, although art 3(1) tackles, in sub-paragraphs (*c*) and (*d*), the problem of both in-term and post-term restraints on the franchisee conducting or participating in a competing business, there are many variants of the way in which this can arise, which may not be adequately covered by the terms of the Regulation. The Regulation does however create a problem in times of enforcement of the post-termination restraints. Sub-paragraph (*c*) permits the franchisor to require the franchisee 'not to engage directly or indirectly in any similar business in a territory where it would compete with a member of the franchised network, including the franchisor; the franchisee may be held to this obligation after termination of the agreement, for a reasonable period which may not exceed one year, in the territory where it has exploited the franchise'. The question arises as to whether the phrase 'in a territory where it would compete with a member of the franchised network' includes the territory allocated to the franchisee. This particular issue is not fully addressed in any of the five Commission decisions. In *Pronuptia* (para 25(i), first indent — *see* Appendix IV) there is a prohibition on the franchisee from competing 'in the same area or in any other area where he would be in competition with another Pronuptia outlet'. In *ServiceMaster* (para 10 — *see* Appendix V) 'the franchisee's obligation during the term of the agreement not to be engaged in a competing business' is without reference to area or other outlets. In *Yves Rocher* (para 26 — *see* Appendix V) 'the franchisee is forbidden to carry on either directly or indirectly, whether in return for payment or not, any business which competes with an Yves Rocher Beauty Centre'. If it was the intention to include the territory allocated to the franchisee in the phrase in question it would have been relatively easy to use the Pronuptia wording and put the matter beyond doubt. It must surely be arguable that the phrase means other members of the franchised network since it would not make sense for the franchisee to compete with himself. However, in sub-paragraph (*d*) the franchisor can only restrain the franchisee during the time from acquiring 'financial interests in the capital of a competing undertaking, which would give the franchisee the power to influence the economic conduct of such undertaking'. These two provisions raise a number of questions to which it is difficult to find a satisfactory answer.

(1)   If the franchisee is prevented under sub-paragraph (c) from having an interest in a business in a territory where it would compete with a member of the franchised network or the franchisor, can he be prevented from having an interest in a competing business which carries on business in such a territory? Or, if sub-paragraph (c) does not include the franchisee's territory as is possible, is the competing business in which the franchisee has an interest limited to one which competes only in the franchisee's territory?

(2)   Since the franchisee can be prevented for a reasonable period not exceeding one year post-termination from being 'engaged directly or indirectly in a similar business . . . in the territory where it has exploited the franchise' does this mean that the franchisee could be in breach if it continues to own an interest in a competing business which it was permitted to own pursuant to sub-paragraph (d)?

The answer to these questions appears to be 'yes', but it may be difficult to persuade a national court to require the franchisee to divest itself of the investment in the competing business post-termination. The answer ultimately will be a matter for the national courts when interpreting the provisions in a franchise agreement. In the meantime, pending the development of case law, the best course is to repeat the provisions in the Regulations so as to benefit from the exemption.

Products

Again, the Regulation leaves unresolved some of the problems, both for the franchisor and for the franchisee, over the choice of products. The combined effect of arts 2(e), 3(1)(b) and 5(c) is to leave unclear in practice the dividing-line between products which the franchisor may insist on the franchisee purchasing and using. Moreover, there are many products to which it is extremely difficult to apply objective tests of equivalence, as art 3(1)(b) recognises; the scope for interpreting subjectively whether goods are equivalent, whether they are necessary for maintaining the common identity or reputation of the franchise network, whether they are no more than accessories, and so on, is almost unlimited. Perhaps these are matters which cannot, in the last event, be determined by the provisions of a Regulation, but only by the Commission or Court of Justice arbitrating on specific cases, although the franchisor is put on notice that the Regulation does not ensure that he is fully protected as regards the choice of products. Article 3(1)(*f*) permits the franchisor to specify the goods or services which are the subject-matter of the franchise which is of course essential if the common identity and reputation of the franchise network are to be protected.

Price recommendations/advertising

It is clear enough from the Regulation that, while price-fixing is prohibited, price recommendations are permissible. It is also clear that the franchisee may carry out advertising, for the nature of which the franchisor's approval must be obtained. What is not so clear is how far advertisements for the franchise goods or services may carry an indication of the prices to be charged. In principle, the franchisee's own advertisements will carry the prices he himself is prepared to charge, irrespective of the prices recommended by the franchisor or charged by other franchisees. In practice, the advertising which the franchisor promotes must not convey the impression that the prices are fixed throughout the franchise network, and the advertising which the individual franchisee, or any group of franchisees, promotes must not convey the impression that there has been a concerted practice in fixing the prices referred to in advertisements. The franchisor may protect his position by specifically referring to recommended prices and by indicating that prices may vary from one area to another or by indicating that prices are only available at participating outlets while leaving franchisees entirely free to decide whether to participate; but, from the provisions of the Regulation, it is not absolutely certain that this wording will suffice. Nor is it certain that franchisees are safe: any reference in an advertisement to a common price, even with local variations, looks rather like the result of a concerted practice. It is, by the way, a weakness of the Regulation that it does not clarify the position on concerted practices; this is probably not the fault of the Commission, which does not have the legal power to change by legislation what has been decided by the Court of Justice. As Appendix VI shows, the rules on concerted practices have been laid down by the Court.

In three other respects, there may be said to be gaps in the Regulation. In the first place, the Regulation defines the franchise agreement between two undertakings, the franchisor and the franchisee. At first sight, this is adequate; but does it allow for the cases in which the franchisee is a company and the directors and shareholders of the franchisee company are joined as parties to the agreement as an additional guarantee to the franchisor of their viability and to accept restrictions on their use of the know-how and their ability unfairly to compete with the franchisor and other franchisees in the franchise network? On this point, the Regulation is bound by the terms of its parent Regulation 19/65, which specifies that the agreements qualifying for block exemption must be between two parties only. Fortunately the issue has been considered by the European Court in *Hydrotherm* (170/83) in which the Court held that the term 'undertaking' as used in the context of competition law must be understood as designating an economic unit for the purposes of the subject-matter of the agreement even if in law that economic unit consists of several parties legal or natural. In that case Regulation 67/67, which had similar wording, was applied on the basis that several contracting undertakings should be treated as one if they constituted a single economic unit for the purposes of the agreement. The Court stated, there is virtually no competition between the undertakings participating concurrently as a single party in the agreement. Provided, therefore, that on the facts the shareholders and directors can be considered as a single economic unit with the franchise there would be no problem.

In the second place, although art 1(3)(c) defines, and art 1(2) makes general provision for, master franchise agreements, it does so on a limited understanding of the use of the term. The definition of 'master franchise agreement' mentions only 'the right to exploit a franchise for the purposes of concluding franchise agreements with third parties, the franchisees'. It would seem clear that if a master franchise agreement provides for the master franchise (sub-franchisor) only to sub-franchise outlets and not to carry on the franchise business itself except for purposes of pilot operations, this is within the definition. The pilot operation would be exploiting the franchise for the purpose of concluding franchise agreements with third parties. However, if, as is often the case, the master franchise agreement authorises the sub-franchisor to carry on the franchised business itself and/or to sub-franchise out its option, that would not meet the requirements of the definition and the benefits of the Regulation could not be obtained. The agreement would have to be for a specific exemption — the opposition procedure would not be available. There is no point in becoming creative by having the sub-franchisor sub-franchise to a subsidiary since in the light of *Hydrotherm* it is arguable that the sub-franchisor and its subsidiary are one undertaking and there is not the third party necessary for the definition exemption.

In the third place, the Regulation makes no provision for development agreements. These are in essence option arrangements under which the developer secures the right to open an agreed number of franchised outlets over an agreed period of time within an exclusive area. They pose the risk of running counter to the EEC rules on competition to the extent that they relate to an exclusive territory within which the developer will have rights. It is common in such agreements to provide that a franchise agreement, as defined in the Regulation, will be entered into once the premises have been found and approved or a territory specific to an identified location has been agreed. In paras 17, 28 and 36 and art 1 of *Computerland* (Appendix V) the issue of development area ageements was discussed and exemption given. Unfortunately the decision does not explain fully the structure which Computerland used for its agreements although it may be inferred from paras 28 and 36. Here, unusually, they contained the usual element of a franchise agreement. The Commission determined in para 28 that:

> The 'Development Area Agreements' referred to above under point 17, which contain similar provisions to the standard form agreement regarding location clause, protected area and sales to end-users, are accordingly deemed to be restrictive of competition.

Notwithstanding, the Commission decided the exemption could be given (para 36):

> Consequently, the provisions of Article 85(1) may, under the terms of Article 85(3), be declared inapplicable to the standard form Computerland franchise agreement. The same arguments referred to in points 29 to 35 apply *mutatis mutandis* to the 'Development Area Agreements'

and other existing franchise agreements which are equally or less restrictive of competition than the standard form agreement.

Unless the Regulation is amended in due course, to take account of development agreements and the various approaches adopted, they will need to be individually notified, according to the circumstances of the case, for a decision on exemption.

Chapter 17

Comment: an American view

by Philip F Zeidman

A: The block exemption concept
B: Comparisons with treatment of franchise agreements under United States law
C: Recognition of franchising as pro-competitive
D: Unresolved issues
E: Conclusion

The franchising block exemption regulation represents a watershed in the development of international franchising. The adoption of this Regulation resolved the serious issues raised in the European Court's *Pronuptia* decision concerning the legality of standard franchise agreements under EC law. Among other significant and troubling holdings, the *Pronuptia* decision held that franchise agreement provisions resulting in market sharing or exclusive territories have the effect of 'prevention, restriction or distortion of competition' within the meaning of art 85(1) of the EEC Treaty, at least where the franchise system is widespread. The typical and familiar franchise agreement, therefore, could be declared void under art 85(2). Absent the availability of a block exemption, franchisors were forced either to take their chances or to turn to the burdensome individual exemption procedure to escape the broad reach of art 85(1). American franchisors, by far the predominant number of such companies operating on an international scale, were dismayed; several entertained serious reservations about entering or further penetrating the European marketplace: a revamping of a tried and tested marketing system seemed to many to make the game not worth the candle.

By enacting a franchising block exemption regulation, the European Commission legitimised the franchising form of distribution, recognised the franchising relationship as a distinct genre, and provided a road map for franchisors doing business in the EC. The Regulation enables franchise agreements that comport with the Regulation's terms to gain exemption from the application of art 85(1) of the EEC Treaty without the need to notify the agreement to the Commission. It is far from perfect, as will be noted. But, if it had not been adopted, even in imperfect form, the course of franchising in Europe would have been materially affected — to the detriment of franchisors, franchisees, and the economies and societies of the Member States.

A: The block exemption concept

While the substantive provisions of the Regulation are significant and reflect many of the positions advanced by franchisors during the drafting of the Regulation, the block exemption procedural device is, in and of itself, an interesting mechanism that warrants a few observations.

The existence of the block exemption regulation lowers the administrative impediments facing franchisors operating in the EC. The Regulation achieves this result by reducing the likelihood that an agreement will need to be submitted to the Commission for approval, and (due to the comprehensive guidelines it provides) by reducing the likelihood that the agreement will be found to violate the EEC Treaty. The Regulation serves as a safe harbour for franchisors navigating through the treacherous waters of the Community's competition policy. Antitrust lawyers in the United States sometimes analogise the block exemption procedure to the Department of Justice (DOJ) antitrust guidelines that are promulgated from time to time on various antitrust subjects (for example Vertical Restraints Guidelines, Merger Guidelines and Antitrust Enforcement Guidelines for International Operations). While the analogy is inexact, both block exemptions and DOJ guidelines provide the business community with a sense of the type of conduct that will be considered actionable for infringements of antitrust law or competition law.

It is important to emphasise two features of the block exemption procedure. First, block exemptions are strictly construed. Thus, one should not assume that an arrangement not specifically addressed by a block exemption will be able to take advantage of the exemption. In this regard, the authors correctly caution that 'development agreements' do not satisfy the Regulation, even though 'master franchise agreements' are covered (albeit without much guidance from the Commission as to how that coverage is to be effected).

Second, block exemptions are offered only as a package, and agreements are permitted to benefit from the provisions of only one block exemption regulation. This means that an agreement unable to satisfy all the requirements of one block exemption cannot escape the application of art 85(1) by 'cherry-picking', the elements of more than one block exemption that are satisfied by the agreement. However, a party utilising an agreement whose provisions are not expressly accepted by the Regulation might be able to fit within one of the other block exemptions, such as those covering exclusive distribution agreements, exclusive purchasing agreements, patent licensing agreements, or know-how licensing agreements. After an election is made to utilise one block exemption, any agreements containing questionable provisions could still be granted an individual exemption by the Commission.

B: Comparison with treatment of franchise agreements under United States law

As the Regulation was drafted, it is able to accommodate most US franchisors without undue hardship. Franchise agreements used in the US generally can be conformed to satisfy the Regulation's requirements without severely altering the system. It should perhaps be noted that this fortunate circumstance did not occur without some effort. American franchisors were in the forefront of those seeking to explain franchising to the Commission, to point out the benefits it affords, and to urge that those benefits not be lost due to the impediments presented by *Pronuptia*.

Franchise agreements containing the following common restrictions may still generally take advantage of the Regulation:

— territorial restrictions such as a location clause, the grant of exclusive territorial rights, and an obligation by the franchisor not to supply goods to others in the franchisee's territory;
— various supply restrictions and purchasing obligations;
— non-competition provisions precluding franchisees from engaging, during the term of the agreement and post-termination for a reasonable period up to one year, in a similar business in the territory in competition with the system;
— confidentiality provisions restricting the franchisee's disclosure and use of know-how, both during and after the term of the agreement (although franchisees cannot be prevented from using know-how post-term if the know-how has become generally known); and
— quality and performance obligations such as requiring franchisees: to sell only goods satisfying objective standards; to attend training courses; to permit franchisor inspections; to apply the franchisor's commercial methods; to carry a minimum range of inventory; to provide warranty services; and to attain a minimum sales level.

Many of these provisions are permissible only if 'necessary to protect the franchisor's industrial or intellectual property rights or to maintain the common identity and reputation of the franchised network'; this standard certainly seems modest, and is likely to be met by virtually every franchisor.

By virtue of the Regulation, the treatment of franchisors under EC law is quite similar to their treatment under US antitrust law. The evaluation of franchise agreements in the US starts with, and, indeed, in some sense can end with, the analysis employed by the US Supreme Court in *Continental TV, Inc v GTE Sylvania, Inc*, 433 US 36 (1977). There, the Court firmly established that vertical non-price distribution restraints, such as those commonly employed in franchise agreements, are to be analysed under a rule of reason that considers the competitive effects of such restraints. The Court held that the antitrust laws are concerned primarily with interbrand competition, and that vertical non-price restraints often enhance interbrand competition by allowing manufacturers to achieve efficiencies in the distribution of their products. The Court explained that the reasons these restraints may be pro-competitive include the following: (1) firms entering a market can use distribution restraints to induce qualified retailers to make the type of investment required to distribute products unknown to consumers; (2) protection of dealers from 'free riding' — that is, protection of dealers who make investments in service and promotion from dealers who do not make such investments but cut their prices and take advantage of full-service dealers' investments; and (3) the restraints allow manufacturers to enforce quality and safety standards, and encourage retailers to engage in promotional activities and to provide services necessary to efficiently market the manufacturers' products. Because the *Sylvania* analysis has been broadly applied to many forms of distribution arrangements, it is easy to overlook the fact that the *Sylvania* opinion actually evaluated the legality of a franchise agreement involving a manufacturer of televisions and its franchised retailers.

Under US antitrust law, therefore, the non-price restraints found in most franchise agreements are valid, at least where the franchisor does not possess market power in a relevant market, which power may be inferred from a franchisor's large market share, or from its unique product or exclusive access to an essential input. A similar result is likely to be obtained under the franchising Regulation, although the application of the Regulation, with its acceptable, conditionally acceptable and unacceptable clauses and circumstances, is perhaps more mechanical than the application of the US's rule of reason.

Perhaps the greatest practical difference between franchise agreements under US and EC law stems from the Commission's overriding concern with market integration and non-discrimination between Member States. This political and social concern manifests itself in several requirements that would not be justified if based solely on antitrust principles. The most important of these requirements are:

—   franchisees must be free to obtain the goods that are the
       subject-matter of the franchise from other franchisees
       and from other authorised distributors, if any (parallel
       imports must be permitted); and
—   franchisees must be free to make passive (unsolicited)
       sales of the goods or services that are the subject-matter
       of the franchise to end users everywhere within the
       common market, including into other franchisees' terri-
       tories. However, franchisees may be prohibited from
       making active, (solicited) sales outside of their terri-
       tories.

Indeed, it is precisely because of the differences between the
degrees of integration of the US and Community Markets
respectively that the EC Commission and Court strongly favour
the principle of intrabrand competition.

However, franchisees and consumers in the Community may
benefit from more intrabrand competition in obtaining the franchisor's goods than do their US counterparts. For franchisors
operating in the US and elsewhere, these requirements will
necessitate some mental adjustments, but no significant structural
changes.

C: Recognition of franchising as pro-competitive

The point of reference for the EC's favourable view of franchising is expressed in several of the recitals to the Regulation. As
noted in the text, Recital 7 asserts that franchise agreements
normally improve the distribution of goods and services, facilitate
market entry (particularly for small and medium-sized undertakings), allow outlets to have a higher chance of success, and
increase the likelihood of more effective competition between
smaller and larger undertakings. Recital 8 pronounces that the
favourable effect of franchising on interbrand competition, and
the fact that consumers are free to deal with any franchisee in
a system, ensures that consumers will derive a share of the
benefits of franchising.

In the US, courts are beginning to grant franchisors greater latitude on the reasonableness of non-price vertical restraints than they grant to other distribution arrangements. This increased flexibility recognises that franchisors have a greater stake in the success of their franchisees than does a manufacturer or distributor who imposes such restraints on independent dealers (*Seagood Trading Corp v Jerrico, Inc*, 924 F.2d 1555, 1565–66 (11th Cir. 1991)). Some courts also recognise that the franchising method of doing business is itself a pro-competitive factor in the marketplace and consequently include this in their analyses of whether a particular action unreasonably affects competition (*Midwestern Waffles, Inc v Waffle House, Inc*, 1983–2 Trade Cas. (CCH) ¶ 65,567 (N.D. Ga. 1982), *aff'd*, 734 F.2d 705 (11th Cir. 1984)). But the recitals of the Regulation go further than has any legislative or executive agency in the US in accepting the pro-competitive benefits of franchising. They provide the basis for national courts, as well as for the legislative and administrative bodies of Member States, to justify actions beneficial to franchising. They also serve as a useful model in the US and elsewhere.

D: Unresolved issues

The Regulation contains numerous ambiguities and presents various problems, as discussed in the text. From the perspective of US franchisors, the principal such issues are as follows.

Application to multi-tier franchises

The inapplicability of the Regulation to area development agreements and wholesale franchise agreements is a serious deficiency. Also, the exemption provided for master franchise agreements is too narrow, as it does not exempt three-party agreements entered by a franchisor, master franchisee and franchisee. For franchisors at a distance, such as those in the US, these are especially troubling, since entering those markets may be feasible only through such vehicles.

Supply issues/tying

Article 2(*e*) allows the franchisor to prohibit franchisees from carrying 'goods competing with the franchisor's goods which are the subject-matter of the franchise', but this prohibition cannot be extended to accessory items or to spare parts for the franchisor's goods. Additionally, art 3(1)(*b*) allows the franchisor, in so far as necessary to protect the franchisor's industrial or intellectual property rights or to maintain the common identity and reputation of the system, to require franchisees 'to sell . . . goods which are manufactured only by the franchisor or by third parties designated by it, where it is impracticable, owing to the nature of the goods which are the subject-matter of the franchise, to apply objective quality specifications'. However, without prejudice to arts 2(*e*) and 3(1)(*b*), the franchisor cannot prevent franchisees from obtaining supplies of goods of a quality equivalent to those offered by the franchisor. The net result of these provisions has been to generate considerable uncertainty as to which of the goods sold by franchisees must be obtained from the franchisor or its designees. The most frequently cited example of this dilemma is whether a fast food franchisee can be required to purchase a particular brand of soft drink. This is not generally thought to be a serious problem in the US, unless the franchisor is deriving a financial benefit from such franchisee purchases.

Under the Regulation, before the franchisor could impose such a purchase requirement, it would need to establish either:

(a)   that the soft drink is produced according to the franchisor's instructions and is an essential subject-matter of the franchise, as opposed to being an accessory item;

(b)   that the purchase requirement is necessary to protect the franchisor's industrial or intellectual property rights, and that it is impracticable, due to the nature of the product, to apply objective quality specifications for soft drinks; or

(c)   that the purchase requirement is necessary to maintain the common identity and reputation of the system, and that it is impracticable, due to the nature of the product, to apply objective quality specifications for soft drinks.

Regrettably, the Commission declined to include, as a possible basis for finding it impracticable to apply objective quality specifications, the fact that the existence of a large number of franchisees might make it impracticable, from a financial point of view, to enforce quality standards. The Commission believed that franchisee numerosity would be too subjective a factor and too easy to circumvent for inclusion in the concept of impracticability. This limitation varies with the decision in *Pronuptia*, where the Court determined that either the nature of the goods *or* the large number of franchisees could provide a basis for permitting the franchisor to limit the sources of supply available to franchisees. There is at least a theoretical possibility that impracticability due to franchisee numerosity could be justified in an opposition procedure or an application for an individual exemption. It also should be recognised, as in *Computerland* (*see* Appendix V), that the impracticability of applying objective quality criteria might be established by the existence of a very large number of *products* that franchisees are required to carry.

It would be desirable to permit franchisors to determine approved products for their systems based on non-objective criteria, in as much as consumers increasingly are using product brands as proxies for product quality and are basing their purchasing decisions upon the availability of desired brands.

Know-how definition

The Regulaton embraces a narrow definition of know-how that some franchisors could have difficulty meeting. This is crucial because the Regulation applies only to franchise agreements in which the franchisor is obligated to communicate know-how to the franchisee. Know-how is defined as 'a package of non-patented practical information, resulting from experience and testing by the franchisor, which is secret, substantial, and identified'.

The definitions of 'secret', 'substantial', and 'identified' are similar to those of the block exemption regulation for know-how licensing agreements. 'Secret' means that the know-how, taken as a whole, is not generally known or easily accessible; 'substantial' means that the know-how includes information that is important for the sale of goods or provision of services to customers, and that can improve the competitive position of the franchise; and 'identified' means that the know-how must be sufficiently described and recorded to verify that it is 'secret' and 'substantial'. These definitions, if interpreted strictly, present serious risks to franchisors of being ineligible for the benefits of the Regulation. Secrecy is difficult to maintain in a commercial environment, and what is considered substantial is very subjective since it is defined in relation to the usefulness that a franchisee will derive from the information.

There does not seem to be a need for such a technical definition of 'know-how' to be considered a franchise. Franchisors provide many forms of assistance and support that are important to the operation of a successful franchise system, but which may not qualify as 'know-how'. Indeed, the cornerstone of many franchise systems is the franchisor's trademarks and other intellectual property rights, and/or innovative or distinctive product. In those situations, the assistance provided by the franchisor to its franchisees may only be of secondary importance, and may fall short of the rarified view of know-how presented in the Regulation.

E: Conclusion

The block exemption regulation provides a valuable framework for franchising in the EC. With modest additional refinement and development, the Regulation should provide franchisors with the certainty and confidence to participate in, and contribute to, the Community economy to the same extent that they have participated in, and contributed to, the American economy.

The author wishes to acknowledge the invaluable contribution of Steven B Feirman of Brownstein Zeidman and Schomer, Washington, DC, in the preparation of this chapter.

Appendix I

Relevant Articles of the EEC Treaty

Article 85

1. The following shall be prohibited as incompatible with the common market: all agreements between undertakings, decisions by associations of undertakings and concerted practices which may affect trade between Member States and which have as their object or effect the prevention, restriction or distortion of competition within the common market, and in particular those which:

(*a*) directly or indirectly fix purchase or selling prices or any other trading conditions;

(*b*) limit or control production, markets, technical development, or investment;

(*c*) share markets or sources of supply;

(*d*) apply dissimilar conditions to equivalent transactions with other trading parties, thereby placing them at a competitive disadvantage;

(*e*) make the conclusion of contracts subject to acceptance by the other parties of supplementary obligations which, by their nature or according to commercial usage, have no connection with the subject of such contracts.

2. Any agreements or decisions prohibited pursuant to this Article shall be automatically void.

3. The provisions of paragraph 1 may, however, be declared inapplicable in the case of:

— any agreement or category of agreements between undertakings;

— any decision or category of decisions by associations of undertakings;

— any concerted practice or category of concerted practices;

which contributes to improving the production or distribution of goods or to promoting technical or economic progress, while allowing consumers a fair share of the resulting benefit, and which does not:

(*a*) impose on the undertakings concerned restrictions which are not indispensable to the attainment of these objectives;

(*b*) afford such undertakings the possibility of eliminating competition in respect of a substantial part of the products in question.

Article 86

Any abuse by one or more undertakings of a dominant position within the common market or in a substantial part of it shall be prohibited as incompatible with the common market in so far as it may affect trade between Member States.

Such abuse may, in particular, consist in:

(*a*) directly or indirectly imposing unfair purchase or selling prices or other unfair trading conditions:

(*b*) limiting production, markets or technical development to the prejudice of consumers;

(*c*) applying dissimilar conditions to equivalent transactions with other trading parties, thereby placing them at a competitive disadvantage;

(*d*) making the conclusion of contracts subject to acceptance by the other parties of supplementary obligations which, by their nature or according to commercial usage, have no connection with the subject of such contracts.

Appendix II

Commission Regulation (EEC) No 4087/88

of 30 November 1988
on the application of Article 85(3) of the Treaty to
categories of franchise agreements

THE COMMISSION OF THE EUROPEAN COMMUNITIES,

Having regard to the Treaty establishing the European Economic Community,

Having regard to Council Regulation No 19/65/EEC of 2 March 1965 on the application of Article 85(3) of the Treaty to certain categories of agreements and concerted practices, as last amended by the Act of Accession of Spain and Portugal, and in particular Article 1 thereof,

Having published a draft of this Regulation,

Having consulted the Advisory Committee on Restrictive Practices and Dominant Positions,

Whereas:

(1) Regulation No 19/65/EEC empowers the Commission to apply Article 85(3) of the Treaty by Regulation to certain categories of bilateral exclusive agreements falling within the scope of Article 85(1) which either have as their object the exclusive distribution or exclusive purchase of goods, or include restrictions imposed in relation to the assignment or use of industrial property rights.

(2) Franchise agreements consist essentially of licences of industrial or intellectual property rights relating to trade marks or signs and know-how, which can be combined with restrictions relating to supply or purchase of goods.

(3) Several types of franchise can be distinguished according to their object: industrial franchise concerns the manufacturing of goods, distribution franchise concerns the sale of goods, and service franchise concerns the supply of services.

(4) It is possible on the basis of the experience of the Commission to define categories of franchise agreements which fall under Article 85(1) but can normally be regarded as satisfying the conditions laid down in Article 85(3). This is the case for franchise agreements whereby one of the parties supplies goods or provides services to end users. On the other hand, industrial franchise agreements should not be covered by this Regulation. Such agreements, which usually govern relationships between producers, present different characteristics than the other types of franchise. They consist of manufacturing licences based on patents and/or technical know-how, combined with trade-mark licences. Some of them may benefit from other block exemptions if they fulfil the necessary conditions.

(5) This Regulation covers franchise agreements between two undertakings, the franchisor and the franchisee, for the retailing of goods or the provision of services to end users, or a combination of these activities, such as the processing or adaptation of goods to fit specific needs of their customers. It also covers cases where the relationship between franchisor and franchisees is made through a third undertaking, the master franchisee. It does not cover wholesale franchise agreements because of the lack of experience of the Commission in that field.

(6) Franchise agreements as defined in this Regulation can fall under Article 85(1). They may in particular affect intra-Community trade where they are concluded between undertakings from different Member States or where they form the basis of a network which extends beyond the boundaries of a single Member State.

(7) Franchise agreements as defined in this Regulation normally improve the distribution of goods and/or the provision of services as they give franchisors the possibility of establishing a uniform network with limited investments, which may assist the entry of new competitors on the market, particularly in the case of small and medium-sized undertakings, thus increasing interbrand competition. They also allow independent traders to set up outlets more rapidly and with higher chance of success than if they had to do so without the franchisor's experience and assistance. They have therefore the possibility of competing more efficiently with large distribution undertakings.

(8) As a rule, franchise agreements also allow consumers and other end users a fair share of the resulting benefit, as they combine the advantage of a uniform network with the existence of traders personally interested in the efficient operation of their business. The homogeneity of the network and the constant cooperation between the franchisor and the franchisees ensures a constant quality of the products and services. The favourable effect of franchising on interbrand competition

and the fact that consumers are free to deal with any franchisee in the network guarantees that a reasonable part of the resulting benefits will be passed on to the consumers.

(9) This Regulation must define the obligations restrictive of competition which may be included in franchise agreements. This is the case in particular for the granting of an exclusive territory to the franchisees combined with the prohibition on actively seeking customers outside that territory, which allows them to concentrate their efforts on their allotted territory. The same applies to the granting of an exclusive territory to a master franchisee combined with the obligation not to conclude franchise agreements with third parties outside that territory. Where the franchisees sell or use in the process of providing services, goods manufactured by the franchisor or according to its instructions and or bearing its trade mark, an obligation on the franchisees not to sell, or use in the process of the provision of services, competing goods, makes it possible to establish a coherent network which is identified with the franchised goods. However, this obligation should only be accepted with respect to the goods which form the essential subject-matter of the franchise. It should notably not relate to accessories or spare parts for these goods.

(10) The obligations referred to above thus do not impose restrictions which are not necessary for the attainment of the abovementioned objectives. In particular, the limited territorial protection granted to the franchisees is indispensable to protect their investment.

(11) It is desirable to list in the Regulation a number of obligations that are commonly found in franchise agreements and are normally not restrictive of competition and to provide that if, because of the particular economic or legal circumstances, they fall under Article 85(1), they are also covered by the exemption. This list, which is not exhaustive, includes in particular clauses which are essential either to preserve the common identity and reputation of the network or to prevent the know-how made available and the assistance given by the franchisor from benefiting competitors.

(12) The Regulation must specify the conditions which must be satisfied for the exemption to apply. To guarantee that competition is not eliminated for a substantial part of the goods which are the subject of the franchise, it is necessary that parallel imports remain possible. Therefore, cross deliveries between franchisees should always be possible. Furthermore, where a franchise network is combined with another distribution system, franchisees should be free to obtain supplies from authorised distributors. To better inform consumers, thereby helping to ensure that they receive a fair share of the resulting benefits, it must

be provided that the franchisee shall be obliged to indicate its status as an independent undertaking, by any appropriate means which does not jeopardise the common identity of the franchised network. Furthermore, where the franchisees have to honour guarantees for the franchisor's goods, this obligation should also apply to goods supplied by the franchisor, other franchisees or other agreed dealers.

(13) The Regulation must also specify restrictions which may not be included in franchise agreements if these are to benefit from the exemption granted by the Regulation, by virtue of the fact that such provisions are restrictions falling under Article 85(1) for which there is no general presumption that they will lead to the positive effects required by Article 85(3). This applies in particular to market sharing between competing manufacturers, to clauses unduly limiting the franchisee's choice of suppliers or customers, and to cases where the franchisee is restricted in determining its prices. However, the franchisor should be free to recommend prices to the franchisees, where it is not prohibited by national laws and to the extent that it does not lead to concerted practices for the effective application of these prices.

(14) Agreements which are not automatically covered by the exemption because they contain provisions that are not expressly exempted by the Regulation and not expressly excluded from exemption may nonetheless generally be presumed to be eligible for application of Article 85(3). It will be possible for the Commission rapidly to establish whether this is the case for a particular agreement. Such agreements should therefore be deemed to be covered by the exemption provided for in this Regulation where they are notified to the Commission and the Commission does not oppose the application of the exemption within a specified period of time.

(15) If individual agreements exempted by this Regulation nevertheless have effects which are incompatible with Article 85(3), in particular as interpreted by the administrative practice of the Commission and the case law of the Court of Justice, the Commission may withdraw the benefit of the block exemption. This applies in particular where competition is significantly restricted because of the structure of the relevant market.

(16) Agreements which are automatically exempted pursuant to this Regulation need not be notified. Undertakings may nevertheless in a particular case request a decision pursuant to Council Regulation No 17 as last amended by the Act of Accession of Spain and Portugal.

(17) Agreements may benefit from the provisions either of this Regulation or of another Regulation, according to their particular nature and provided that they fulfil the necessary conditions of application. They

may not benefit from a combination of the provisions of this Regulation with those of another block exemption Regulation,

HAS ADOPTED THIS REGULATION:

Article 1

1. Pursuant to Article 85(3) of the Treaty and subject to the provisions of this Regulation, it is hereby declared that Article 85(1) of the Treaty shall not apply to franchise agreements to which two undertakings are party, which include one or more of the restrictions listed in Article 2.

2. The exemption provided for in paragraph 1 shall also apply to master franchise agreements to which two undertakings are party. Where applicable, the provisions of this Regulation concerning the relationship between franchisor and franchisee shall apply *mutatis mutandis* to the relationship between franchisor and master franchisee and between master franchisee and franchisee.

3. For the purposes of this Regulation:

(*a*) 'franchise' means a package of industrial or intellectual property rights relating to trade marks, trade names, shop signs, utility models, designs, copyrights, know-how or patents, to be exploited for the resale of goods or the provision of services to end users;

(*b*) 'franchise agreement' means an agreement whereby one undertaking, the franchisor, grants the other, the franchisee, in exchange for direct or indirect financial consideration, the right to exploit a franchise for the purposes of marketing specified types of goods and/or services; it includes at least obligations relating to:
   — the use of a common name or shop sign and a uniform presentation of contract premises and/or means of transport,
   — the communication by the franchisor to the franchisee of know-how,
   — the continuing provision by the franchisor to the franchisee of commercial or technical assistance during the life of the agreement;

(*c*) 'master franchise agreement' means an agreement whereby one undertaking, the franchisor, grants the other, the master franchisee, in exchange of direct or indirect financial consideration, the right to exploit a franchise for the purposes of concluding franchise agreements with third parties, the franchisees;

(*d*) 'franchisor's goods' means goods produced by the franchisor or according to its instructions, and/or bearing the franchisor's name or trade mark;

(*e*) 'contract premises' means the premises used for the exploitation of the franchise or, when the franchise is exploited outside those premises, the base from which the franchisee operates the means of transport used for the exploitation of the franchise (contract means of transport);

(*f*) 'know-how' means a package of non-patented practical information, resulting from experience and testing by the franchisor, which is secret, substantial and identified;

(*g*) 'secret' means that the know-how, as a body or in the precise configuration and assembly of its components, is not generally known or easily accessible, it is not limited in the narrow sense that each individual component of the know-how should be totally unknown or unobtainable outside the franchisor's business;

(*h*) 'substantial' means that the know-how includes information which is of importance for the sale of goods or the provision of services to end users, and in particular for the presentation of goods for sale, the processing of goods in connection which the provision of services, methods of dealing with customers, and administration and financial management; the know-how must be useful for the franchisee by being capable, at the date of conclusion of the agreement, of improving the competitive position of the franchisee, in particular by improving the franchisee's performance or helping it to enter a new market;

(*i*) 'identified' means that the know-how must be described in a sufficiently comprehensive manner so as to make it possible to verify that it fulfils the criteria of secrecy and substantiality; the description of the know-how can either be set out in the franchise agreement or in a separate document or recorded in any other appropriate form.

Article 2

The exemption provided for in Article 1 shall apply to the following restrictions of competition:

(*a*) an obligation on the franchisor, in a defined area of the common market, the contract territory, not to:
  — grant the right to exploit all or part of the franchise to third parties,
  — itself exploit the franchise, or itself market the goods or services which are the subject-matter of the franchise under a similar formula,
  — itself supply the franchisor's goods to third parties;

(*b*) an obligation to the master franchisee not to conclude franchise agreement with third parties outside its contract territory;

(c) an obligation on the franchisee to exploit the franchise only from the contract premises;

(d) an obligation on the franchisee to refrain, outside the contract territory, from seeking customers for the goods or the services which are the subject-matter of the franchise;

(e) an obligation on the franchisee not to manufacture, sell or use in the course of the provision of services, goods competing with the franchisor's goods which are the subject-matter of the franchise; where the subject-matter of the franchise is the sale or use in the course of the provision of services both certain types of goods and spare parts or accessories therefor, that obligation may not be imposed in respect of these spare parts or accessories.

Article 3

1. Article 1 shall apply notwithstanding the presence of any of the following obligations on the franchisee, in so far as they are necessary to protect the franchisor's industrial or intellectual property rights or to maintain the common identity and reputation of the franchised network:

(a) to sell, or use in the course of the provision of services, exclusively goods matching minimum objective quality specifications laid down by the franchisor;

(b) to sell, or use in the course of the provision of services, goods which are manufactured only by the franchisor or by third parties designed by it, where it is impracticable, owing to the nature of the goods which are the subject-matter of the franchise, to apply objective quality specifications;

(c) not to engage, directly or indirectly, in any similar business in a territory where it would compete with a member of the franchised network, including the franchisor; the franchisee may be held to this obligation after termination of the agreement, for a reasonable period which may not exceed one year, in the territory where it has exploited the franchise;

(d) not to acquire financial interests in the capital of a competing undertaking, which would give the franchisee the power to influence the economic conduct of such undertaking;

(e) to sell the goods which are the subject-matter of the franchise only to end users, to other franchisees and to resellers within other channels of distribution supplied by the manufacturer of these goods or with its consent;

(f) to use its best endeavours to sell the goods or provide the services that are the subject-matter of the franchise; to offer for sale a minimum range of goods, achieve a minimum turnover, plan its orders in advance, keep minimum stocks and provide customer and warranty services;

(*g*) to pay to the franchisor a specified proportion of its revenue for advertising and itself carry out advertising for the nature of which it shall obtain the franchisor's approval.

2. Article 1 shall apply notwithstanding the presence of any of the following obligations on the franchisee:

(*a*) not to disclose to third parties the know-how provided by the franchisor; the franchisee may be held to this obligation after termination of the agreement;

(*b*) to communicate to the franchisor any experience gained in exploiting the franchise and to grant it, and other franchisees, a non-exclusive licence for the know-how resulting from that experience;

(*c*) to inform the franchisor of infringements of licensed industrial or intellectual property rights, to take legal action against infringers or to assist the franchisor in any legal actions against infringers;

(*d*) not to use know-how licensed by the franchisor for purposes other than the exploitation of the franchise; the franchisee may be held to this obligation after termination of the agreement;

(*e*) to attend or have its staff attend training courses arranged by the franchisor;

(*f*) to apply the commercial methods devised by the franchisor, including any subsequent modification thereof, and use the licensed industrial or intellectual property rights;

(*g*) to comply with the franchisor's standards for the equipment and presentation of the contract premises and/or means of transport;

(*h*) to allow the franchisor to carry out checks of the contract premises and/or means of transport, including the goods sold and the services provided, and the inventory and accounts of the franchisee;

(*i*) not without the franchisor's consent to change the location of the contract premises;

(*j*) not without the franchisor's consent to assign the rights and obligations under the franchise agreement.

3. In the event that, because of particular circumstances, obligations referred to in paragraph 2 fall within the scope of Article 85(1), they shall also be exempted even if they are not accompanied by any of the obligations exempted by Article 1.

Article 4

The exemption provided for in Article 1 shall apply on condition that:

(*a*) the franchisee is free to obtain the goods that are the subject-matter of the franchise from other franchisees; where such goods are also distributed through another network of authorised distributors, the franchisee must be free to obtain the goods from the latter;

(*b*) where the franchisor obliges the franchisee to honour guarantees for the franchisor's goods, that obligation shall apply in respect of such goods supplied by any member of the franchised network or other distributors which give a similar guarantee, in the common market;

(*c*) the franchisee is obliged to indicate its status as an independent undertaking; this indication shall however not interfere with the common identity of the franchised network resulting in particular from the common name or shop sign and uniform appearance of the contract premises and/or means of transport.

Article 5

The exemption granted by Article 1 shall not apply where:

(*a*) undertakings producing goods or providing services which are identical or are considered by users as equivalent in view of their characteristics, price and intended use, enter into franchise agreements in respect of such goods or services;

(*b*) without prejudice to Article 2(*e*) and Article 3(1)(*b*), the franchisee is prevented from obtaining supplies of goods of a quality equivalent to those offered by the franchisor;

(*c*) without prejudice to Article 2(*c*), the franchisee is obliged to sell, or use in the process of providing services, goods manufactured by the franchisor or third parties designated by the franchisor and the franchisor refuses, for reasons other than protecting the franchisor's industrial or intellectual property rights, or maintaining the common identity and reputation of the franchised network, to designate as authorised manufacturers third parties proposed by the franchisee;

(*d*) the franchisee is prevented from continuing to use the licensed know-how after termination of the agreement where the know-how has become generally known or easily accessible, other than by breach of an obligation by the franchisee;

(*e*) the franchisee is restricted by the franchisor, directly or indirectly, in the determination of sale prices for the goods or services which are the subject-matter of the franchise, without prejudice to the possibility for the franchisor of recommending sale prices;

(*f*) the franchisor prohibits the franchisee from challenging the validity of the industrial or intellectual property rights which form part of the franchise, without prejudice to the possibility for the franchisor of terminating the agreement in such a case;

(g) franchisees are obliged not to supply within the common market the goods or services which are the subject-matter of the franchise to end users because of their place of residence.

Article 6

1. The exemption provided for in Article 1 shall also apply to franchise agreements which fulfil the conditions laid down in Article 4 and include obligations restrictive of competition which are not covered by Articles 2 and 3(3) and do not fall within the scope of Article 5, on condition that the agreements in question are notified to the Commission in accordance with the provisions of Commission Regulation No 27 and that the Commission does not oppose such exemption within a period of six months.

2. The period of six months shall run from the date on which the notification is received by the Commission. Where, however, the notification is made by registered post, the period shall run from the date shown on the postmark of the place of posting.

3. Paragraph 1 shall apply only if:

(a) express reference is made to this Article in the notification or in a communication accompanying it; and

(b) the information furnished with the notification is complete and in accordance with the facts.

4. The benefit of paragraph 1 can be claimed for agreements notified before the entry into force of this Regulation by submitting a communication to the Commission referring expressly to this Article and to the notification. Paragraphs 2 and 3(b) shall apply *mutatis mutandis*.

5. The Commission may oppose exemption. It shall oppose exemption if it receives a request to do so from a Member State within three months of the forwarding to the Member State of the notification referred to in paragraph 1 or the communication referred to in paragraph 4. This request must be justified on the basis of considerations relating to the competition rules of the Treaty.

6. The Commission may withdraw its opposition to the exemption at any time. However, where that opposition was raised at the request of a Member State, it may be withdrawn only after consultation of the advisory Committee on Restrictive Practices and Dominant Positions.

7. If the opposition is withdrawn because the undertakings concerned

have shown that the conditions of Article 85(3) are fulfilled, the exemption shall apply from the date of the notification.

8. If the opposition is withdrawn because the undertakings concerned have amended the agreement so that the conditions of Article 85(3) are fulfilled, the exemption shall apply from the date on which the amendments take effect.

9. If the Commission opposes exemption and its opposition is not withdrawn, the effects of the notification shall be governed by the provisions of Regulation No 17.

Article 7

1. Information acquired pursuant to Article 6 shall be used only for the purposes of this Regulation.

2. The Commission and the authorities of the Member States, their officials and other servants shall not disclose information acquired by them pursuant to this Regulation of a kind that is covered by the obligation of professional secrecy.

3. Paragraphs 1 and 2 shall not prevent publication of general information or surveys which do not contain information relating to particular undertakings or associations of undertakings.

Article 8

The Commission may withdraw the benefit of this Regulation, pursuant to Article 7 of Regulation No 19/65/EEC, where it finds in a particular case that an agreement exempted by this Regulation nevertheless has certain effects which are incompatible with the conditions laid down in Article 85(3) of the EEC Treaty, and in particular where territorial protection is awarded to the franchisee and:

(*a*) access to the relevant market or competition therein is significantly restricted by the cumulative effect of parallel networks of similar agreements established by competing manufacturers or distributors;

(*b*) the goods or services which are the subject-matter of the franchise do not face, in a substantial part of the common market, effective competition from goods or services which are identical or considered by users as equivalent in view of their characteristics, price and intended use;

(*c*) the parties, or one of them, prevent end users, because of their place of residence, from obtaining, directly or through intermediaries, the goods or services which are the subject-matter of the franchise within the common market, or use differences in specifications concerning those goods or services in different Member States, to isolate markets;

(*d*) franchisees engage in concerted practices relating to the sale prices of the goods or services which are the subject-matter of the franchise;

(*e*) the franchisor uses its right to check the contract premises and means of transport, or refuses its agreement to requests by the franchisee to move the contract premises or assign its rights and obligations under the franchise agreement, for reasons other than protecting the franchisor's industrial or intellectual property rights, maintaining the common identity and reputation of the franchised network or verifying that the franchisee abides by its obligations under the agreement.

Article 9

This Regulation shall enter into force on 1 February 1989.

It shall remain in force until 31 December 1999.

This Regulation shall be binding in its entirety and directly applicable in all Member States.

Done at Brussels, 30 November 1988.

For the Commission
Peter SUTHERLAND
Member of the Commission

Appendix III

De minimis rules

Commission notice of 3 September 1986 on agreements of minor importance which do not fall under Article 85(1) of the Treaty establishing the European Economic Community

(86/C 231/02)

I

1. The Commission considers it important to facilitate cooperation between undertakings where such cooperation is economically desirable without presenting difficulties from the point of view of competition policy, which is particularly true of cooperation between small and medium-sized undertakings. To this end it published the 'Notice concerning agreements, decisions and concerted practices in the field of cooperation between undertakings' listing a number of agreements that by their nature cannot be regarded as restraints of competition. Furthermore, in the Notice concerning its assessment of certain subcontracting agreements the Commission considered that this type of contract which offers opportunities for development, in particular, to small and medium-sized undertakings is not in itself caught by the prohibition in Article 85(1). By issuing the present Notice, the Commission is taking a further step towards defining the field of application of Article 85(1), in order to facilitate cooperation between small and medium-sized undertakings.

2. In the Commission's opinion, agreements whose effects on trade between Member States or on competition are negligible do not fall under the ban on restrictive agreements contained in Article 85(1). Only those agreements are prohibited which have an appreciable impact on market conditions, in that they appreciably alter the market position, in other words the sales or supply possibilities, of third undertakings and of users.

3. In the present Notice the Commission, by setting quantitative criteria and by explaining their application, has given a sufficiently concrete meaning to the concept 'appreciable' for undertakings to be able to

judge for themselves whether the agreements they have concluded with
other undertakings, being of minor importance, do not fall under Article
85(1). The quantitative definition of 'appreciable' given by the Commission is, however, no absolute yardstick, in fact, in individual cases
even agreements between undertakings which exceed these limits may
still have only a negligible effect on trade between Member States or
on competition, and are therefore not caught by Article 85(1).

4. As a result of this Notice, there should no longer be any point in
undertakings obtaining negative clearance, as defined by Article 2 of
Council Regulation No 17, for the agreements covered, nor should it
be necessary to have the legal position established through Commission
decisions in individual cases; notification with this end in view will no
longer be necessary for such agreements. However, if it is doubtful
whether in an individual case an agreement appreciably affects trade
between Member States or competition, the undertakings are free to
apply for negative clearance or to notify the agreement.

5. In cases covered by the present Notice the Commission, as a
general rule, will not open proceedings under Regulation No 17, either
upon application or upon its own initiative. Where, due to exceptional
circumstances, an agreement which is covered by the present Notice
nevertheless falls under Article 85(1), the Commission will not impose
fines. Where undertakings have failed to notify an agreement falling
under Article 85(1) because they wrongly assumed, owing to a mistake
in calculating their market share or aggregate turnover, that the agreement was covered by the present Notice, the Commission will not
consider imposing fines unless the mistake was due to negligence.

6. This Notice is without prejudice to the competence of national
courts to apply Article 85(1) on the basis of their own jurisdiction,
although it constitutes a factor which such courts may take into account
when deciding a pending case. It is also without prejudice to any interpretation which may be given by the Court of Justice of the European
Communities.

II

7. The Commission holds the view that agreements between undertakings engaged in the production or distribution of goods or in the
provision of services generally do not fall under the prohibition of
Article 81(1) if:

— the goods or services which are the subject of the agreement
   (hereinafter referred to as 'the contract products') together with
   the participation undertakings' other goods or services which are

considered by users to be equivalent in view of their characteristics, price and intended use, do not represent more than 5% of
the total market for such goods or services (hereinafter referred
to as 'products') in the area of the common market affected by
the agreement and
— the aggregate annual turnover of the participating undertakings
  does not exceed 200 million ECU.

8. The Commission also holds the view that the said agreements do
not fall under the prohibition of Article 85(1) if the abovementioned
market share or turnover is exceeded by not more than one tenth during
two successive financial years.

9. For the purposes of this Notice, participating undertakings are:

(a) undertakings party to the agreement;
(b) undertakings in which a party to the agreement, directly or
indirectly,
— owns more than half the capital or business assets or
— has the power to exercise more than half the voting rights, or
— has the power to appoint more than half the members of the
  supervisory board, board of management or bodies legally
  representing the undertakings, or
— has the right to manage the affairs;
(c) undertakings which directly or indirectly have in or over a party
to the agreement the rights or powers listed in (b);
(d) undertakings in or over which an undertaking referred to in (c)
directly or indirectly has the rights or powers listed in (b).

Undertakings in which several undertakings as referred to in (a) to
(d) jointly have, directly or indirectly, the rights or powers set out in
(b) shall also be considered to be participating undertakings.

10. In order to calculate the market share, it is necessary to determine
the relevant market. This implies the definition of the relevant product
market and the relevant geographical market.

11. The relevant product market includes besides the contract products any other products which are identical or equivalent to them. This
rule applies to the products of the participating undertakings as well as
to the market for such products. The products in question must be
interchangeable. Whether or not this is the case must be judged from
the vantage point of the user, normally taking the characteristics, price
and intended use of the goods together. In certain cases, however,
products can form a separate market on the basis of their characteristics,
their price or their intended use alone. This is true especially where
consumer preferences have developed.

12. Where the contract products are components which are incorporated into another product by the participating undertakings, reference should be made to the market for the latter product, provided that the components represent a significant part of it. Where the contract products are components which are sold to third undertakings, reference should be made to the market for the components. In cases where both conditions apply, both markets should be considered separately.

13. The relevant geographical market is the area within the Community in which the agreement produces its effects. This area will be the whole common market where the contract products are regularly bought and sold in all Member States. Where the contract products cannot be bought and sold in a part of the common market, or are bought and sold only in limited quantities or at irregular intervals in such a part, that part should be disregarded.

14. The relevant geographical market will be narrower than the whole common market in particular where:

— the nature and characteristics of the contract product, e.g. high transport costs in relation to the value of the product, restrict its mobility; or
— movement of the contract product within the common market is hindered by barriers to entry to national markets resulting from State intervention, such as quantitative restrictions, severe taxation differentials and non-tariff barriers, e.g. type approvals or safety standard certifications. In such cases the national territory may have to be considered as the relevant geographical market. However, this will only be justified if the existing barriers to entry cannot be overcome by reasonable effort and at an acceptable cost.

15. Aggregate turnover includes the turnover in all goods and services, excluding tax, achieved during the last financial year by the participating undertaking. In cases where an undertaking has concluded similar agreements with various other undertakings in the relevant market, the turnover of all participating undertakings should be taken together. The aggregate turnover shall not include dealings between participating undertakings.

16. The present Notice shall not apply where in a relevant market competition is restricted by the cumulative effects of parallel networks of similar agreements established by several manufacturers or dealers.

17. The present Notice is likewise applicable to decisions by associations of undertakings and to concerted practices.

Appendix IV

The Pronuptia case

This version of the case is taken from *The Journal of International Franchising and Distribution Law*, September 1986, translated by Bryan Harris.

In Case 161/84 whose object is a request to the Court by the Federal Court, applying Article 177 of the EEC Treaty, and seeking in the litigation taking place within that jurisdiction between Pronuptia de Paris GmbH, Frankfurt am Main and Pronuptia de Paris, Irmgard Schillgallis, Hamburg, a preliminary ruling on the interpretation of Article 85 of the EEC Treaty and of Commission Regulation 67/67 of 22 March 1967, relating to the application of Article 85(3) of the EEC Treaty to categories of exclusive agreements, The Court consisting of:

Lord Mackenzie Stuart, **President**.
Messrs U. Everling, K. Bahlmann and R. Joilet, **Presidents of Chambers**.
Messrs T. Koopmans, I Due and Y. Galmot. **Judges**.
Advocate-General: Mr Verloren Van Themaat.
Clerk: Miss D. Louterman, Administrator.

Considering the observations submitted for the appellant by Dr Rainer Bechtold; for the respondent by Dr Eberhard Kolonko; for the Republic of France by Mrs S.C. de Margerie, as agent; for the Commission of the European Communities by Dr Norbert Koch, as agent.
Having heard the Advocate-General's conclusions in audience on 19 June 1985, gives the present decision. (*the facts not being reproduced here*)

1. By an order dated 15 May 1984, received at the Court on 25 June 1984, the Federal Court submitted, in accordance with Article 177 of the EEC Treaty, several questions relating to the interpretation of Article 85 of the EEC Treaty and of Commission Regulations 67/67 of 22 March 1967, concerning the application of Article 85(3) to categories of exclusive agreements, so that the question should be examined whether these provisions were applicable to franchise contracts.

2. These questions have been raised in the context of litigation between the firm Pronuptia de Paris GmbH from Frankfurt am Main (hereafter the franchisor), a subsidiary of a French society of the same name, and Madam Schillgallis from Hamburg who carries on business under the name Pronuptia de Paris (hereafter the franchisee). This litigation relates to the franchisee's obligation to pay the franchisor arrears of fees based on her turnover during the years 1978 to 1980.

3. The French parent company of the franchisor distributes, under the trade mark Pronuptia de Paris wedding dresses and other clothes worn at weddings. In the Federal German Republic the distribution of these products is undertaken either by shops dealing directly with its subsidiary, or in shops belonging to the independent retailers which are linked to it by franchise contracts concluded in its name by its subsidiary and acting at the same time in its own name.

4. By three contracts which were signed on the 24 February 1980, the franchisee obtained a franchise for three distinct areas, those of Hamburg, Oldenburg and Hanover. The three contracts are drafted in practically identical terms. They include more particularly the following elements.

5. The franchisor:

- grants to the franchisee, in respect of a certain territory which is defined in a map annexed to the contract, the exclusive right to the use of the sign Pronuptia de Paris with a view to the sale of its products and services, as well as the right of advertising within this territory;

- undertakes not to open any other shop called Pronuptia in the territory in question nor to provide any product or service to third parties in this territory;

- undertakes to help the franchisee as regards the business and advertising aspects of his enterprise, the furnishing and decoration of the shop, the training of staff, the techniques of sale, fashion and the goods, purchasing, marketing and, in a general way, everything which, according to its experience, could contribute to improving the turnover and profitability of the franchisee's business.

6. The franchisee, who remains the sole owner of his business and assumes the risks, is required:

- to sell the goods, using the trade name and trade mark Pronuptia de Paris, only in the shop specified in the contract, which must be furnished and decorated mainly for the sale of wedding goods according to the franchisor's directions, with a view to taking full advantage of the image of the trade mark belonging to the Pronuptia distribution chain, and must not be transferred to another location or changed except with the franchisor's agreement;

- to buy from the franchisor 80 per cent of the wedding dresses and accessories, as well as a proportion to be determined by the franchisor himself of cocktail dresses and evening gowns, and not otherwise to take stocks except from suppliers approved by the franchisor;

- to pay the franchisor, in consideration of the agreed advantages, a single entry fee for the contract territory of DM 15,000 and, during the whole period of the contract, a fee equal to 10 per cent of the whole turnover achieved by the sale of Pronuptia products, evening clothes purchased from suppliers other than Pronuptia not, however, being counted for this fee;

- to consider, without prejudice to his freedom to fix his resale prices himself, the prices proposed by the franchisor as resale recommendations;

- to advertise in the contract territory only with the agreement of the franchisor and, in any case, to bring this advertising into line with that carried out both internationally and nationally by the franchisor; to distribute in the most conscientious way possible the catalogues and other advertising materials supplied by the franchisor; and, generally, to apply the business methods of which she has been informed by the franchisor;

- to make the sale of wedding goods the principal object of the business;

- to abstain from any act of competition with the Pronuptia business, and in particular not to open a business having similar or identical objects to those carried on in the context of the contract; nor to participate directly or indirectly in such a business within the territory of the Federal German Republic, including West Berlin, nor in a territory where Pronuptia is represented in any way, this undertaking to apply for the duration of the contract as well as for a period of one year after it has come to an end;

- not to grant to third parties the rights and obligations stemming from the contract, not its business, without the prior agreement of the franchisor, it being understood that this agreement will be given if the transfer arises for reasons of health and if the new party to the contract establishes his solvency and proves that he is not, in any sense whatever, a competitor of the franchisor.

7. Having been ordered by the Court of first instance to pay DM 158,503 in respect of the arrears of fees on turnover for the years 1978 to 1980, the franchisee lodged an appeal against this judgment to the Provincial Court of Appeal of Frankfurt am Main, arguing, in order to escape payment of these arrears, that the contracts in question violated

Article 85(1) of the Treaty and did not benefit from the block exemption for exclusive agreements under Commission Regulation 67/67. By a decision dated 2 December 1982, the Provincial Court of Appeal upheld the franchisee's argument. It decided that the reciprocal exclusivity undertakings constituted restrictions on competition within the Common Market, inasmuch as the franchisor could not supply any other business within the contract territory and the franchisee could not buy and resell other goods originating from other member states, except to a limited degree. Since these contracts do not benefit from an exemption by virtue of Article 85(3), they must, according to that Court, be considered void by virtue of Article 85(2). With regard to exemption, the Provincial Court of Appeal reckoned in particular that it was not necessary for it to decide whether franchise contracts were excluded in principle from the scope of Commission Regulation 67/67, already mentioned. Indeed, according to the Provincial Court of Appeal, the contracts in question do in any case contain commitments which go beyond those described in Article 1 of the Regulation and which constitute restrictions of competition which are not covered by Article 2.

8. Against this decision the franchisor submitted an appeal to the Federal Court directed towards the reinstatement of the judgment given at first instance. The Federal Court considered that the decision to be taken on appeal would depend on the interpretation of Community law. Consequently it referred the following questions to this Court for a preliminary decision:

(1) Is Article 85(1) of the EEC Treaty applicable to franchise agreements such as the contracts between the parties, which have as their object the establishment of a special distribution system whereby the franchisor provides to the franchisee, in addition to goods, certain trade names, trade marks, merchandising material and services?

(2) If the first question is answered in the affirmative:
   Is Regulation No 67/67/EEC of the Commission of 22 March 1967 on the application of Article 85(3) of the Treaty to certain categories of exclusive dealing agreements (block exemption) applicable to such contracts?

(3) If the second question is answered in the affirmative:
   a. Is Regulation No 67/67/EEC still applicable if several undertakings which, though legally independent, are bound together by commercial ties and form a single economic entity for the purposes of the contract participate on one side of the agreement?
   b. Does Regulation No 67/67/EEC, and in particular Article 2(2)(c) thereof, apply to an obligation on the part of the

franchisee to advertise solely with the prior agreement of the franchisor and in a manner that is in keeping with the latter's advertising, using the publicity material supplied by him, and in general to use the same business methods? Is it relevant in this connection that the franchisor's publicity material contains price recommendations which are not binding?

c. Does Regulation No 67/67/EEC, and in particular Articles 1(1)(b), 2(1)(a) and 2(b) thereof, apply to an obligation on the part of the franchisee to confine the sale of the contract goods exclusively or at least for the most part to particular business premises specially adapted for the purpose?

d. Does Regulation No 67/67/EEC, and in particular Article 1(1)(b) thereof, apply to an obligation on the part of the franchisee—who is bound to purchase most of his supplies from the franchisor—to make the rest of his purchases of goods covered by the contract solely from suppliers approved by the franchisor?

e. Does Regulation No 67/67/EEC sanction an obligation on the franchisor to give the franchisee commercial, advertising and professional support?

First question

9. The firm Pronuptia de Paris GmbH from Frankfurt am Main, the franchisor, submitted that a system of franchise contracts allowed a combination of the advantages of a form of distribution presenting a homogeneous appearance (like subsidiaries) to outside persons and distribution by independent retailers who themselves assumed the business risks. Made up of a network of vertical agreements, which were intended to guarantee a uniform presentation to outside persons, the system of contracts reinforced the competitive capacity of the franchisor at the horizontal level, that is to say, in relation to other forms of distribution. It made it possible for an undertaking, which would not otherwise dispose of the requisite financial resources, to establish a distribution network which was supraregional, a network in which small undertakings, as franchisees keeping their autonomy, also took part. In view of these advantages, Article 85(1) did not apply provided that franchise contracts contained no restrictions on the contracting parties' freedom, other than those which stemmed from the nature of a franchise system. Exclusive obligations of delivery and supply, to the extent that they were intended to ensure uniform stocks, obligations concerned with homogeneous advertising and with a uniform management of commercial locations and the prohibition of selling in other shops the goods delivered in accordance with the contract, were inherent in the very nature of the franchise contract and would escape the application of Article 85(1).

10. Madam Schillgallis, the franchisee, suggested an affirmative answer to the question which had been referred. The disputed contracts were characterised by the territorial protection granted to the franchisee. They could not be compared to contracts with commercial agents, in view of the differences between them and the latter, since franchisees acted in their own name and on their own account and assumed the business risks. The franchise contract system in question involved perceptible restrictions on competition, bearing in mind that Pronuptia was, as it claimed itself, the French world leader in wedding dresses and accessories.

11. The French Government submitted that Article 85(1) was capable of applying to franchise contracts which were agreements relating to the distribution of a product and concluded with independent business people, but did not necessarily apply to them, having regard to the positive aspects of these contracts.

12. The Commission emphasised that the scope of Article 85(1) was not limited to certain types of contracts, from which it deduced that, when certain conditions were fulfilled, Article 85(1) applied also to contracts which, apart from the supply of goods, were intended to make available a trade name and a trade mark, whether registered or not, for products as well as for services.

13. It is appropriate then to note that franchise contracts whose legality has not hitherto been submitted to the Court's examination, are of great variety. It emerges from the discussion before the Court that a distinction must be drawn between different types of franchise contract and particularly franchise contracts for services by virtue of which the franchisee offers a service under the sign, trade name or trade mark of the franchisor and conforms with the requirements of the latter; production franchise contracts, by virtue of which the franchisee himself manufactures, in accordance with the franchisor's directions, the goods which he sells under the latter's trade mark; and finally, distribution franchise contracts by virtue of which the franchisee undertakes to sell certain goods in a shop which carries the franchisor's sign. The Court will pronounce only on this third category of contracts, to which the question from the national court expressly relates.

14. It should then be observed that the compatibility of distribution franchise contracts with Article 85(1) cannot be assessed in an abstract way but only by reference to the clauses contained in these contracts. To ensure that its reply is fully helpful to the national court, this Court will be concerned with contracts which have contents such as those which have already been described.

15. In a system of distribution franchises such as this, a firm which is established in a market as a distributor and which is thus able to develop a scheme of commercial methods, grants independent business men — for consideration — the opportunity to establish themselves in other markets using its sign and its business methods on which its success has been based. Rather than a system of distribution, it concerns a way of exploiting financially, without committing its own capital, a collection of skills. Moreover, this system makes available to business men, who do not have the necessary experience, access to methods which they would have acquired only after long efforts of trial and error and allows them to benefit from the reputation of the sign. Distribution franchise contracts are in this respect different from sales concession contracts or from those which link the appointed retailer in a system of selective distribution which includes neither the use of the same sign nor the application of uniform business methods nor the payment of royalties in respect of agreed advantages. Such a system, which allows the franchisor to share the success, does not in itself jeopardise competition. To enable it to function, a double condition has to be fulfilled.

16. In the first place, the franchisor has to be able to communicate to franchisees his know-how and to provide them with the necessary help in implementing his methods, without running the risk that this know-how and this help benefit, however indirectly, his competitors. Consequently the clauses which are indispensable to avoid this risk do not constitute restrictions on competition in the sense of Article 85(1). From this follows the prohibition on the franchisee on opening, during the period of the contract or during a reasonable period after its expiration, a shop having a similar or identical purpose, in a region in which it could compete with members of the network. Similarly, from this flows the obligation imposed on the franchisee not to transfer his shop without the prior agreement of the franchisor; this clause helps to avoid the benefit of the know-how provided and the help given passing indirectly to a competitor.

17. In the second place, the franchisor must be able to take appropriate measures to preserve the identity and the reputation of the network symbolised by the sign. It follows from this that the clauses which institute controls indispensable for this purpose do not constitute restrictions of competition in the sense of Article 85(1).

18. Similar considerations apply to the obligation on the franchisee to apply the business methods developed by the franchisor and to make use of the know-how which has been provided.

19. This is also the case regarding the obligation on the franchisee not to sell the goods covered by the contract except in a location furnished and decorated according to the franchisor's instructions, an obligation whose object is to guarantee a uniform presentation meeting certain requirements. These same requirements apply to the positioning of the shop, whose choice is also liable to influence the reputation of the network. This also explains why the franchisee cannot transfer his shop to another location without the agreement of the franchisor.

20. The prohibition on the franchisee transferring the rights and obligations resulting from the contract without the franchisor's agreement safeguards the latter's right to choose freely the franchisees whose commercial qualifications are a condition on which the reputation of the network is founded and maintained.

21. Thanks to the control exercised by the franchisor over the stock offered by the franchisee, the public can find at each franchisee's establishment goods of the same quality. It may be impracticable in certain cases, as in the field of fashion goods, to formulate objective quality specifications. Ensuring respect for these specifications may also, in view of the large number of franchisees, involve too great a cost. The clause providing that the franchisee should sell only those goods originating with the franchisor or with suppliers chosen by the franchisor may, in such conditions, be considered necessary by way of protection for the network's reputation. It should not, however, lead to a situation in which the franchisee is prevented from acquiring those goods from other franchisees.

22. Finally, as advertising contributes towards forming the image which the public has of the sign symbolising the network, the clause which subjects all advertising by the franchisee to the franchisor's consent is also indispensable for the preservation of the network's identity, provided that it concerns only the nature of the advertising.

23. It is appropriate, on the other hand, to emphasise that, far from being necessary for the protection of the know-how provided or the preservation of the identity and reputation of the network, certain clauses restrict competition between its members. This is the case with clauses which attain a sharing of markets between franchisor and franchisees or between franchisees or which prevent the latter from competing among themselves on prices.

24. In this respect it is necessary to draw the attention of the national court to the clause which obliges the franchisee to sell the contract goods only from the location specified in the contract. This clause prohibits a franchisee from opening a second shop. Its real significance appears if it is related to the commitment entered into by the franchisor to ensure that the franchisee has within a certain territory the exclusive use of the licensed sign. To fulfill the promise thus made to a franchisee, the franchisor must not only undertake not to become established himself in the territory but also to require from other franchisees an undertaking not to open another shop beyond their own. The juxtaposition of clauses of this type leads to a certain sharing of markets between the franchisor and the franchisee or between the franchisees and thereby restricts competition within the network. Moreover, it follows from the judgment of 13 July 1966, in *Consten and Grundig v. the Commission* (cases 36–8/64), that this type of restriction constitutes a limitation of competition in the sense of Article 85(1), inasmuch as it concerns a sign which has already been widely broadcast. It is certainly possible that a candidate franchisee would not take the risk of becoming integrated in a chain of shops, by making his own investment, by paying a relatively high fee for entry and by undertaking to pay a substantial annual fee, if he could not, thanks to a certain protection against competition by the franchisor and by other franchisees, have some hope that his business could be profitable. This consideration can always apply, but only in the context of the possible examination of the agreement in the light of the conditions of Article 85(3).

25. If clauses which limit the franchisee's freedom to determine his prices are restrictive of competition, the same is not true of the fact that the franchisor may communicate indicative prices to franchisees, always on condition that, as between the franchisor and franchisees or between franchisees, there is no concerted practice with a view to the effective application of these prices. It is up to the national court to verify whether this condition exists.

26. It is important to conclude by saying that the distribution franchise contracts which contain clauses leading to a sharing of markets between the franchisor and franchisees or between franchisees are in any event liable to affect trade between member states, even if they are concluded between firms established within the same member state, to the extent that they prevent franchisees from setting up in another member state.

27. In view of the foregoing considerations, the first question has to be answered as follows:

(1) The compatibility of distribution franchise contracts with Article 85(1) depends on the clauses contained in those contracts and on the economic context in which they have been included.

(2) Clauses which are indispensable for the purpose of preventing the know-how provided and the help given by the franchisor from benefiting competitors do not constitute restrictions of competition within the meaning of Article 85(1).

(3) Clauses which institute controls indispensable for the preservation of the identity and reputation of the network symbolised by the sign do not constitute restrictions of competition within the meaning of Article 85(1).

(4) Clauses which result in a sharing of markets between franchisor and franchisees or between franchisees constitute restrictions of competition within the meaning of Article 85(1).

(5) The fact that the franchisor may communicate to the franchisee indicative prices does not constitute a restriction of competition, provided that, as between the franchisor and the franchisees or between the franchisees, there is no concerted practice with a view to the effective application of these prices.

(6) Distribution franchise contracts which contain clauses leading to market sharing between franchisor and franchisee or between franchisees are liable to affect trade between member states.

Second question

28. The second question, which was put only in case an affirmative response was given to the first, raises the question whether Commission Regulation 67/67, of 22 March 1967, concerning the application of Article 85(3) of the Treaty to certain categories of exclusive agreements applies in the case of distribution franchise contracts. Having regard to the foregoing considerations relating to the clauses which lead to a sharing of markets between franchisor and franchisees and between franchisees, it does still have some interest; and it is appropriate to examine it.

29. The firm Pronuptia de Paris, the franchisor, suggested that the Court should give a positive response to the second question. Regulation 67/67 applied to exclusive supply and delivery obligations when the undertakings were contained in agreements comprising in addition the grant of a licence to use trade mark or other signs distinctive of the firm. In a franchise contract, the exclusive obligations of delivery and supply also presented certain advantages which were set out in the sixth recital of Regulation 67/67. Clauses other than those covered by Article 2 of Regulation 67/67 were not an obstacle to the application of exemption, inasmuch as they did not restrict competition within the meaning of Article 85(1).

30. Madam Schillgallis, the franchisee, concluded that Regulation 67/67 was inapplicable to franchise contracts. In the first place, the Regulation had been drafted on the basis of the experience acquired at the time by the Commission, an experience which concerned only sales concession agreements. In the second place, the franchisor had considerably greater powers over the franchisee than the licensor over his concessionaire. In the third place, the restriction of competition inherent in franchise contacts also applied at the horizontal level, since the franchisor himself generally exploited the subsidiaries which intervened at the same stage in the economic process as the franchisees.

31. The French Government submitted that Regulation 67/67 did not appear to be applicable to this type of contract.

32. The Commission admitted at the outset that it did not have sufficient experience to define the concept of the franchise contract. It added that it was not the object of Regulation 67/67 to exempt restrictions on competition contained in agreements which included the licensing of the sign, a trade name or a trade mark, forms of licensing which, taken together with the transfer of know-how and business help, seemed to it to be the essential element of franchise contracts. Nevertheless, if licence agreements of this type included agreements on the supply of goods with a view to resale, and if these supply agreements could be separated from the licensing agreements, Regulation 67/67 could then apply to supply agreements, provided that its conditions had been complied with. In this respect, the exclusive concessionaire should not be seen to impose, in his capacity as exclusive concessionaire, restrictions of competition other than those covered by Article 1(1) and Article 2(1). In the contracts which were the subject of the questions by the German Court, the location clause contained in the franchise contract established such a close link between the elements of exclusive distribution and the elements constituted an indivisible whole; and this made block exemption inapplicable even in respect of that part of the contract relating to the exclusive sales concession.

33. It is appropriate in this respect to consider several elements in the text of Regulation 67/67. In the first place, the category of contracts benefiting from block exemption is defined by reference to undertakings, whether reciprocal or not, of supply and sale and not by reference to factors such as the use of the same sign, the application of uniform business methods and the payment of fees by way of consideration for agreed advantages, which are characteristic of distribution franchise contracts. In the second place, the exact terms of Article 2 cover expressly only contracts for exclusive sales concessions, which have, as in the case already mentioned above, a different nature from distribution franchise contrasts. In the third place, the same Article lists the restrictions and obligations which may be imposed on the exclusive concessionaire, without making reference to those which may be stipulated by the other party to the contract; while, in the case of the distribution franchise contract, the obligations assumed by the franchisor, and particularly those governing the provision of know-how and help to the franchisee, acquire a special importance. In the fourth place, the list of obligations on the part of the concessionaire, covered by Article 2(2), allow for the inclusion neither of the obligation to pay fees nor of clauses which set up controls indispensable for preserving the identity and reputation of the network.

34. It must therefore be concluded that for these reasons Regulation 67/67 does not apply to distribution franchise contracts such as those which have been examined in the context of the present proceedings.

Third question

35. Taking into account the replies given to the second question from the national court, the third question becomes superfluous.

Costs

36. The costs incurred by the French Government and by the Commission of the European Communities, which have submitted observations to the Court, cannot be recovered. Since, as regards the principal parties in the case, the proceedings stem from matters raised before the national court, it is for the latter to decide on the costs.

For these reasons, the Court deciding on the questions submitted to it by the Federal Court, by order dated 15 May 1984, states the law as follows:

1. (a) The compatibility of distribution franchise contracts with Article 85(1) depends on the clauses contained in those contracts and on the economic context in which they have been included.

   (b) Clauses which are indispensable for the purpose of preventing the know-how provided and the help given by the franchisor from benefiting competitors do not constitute restrictions of competition within the meaning of Article 85(1).

   (c) Clauses which institute controls indispensable for the preservation of the identity and reputation of the network symbolised by the sign do not constitute restrictions of competition within the meaning of Article 85(1).

   (d) Clauses which result in a sharing of markets between franchisor and franchisees or between franchisees constitute restrictions of competition within the meaning of Article 85(1).

   (e) The fact that the franchisor may communicate to the franchisee indicative prices does not constitute a restriction of competition, provided that, as between the franchisor and the franchisees or between the franchisees, there is no concerted practice with a view to the effective application of these prices.

(f) Distribution franchise contracts which contain clauses leading to market sharing between franchisor and franchisee or between franchisees are liable to affect trade between member states.

2. Regulation 67/67 does not apply to distribution franchise contracts such as those which have been examined in the context of the present proceedings.

Mackenzie Stuart, Everling, Bahlmann, Joilet, Koopmans, Due, Galmot.

Delivered publicly in Luxembourg on 28 January 1986.

A. J. Mackenzie Stuart President.

Appendix V

Commission Decisions

Yves Rocher

(87/14/EEC)

1. Facts

A. The undertaking

(1) Société d'études de chimie et de thérapie appliquées (SECTA) Laboratoires de Cosmétologie Yves Rocher, whose registered office is in La Gacilly, France, is one of the leading European producers of cosmetics. Its equity capital is held 35% by the Yves Rocher family and 65% by Sanofi, a subsidiary of Elf Aquitaine, whose cosmetics production accounts for a quarter of its total turnover.

(2) Yves Rocher markets its products in 50 countries and has 15 wholly-owned marketing subsidiaries abroad. It originally sold its products by mail order but, starting in 1970, has set up in seven Community Member States (France, Germany, Belgium, Luxembourg, the Netherlands, the United Kingdom and Spain) a network of franchised retail outlets known as 'Yves Rocher Beauty Centres'. These Centres sell only Yves Rocher products. The Yves Rocher group now has some 10 million mail-order customers. Its network of shops consists of about a thousand franchise businesses of which a little over 600 are in France. Their average annual turnover is less than 300 000 ECU. Yves Rocher also operates a number of pilot schemes on its own account.

B. The product and the market

(3) Cosmetics in the broad sense, i.e. that of substance used in beauty care, can be broken down into 42 groups comprising some 100 000 different products. This extreme diversity selects the public's many requirements, the creativity of perfumers and cosmeticians, and the high level of technical expertise attained which makes it possible to satisfy those requirements.

(4) Nevertheless, the general statistics published by the business circles concerned all distinguish beween four main categories of products:
— beauty products (make-up and skin-care products),
— alcohol-based perfumes,
— hair-care products,
— toiletries.

(5) In all the Member States in which the Yves Rocher network is established cosmetics are a growth market, albeit to differing degrees for each of the four segments referred to above. Most customers are women (90% of sales).

(6) On the supply side, the number of both producers and distributors of cosmetics is fairly large. The industry is characterised by the presence of subsidiaries of major industrial groups, being an attractive means of diversification for many groups whose principal line of business is technically similar (pharmaceutical groups in particular). The financial ties between cosmetics manufacturers are therefore global and complex.

(7) The degree of concentration in the industry is comparatively low. The largest European firm holds a 15% share of the Community market, and none of the others has a share exceeding 5%.

(8) If one compares the ranking, over a period of time, of producers in terms of market share, a fair amount of movement is apparent, which is itself an indication of the effort made by each firm to promote its image, and of the severity of competition between suppliers.

(9) In the cosmetics sector as a whole, Yves Rocher holds 7,5% of the French market, 6% of the Belgian market, and a share of less than 5% in every other Member State in which the network is established. Unlike some producers who specialise in one or other of the abovementioned four categories of cosmetics, Yves Rocher is active in every segment of the market. Its business is oriented more towards the production of beauty products and alcohol-based perfumes, but even in France, the country in which the Yves Rocher network is most extensive, its sales do not exceed 15% of total sales in any particular category of products.

(10) The channels through which cosmetics are distributed are many in number and complementary in character in every Member State in which the Yves Rocher chain is established. A distinction may be drawn between general retail outlets and specialist (or selective, exclusive or franchise) retail outlets.

(11) In France, about half the cosmetics sold are marketed through some 100 000 general retail outlets (stores selling household products

and cosmetics — *drogueries*), grocers' shops, self-service stores, etc.). A third of all sales are made through some 7 500 specialist retail outlets, including about a thousand franchise shops. Direct selling by the manufacturer (selling by mail order, door-to-door sales or own shops) and sales in chemist's shops each account for about 10% of the industry's total turnover. The respective share of sales accounted for by various forms of distribution varies, however, according to the market segment, as can be seen from the table below showing the proportion of each category of products sold by each distribution method.

(12) The percentage of overall cosmetics sales effected by general retailers is comparable in the other Member States concerned.

(13) Retail selling prices vary considerable from one Member State in which the network is established to another. Compared with the prices charged by its competitors, Yves Rocher, whose marketing method is a combination of selling by mail order and specialist retailing, fixes its prices at a level somewhere between those of specialist retailers and those of general retailers.

Yves Rocher sells its products to its franchisees at an average discount of 30% on its recommended selling prices as published in its catalogues, excluding VAT.

C. The system of notified agreements

(14) As well as selling by mail order, the Yves Rocher group markets its products in the seven Member States concerned through a thousand or so franchised retailers, supplied, in France, direct from the Yves Rocher company and, in the other Member States, by the marketing subsidiaries wholly owned by the company.

(15) The notified standard from franchise contracts are geared mainly to retailing: the beauty treatments that franchisees undertake to give under the notified contracts account for only a small proportion of their turnover.

The notified contracts all display basically the same features, with the exception of special arrangements for Belgian franchisees, particular provisions based on local commercial practice and the presence in the first few franchise contracts, concluded when the network was originally set up, of clauses prescribing resale prices and prohibiting cross supplies between Yves Rocher franchisees.

Methods of choosing franchisees used by Yves Rocher

(16) Yves Rocher selects its franchisees in the light of their personality, their apparent overall aptitude for running a cosmetics retailing business, and their performance in a training programme.

(in %)

Channels	Product					Total
	Alcohol-based perfumes	Beauty products	Toiletries	Hair-care products	Others	
General retailers	6,6	7,8	12,3	21,8	—	48,5
Specialist retailers	15,9	14,0	1,7	0,4	0,4	32,4
Direct selling	2,7	5,1	1,4	1,0	0,4	10,6
Sale in chemist's shops	0,1	5,4	1,2	1,7	—	8,4
Miscellaneous	0,1	—	—	—	—	0,1
Total	25,4	32,3	16,6	24,9	0,8	100,0

(Taken from a survey by DAFSA entitled 'The world perfume and cosmetics industry'.)

Contracts are concluded with the franchise personally and may not be assigned or transferred either in whole or in part without Yves Rocher's previous writtten consent, otherwise the agreement is cancelled without prior notice.

The franchisee undertakes to employ at his Centre a sufficient number of qualified staff.

Legal independence of franchisees

(17) All Yves Rocher franchisees are proprietors of their business, which they carry on at their own risk. They are responsible for the cost of fitting out their premises in accordance with plans and specifications which Yves Rocher causes to be drawn up at its own expense.

All commercial documents issued by the franchisee must carry the franchisee's name and the words 'Yves Rocher Beauty Center'. Yves Rocher have circulated a directive to franchisees requiring them to display an appropriate notice indicating their status of independent franchisees within the Yves Rocher chain.

Franchisees are required to take out insurance covering their civil liability and employer's liability throughout the period of the contract.

Clause concerning the location of the Beauty Centre

(18) Each contract defines the exact location of the franchisee's shop. In practice, Yves Rocher carries out a preliminary market and location study and proposes to the franchisee the most promising shopping district, within which the franchisee determines the exact location of his beauty centre with the franchisor's consent. The contract stipulates that the shop may not be transferred to another place without Yves Rocher's consent and that the use of Yves Rocher identifying marks is not authorised in any other place.

Exclusive territory of the franchisee

(19) Yves Rocher grants the franchisee an exclusive right within an area defined in the contract to use the franchisor's identifying marks and know-how with a view to selling its products through a retail outlet. The franchisor undertakes not to authorise third parties to open another Yves Rocher Beauty Centre in that territory and not to establish such Centres there itself.

Yves Rocher reserves the right to sell its products to consumers by other means (in particular by mail order).

Grant by Yves Rocher of the right to use their identifying marks (shop sign, trademarks, symbols), and their designs and models

(20) Yves Rocher grants the franchisee the right to use the sign, trademarks, symbols, designs and models of which it is the owner, in particular for the bottles, packages and furnishings of the Beauty Centre.

(21) These rights may be exercised only in connection with the operation of the Beauty Centre and its purpose; the franchisee may not exercise them in any other place or for any other purpose and recognises moreover that the right to use the present and future trade name, marks and symbols of Yves Rocher belongs exclusively to the company. The contract does not however restrict the right of franchisees to contract the franchisor's industrial property rights.

The grant by Yves Rocher of the above rights ceases on termination of the contract.

Transfer by Yves Rocher to the franchisee of commercial and beauty treatment know-how

(22) The know-how Yves Rocher undertakes to communicate to the franchisee encompasses every aspect of the franchise business, and in particular technical, commercial, promotional, publicity, administrative and financial matters, staff training and general administration.

Before the Centre is opened, Yves Rocher arranges training sessions for the franchisee on the organisation and running of a Centre and on the beauty products and treatments available there. It provides further training from time to time during the currency of the contract.

The franchisee undertakes not to divulge any confidential information and instructions to third parties, and not to use Yves Rocher's commercial secrets in any place or for any purpose other than the Beauty Centre.

Provision of technical and commercial assistance to the franchisee by Yves Rocher

(23) When the Centre is opened, Yves Rocher provides the franchise with all the aid it considers appropriate in order that the Centre be established and operated in accordance with its policy and image, and places at the franchisee's disposal all its technical knowledge.

During the currency of the contract, the company advises and assists the franchisee on request in the operation of the Beauty Centre: procedures, purchase of products and supplies, publicity (publicity campaign at the time of launch, and periodical sales support and promotion activities, either in the shop or aimed directly at the consumer).

Financial obligations of the franchisee towards the franchisor

(24) In all countries, the franchisee must pay an initial licence fee. In the Netherlands, in addition to an initial licence fee at a lower amount, he must pay an annual royalty of 1% of his turnover net of tax, excluding beauty treatment services.

The franchisee also pays Yves Rocher at regular intervals a fixed proportion of publicity costs.

Use by franchisees of uniform trading methods under Yves Rocher's supervision

(25) The method contracts require franchisees to employ uniform trading methods. The franchisee undertakes to operate his Centre in accordance with the procedures laid down by the company in an operating manual. This covers the following aspects of running the business: decor, lighting, fitting-out in accordance with plans and specifications which Yves Rocher causes to be drawn up at its own expense, layout and furnishing of Centres, presentation of products, sales techniques, publicity campaigns, nature and quality of beauty treatment services, accounts, insurance, etc.

The franchisee is obliged to submit for the prior approval of Yves Rocher all forms of publicity and promotion which he wishes to undertake on his own account. The control exercised by the franchisor extends only to the nature of the publicity and not to the retail prices quoted therein.

The franchisee also undertakes to operate one or more beauty treatment cabines in which only products and treatments authorised by the company may be used or given.

The franchisor reserves the right to carry out checks on stock levels and obtain from the franchisee a copy of his accounts or balance sheet.

Non-competition covenant

(a)   During the lifetime of the contract

(26) The franchisee is expressly forbidden to carry on either directly or indirectly, whether in return for payment or not, any business which competes with an Yves Rocher Beauty Centre. The franchisee is free to acquire financial interests in the capital of a competitor of Yves Rocher, provided this investment does not involve him personally in carrying on competing activities.

He is obliged to sell only products bearing the Yves Rocher trademark, although he may sell accessories (brushes, tweezers, nail scissors, etc.) with Yves Rocher's previous consent.

(b) On termination of the contract

(27) The franchisee is forbidden to compete with Yves Rocher, whether directly or indirectly, even as an employee, for a period of one year within the exclusive territory, whether on his own account or with the help of a rival firm.

Supply arrangements

(28) The franchisee may purchase Yves Rocher products not only from Yves Rocher but also from other franchisees, whether or not the latter are located in the same Member State.

He may buy approved accessories, shop furnishings and products for beauty treatment purposes from any supplier.

Sales promotion obligation

(29) The franchisee undertakes to devote all his energy and as much time as necessary to promoting the sale of Yves Rocher products and beauty treatments and agrees not to carry on any activities incompatible with those of a Beauty Centre.

Franchisees selling prices

(30) Yves Rocher circulates to its franchisees a list of recommended resale prices. All franchisees, including those in Belgium, are free to fix their retail selling prices at a lower or higher level, it being understood that it is recommended to them not to sell at a higher price than that given in the catalogue.

As a result of observations made by the Commission, Yves Rocher has expressly deleted with effect from 1 December 1986 the resale price maintenance provisions — which were not applied in practice — contained in the first contracts concluded when the network was originally set up.

Cross supplies between Yves Rocher franchisees

(31) The franchisee is prohibited from selling, whether directly or indirectly, Yves Rocher products to resellers other than Yves Rocher franchisees.

The first contracts forbade the franchisee to sell products even to other Yves Rocher franchisees. This provision has been deleted with effect from 1 December 1986 as a result of observations made by the Commission. Yves Rocher now authorises in all its contracts cross supplies, both national and transnational, between its franchisees.

Duration of contracts

(32) All Yves Rocher contracts are normally concluded and renewed for not more than five years.

Legal status of the Belgian franchisees

(33) Yves Rocher franchisees resell Yves Rocher products and approved accessories (cf. point 26) and give beauty treatments entirely in their own name and for their own account.

However, under the terms of their contracts, the Belgian franchisees sell, in Yves Rocher's name and for its account, Yves Rocher products supplied by the franchisor or by the other Belgian franchisees by way of cross supplies (cf. point 31) and receive a commission.

In each case, Belgian franchisees are free to fix their selling price to consumers (cf. point 30), it being understood that the amount of the 30% commission owed to them by the franchisor when they sell in its name and on its account, varies accordingly.

Third parties' observations

(34) In response to publication of a notice pursuant to Article 19(3) of Regulation No 17, the Commission received comments from several third parties. Some approved in substance the exemption of the notified standard form contracts, subject to certain objections of principle to the practice of recommending maximum resale prices, the effect of which could be to bring consumer prices to a uniform level. For the purpose of clarification, Yves Rocher has, at the request of the Commission, issued a circular to franchisees stressing that the recommended prices are purely guidelines and has undertaken to avoid any reference in its circulars to the notion of a maximum price. From now on the catalogues circulated by Yves Rocher will mention that the prices are recommended prices.

II   Legal Assessment

A.   Article 85(1)

(35) Article 85(1) prohibits as incompatible with the common market all agreements between undertakings which may affect trade between Member States and which have as their object or effect the prevention, restriction or distortion of competition within the common market.

Characteristics of the franchise contracts at issue

(36) By the notified standard form retail franchise contracts, Yves Rocher grants to its franchisees the exclusive right within an area defined in the contract, to use in a retail shop Yves Rocher identifying marks (sign, trademark and trade name) and its designs and models for the sale of its products.

Yves Rocher transfers to them know-how, consisting in a body of technical and commercial knowledge, previously tested by the franchisor itself, which is not divulged to third parties and therefore constitutes a competitive advantage. This know-how, which is set out in an operating manual and backed up by continuing technical and commercial assistance, is constantly updated in the light of experience gained by the franchisor through its mail-order business and pilot schemes.

The close association between these two forms of support provided by the franchisor helps create an original formula for the retailing of a range of cosmetics based on the theme of natural beauty from plants and sold under a single brand, which franchisees agree to promote exclusively.

(37) These rights of user are not granted unconditionally. Franchisees may exploit the industrial property rights granted and the knowledge communicated only in strict accordance with their subject matter: the original and constantly evolving formula for the retailing of Yves Rocher products using the franchisor's proven trading methods.

(38) Inasmuch as the members of the Yves Rocher network are thus bound together by close *de facto* commercial ties, the franchise contracts at issue are the expression of a closely integrated form of distribution. They nonetheless constitute agreements between undertakings within the meaning of Article 85(1), since the franchisees are the proprietors of their businesses, of which they bear the start-up costs and which they operate at their own risk.

Contractual obligations not restrictive of competition

(39) The original distribution formula translated into action by the contracts at issue does not in itself interfere with competition having regard to existing structures of production and supply in the relevant market (*see* point 15 of the *Pronuptia* case at Appendix IV above). It enables Yves Rocher to establish a uniform distribution network without investing its own capital in the fitting-out of retail shops and at the same time gives non-specialists access to the use of well-known identifying marks and proven trading methods.

(40) The obligations imposed by the franchisor on its franchisees to ensure that they exploit its proprietary industrial property rights and

know-how in a manner in keeping with their subject matter are inherent in the very existence of its right in its intellectual creations and fall outside the scope of the contractual and concerted practice of Article 85(1). Consequently, the restrictions on the commerical freedom of franchisees, without which the transfer of the distribution formula concerned could not be envisaged, do not constitute restrictions of competition within the meaning of Article 85(1).

(41) The absence of any contractual obligation on the part of Yves Rocher to apply selection criteria in the choice of its franchisees is explained by the fact that Yves Rocher itself trains franchisees during an induction course with a view to setting up new franchise shops. It is logically entitled to choose its partners freely and turn down applicants who do not, in its view, have the personal qualities and business qualifications which it requires for the application of the formula it has developed.

(42) The franchisor must also be able to participate in determining the location of the Beauty Centre with the franchisee, in their mutual interest: a bad choice might cause the franchisee to fail in business and indirectly damage the network's reputation. In practice, Yves Rocher carries out a preliminary market and location survey, and proposes to the franchisee the most promising area. The exact location of the shop is determined by the franchisee with the franchisor's consent. In any event, the shop's location is agreed upon in the general interest of all members of the chain. For the same reasons, any change in the Beauty Centre's location is subject to Yves Rocher's consent. Article 85(1) is not applicable to this clause to the extent that the relocation of a Beauty Centre may only be refused for reasons of the network's reputation.

(43) The obligation on the part of the franchisee to sell Yves Rocher products only in a Beauty Centre fitted out and decorated in accordance with plans and specifications which Yves Rocher causes to be drawn up at its own expense is also intended to ensure compliance with the original distribution formula communicated by the franchisor. The exterior appearance and interior lay-out of a Beauty Centre and the presentation of products are not factors which can be divorced from the methods and procedures transmitted by Yves Rocher or from the network's brand image.

The same is true of the franchisee's obligation to use know-how transferred by the franchisor and to apply the trading methods developed by the franchisor.

(44) The clause whereby any local publicity undertaken by the licensee on his own account must be submitted for the previous approval of Yves Rocher is, so far as it concerns only the nature of the publicity

to the exclusion of selling prices, intended to ensure a qualitative control by the franchisor over individual publicity measures in order to avoid any possible deviation from the theme of natural beauty from plants, on which the network's image is based.

(45) The obligation on the franchisee to sell only products bearing the Yves Rocher trademark — except in the case of accessories previously approved by the franchisor — is inherent in the very nature of the Yves Rocher distribution formula, the purpose of which is to enable independent traders to sell the complete range of Yves Rocher products using a sign, a trademark and symbols, as well as trading methods which have proved effective. The retailing of products bearing trademarks other than that of the franchisor exposes Yves Rocher to the risk of the use of their know-how for the benefit of competing producers and would detract from the identity of the network, which is symbolized by the Yves Rocher sign.

This implies that the franchisee may obtain supplies only from Yves Rocher or from other franchisees.

(46) The prohibition on the resale by franchisees of Yves Rocher products to resellers who do not belong to the Yves Rocher network is in this case inherent in franchisee's obligations to comply with the franchisor's procedures and methods and to offer products for sale under the Yves Rocher sign. These obligations would be made meaningless if Yves Rocher franchisees could freely pass over the goods covered by the contract to resellers who by definition have no access to the Yves Rocher know-how and are not bound by the same obligations, which are necessary in order to establish and maintain the originality and reputation of the network and its identifying marks.

(47) The provision under which the franchisee agrees not to carry on competing activities for the duration of the contract, in the same way as the prohibition on the assignment or transfer in whole or in part of the franchise contract, without the prior written consent of the franchisor, and on the divulgence of the know-how made available, is indispensable to protect the know-how and assistance provided by the franchisor. By their nature, the know-how and assistance provided are of a kind which could be used for the benefit of other beauty products or services, which would, even if only indirectly, enable competitors to benefit from the trading methods employed. Other means to avoid the same risks might not be as effective.

The clause which requires that the acquisition of a financial interest in the capital of an undertaking competing with Yves Rocher should not involve the franchisee in personally taking part in competing activities pursues the same aim and is considered in the same way.

(48) The same is true of the clause forbidding former Yves Rocher franchisees from carrying on a retail cosmetics business in their former exclusive territories for one year after the contract's termination. This is simply intended to prevent Yves Rocher's competitors from benefiting from the know-how which has been communicated by Yves Rocher to the former franchisee, and from the clientele acquired as a result of that know-how and Yves Rocher's identifying marks at a time when, owing to the exclusivity of the territory allotted to the franchisee during the currency of the contract, Yves Rocher has no retail outlet in that territory after the contract's expiry and must therefore be allowed a reasonable period in which to establish a new Beauty Centre.

In the present case, the clause does not go beyond what is strictly necessary to achieve its purpose, since a former franchisee can compete with Yves Rocher as soon as the contract expires by setting up in business outside his former exclusive territory, possibly in the territory of other Yves Rocher franchisees. Under the circumstances, this provision cannot be considered as restrictive of competition under Article 85(1).

This assessment is without prejudice to the rights of franchisees under national law on termination of contract.

(49) The general sales promotion obligation imposed on franchisees, in that they undertake to devote all their energy and as much time as necessary to promoting the sale of Yves Rocher products and beauty treatments, and agree in consequence not to carry on any activities incompatible with those of their Centre does not in this case amount to a restriction of competition. The success of the distribution formula adopted by Yves Rocher depends on the presence and the personal commitment of the franchisee in the operation of the business, the franchisee being selected on the basis of his/her personal qualities after having undergone appropriate training by Yves Rocher. Subject to this reservation, the clause does not prohibit the franchisee from carrying on a non-competing business provided the franchisee's personal commitment to the distribution of the Yves Rocher products is ensured.

(50) The right which the franchisee reserves to inspect franchisees' stock levels, accounts and balance sheets, is to enable the franchisor to verify, if the need arises, whether franchisees are discharging their obligations. Insofar as this right serves only to enable checks to be carried out on franchisees' compliance with obligations not covered by Article 85(1), it likewise cannot be considered restrictive of competition without prejudice to any legal consequences under national law of interference by the franchisor.

In particular, the franchisor's right to inspect stock levels allows him to avoid the unduly long stocking of products which could affect their quality.

The Commission reserves its right to intervene in case these controls would be used by the franchisor to affect the freedom of the franchisees to fix their selling prices.

(51) The recommended prices shown on the catalogues issued by Yves Rocher to franchisees are legitimate, since franchisees remain entirely free to determine their own prices and since, during the procedure, no evidence has been found of any concerted practice beween the franchisor and franchisees, or among franchisees, to the effect that the recommended prices should be applied (*see* point 25 of the *Pronuptia* case at Appendix IV above).

No anti-competitive effects from the point of view of competing producers and distributors

(52) From the point of view of competing producers and distributors, the Yves Rocher network cannot have appreciable horizontal anti-competitive effects as against other brands in view of the large number of both producers and distributors of cosmetics.

(53) Although it is one of the leading European producers, Yves Rocher holds just over 5% of the entire cosmetics market in only two Member States, and in its principal geographical market it controls no more than 15% of one of the four market segments. Its 600 or so franchised retail outlets in France cannot, with the approximately 7 000 specialist retailers in that country, have the effect of freezing the structures of distribution and rendering access to the market appreciably more difficult for competing producers compared with the 100 000 general retail outlets in that country and the relatively large volume of their sales in each of the four categories of cosmetics. The same holds true for the other Member States, where the total number of Yves Rocher sales outlets is less than 500 and non-specialist retailers account for a similar proportion of the industry's sales.

Contractual obligations restrictive of competition

(54) On the other hand, Yves Rocher's selection of only one franchisee for a given territory within which the franchisee has an exclusive right to use the franchisor's identifying marks and know-how for the sale of Yves Rocher products in a Beauty Centre, the franchisor's undertaking not to establish a shop itself in the territory of each of its franchisees, combined with the prohibition on the opening by franchisees of a second shop stemming from the prohibition on using Yves Rocher's identifying marks in a location other than that specified in the contract,

results in a degree of sharing of markets between the franchisor and the franchisees or between franchisees, thereby restricting competition within the distribution network.

(55) By virtue of such clauses, Yves Rocher's franchise contracts prevent franchisees from setting up in business in another Member State and may thus affect trade between Member States to an appreciable extent in view of the size of the Yves Rocher group, its market share — greater than 5% in two of the Member States concerned — the reputation of its products, the expansion of the Yves Rocher chain of shops throughout a substantial part of the common market and the existence alongside that chain of a highly developed mail-order business. The notified contracts therefore fall within Article 85(1).

B.   Article 85(3)

(56) Under Article 85(3), the provisions of Article 85(1) may be declared inapplicable in the case of any agreement which contributes to improving the production of distribution of goods or to promoting technical or economic progress, while allowing consumers a fair share of the resulting benefit, and which does not:

(a) impose on the undertakings concerned restrictions which are not indispensable to the attainment of these objectives;
(b) afford such undertakings the possibility of eliminating competition in respect of a substantial part of the products in question.

(57) Commission Regulations No 67/67/EEC and (EEC) No 1983/83, as last amended by the Act of Accession of Spain and Portugal, on the block exemption of exclusive dealing and exclusive distribution agreements are not applicable to the standard form franchise at issue, the legal nature of which is different(*see* points 15 and 33 of the *Pronuptia* case at Appendix IV above). The franchise contracts go beyond mere distribution agreements, for the franchisor undertakes to grant rights to use its identifying marks and its proven trading methods with a view to the application of an original and changing distribution formula. It must therefore be decided whether the contracts at issue qualify for an individual exemption under Article 85(3).

(58) Yves Rocher's franchise contracts contribute to improving the distribution of the goods in question, since they help the producer to penetrate new markets by enabling him to expand his network without having to undertake any investment in the fitting-out of new shops. Moreover, the development of a chain of identical retail outlets strengthens competition *vis-à-vis* large retail organisations with a branch network. By its policy of selection and training, directed mainly at prospective franchisees with no experience of running a retail establishment

selling beauty products, whose sales outlets thus supplement existing specialist sales outlets, Yves Rocher increases interbrand competition and accordingly improves the structure of cosmetics distribution.

(59) The close integration of independent traders within the Yves Rocher network leads to a rationalisation of distribution through a standardisation of trading methods covering every aspect of retailing. The direct nature — there being no wholesalers — of the relationship between franchisor and franchisees facilitates consumer feedback and the adjustment of supply to a constantly changing demand, the fickleness of which is a feature of the market concerned.

(60) The grant to franchisees of an exclusive territory, combined with the prohibition on setting up outside this territory, enables them to pursue a more intensive policy of selling Yves Rocher products by concentrating on their alloted territory, helped in this by the fact that the Yves Rocher retailing formula is based on a single brand. Territorial exclusivity also simplifies planning and ensures the continuity of supplies.

(61) The agreements at issue allow consumers a fair share of the benefit resulting from these improvements in distribution, as a wide range of the same cosmetics is more readily available in a number of Member States. Moreover, because they are running their own business and are therefore motivated by the desire for maximum efficiency, franchisees make dynamic and hard-working retailers, which is to the consumer's advantage. The homogeneity of the network, the standardisation of trading methods and the direct link between franchisor and franchisee all ensure that the consumer benefits in full from the know-how passed on by the franchisor and ensure the quality and freshness of the products, which are liable to deteriorate rapidly with time. Lastly, Yves Rocher's policy of charging prices mid-way between those of specialist and non-specialist retailers helps to widen the circle of cosmetics users.

(62) Finally, the commercial practice of the Yves Rocher network and the civil liability insurance taken out by the Yves Rocher group and by franchisees ensure that any product which may be defective is replaced and that any damage which might be sustained as a result of using an Yves Rocher product or undergoing beauty treatment by a franchisee will be covered. Further, consumers will be in a position to know that they are dealing with independent traders whose individual liability may be called upon.

(63) Yves Rocher's contracts have not imposed any restrictions which are not indispensable to the attainment of the abovementioned objective since the resale-price-maintenance clauses and the prohibition on cross supplies between franchisees, which prevented the machinery for cor-

recting price differences within the network from operating, were deleted from old contracts. The remaining obligations caught by Article 85(1) are indispensable to the establishment of the network: none of the Yves Rocher franchisees would, in all probability, have agreed to undertake the investment needed to set up an independent business had he not been certain of receiving a degree of protection against competition from another Centre set up in his territory by the franchisor or another franchisee.

(64) The agreement between Yves Rocher and each of its franchisees does not afford them the possibility of eliminating competition in respect of a substantial part of cosmetics, as competition between franchisees is sufficiently ensured by the smallness of the exclusive territory alloted and the possibility for each franchisee to sell to any customer, from whatever area, entering his shop.

The loosening-up of the system, adjusted by Yves Rocher at the Commission's request, has brought about a degree of price competition within the network in that franchisees can now freely obtain supplies from any other franchisee and profit from any difference between the selling prices which Yves Rocher fixes in each Member State at a level somewhere between those charged by its major local competitors. Yves Rocher will be unable to prevent or hinder, on pain of revocation of the exemption pursuant to Article 8(3) of Regulation No 17, recourse by franchisees to the transnational cross supplies which the price differences between certain Member States are likely to encourage, especially in the case of franchisees operating near national frontiers.

(65) Even the combined effect of all Yves Rocher franchise contracts is not enough to afford the network the possibility of eliminating competition between brands, in view of the breadth and competitive structure of the supply side and the modest share of the cosmetics market held by Yves Rocher.

(66) The provisions of Article 85(1) may therefore be declared not applicable to the standard form Yves Rocher franchise contracts, under the terms of Article 85(3). Accordingly it is not necessary to examine further the legal status of the Belgian franchisees. Assuming that they fall within the scope of Article 85(1) they benefit from the exemption in any event.

C.   Articles 6 and 8 of Regulation No 17

(67) The first franchise contracts concluded by Yves Rocher when its network was originally set up did not satisfy the requirements of Article 85(3) in the form in which they were notified, in that they contained resale-price-maintenance clauses and a prohibition on cross supplies

between Yves Rocher franchisees. These obligations have been deleted with effect from 1 December 1986 at the Commission's request. It is therefore possible, by virtue of Article 6(1) of Regulation No 17, to make the date on which the exemption takes effect with regard to the old, amended contracts coincide with the date of coming into force of the amendments, namely 1 December 1986.

(68) The other contracts fulfilled the exemption conditions from the date on which they were notified, namely 15 January 1985. In accordance with the second sentence of Article 6(1) of Regulation No 17, the exemption may take effect on that date with regard to these contracts.

(69) In view of the novel character of the notified standard form contracts and the speed at which the structure and methods of cosmetics distribution are liable to change, it is desirable to limit the period of validity of this Decision to 14 January 1992.

(70) Furthermore, it is appropriate that an obligation should be attached to the decision under Article 8(1) of Regulation No 17, requiring Yves Rocher to communicate to the Commission each year the recommended sales prices and prices charged to franchisees for Yves Rocher products on the date of such communication in each Member State where the network is established. This obligation will permit the Commission to assess the economic interest of franchisees in making transnational cross sales which should in the normal course of things be brought about by price differences between Member States, and thus contribute, allowing a reduction in these differences, to allowing consumers a fair share of the benefit resulting from the improvement in distribution. The obligation imposed should also permit the Commission to evaluate the risk of direct or indirect obstacles, whether concerted or unilateral, to transnational cross deliveries, with a view to the possible application of Article 8(3) of Regulation No 17.

Pronuptia

(87/17/EEC)

1. Facts

A. Pronuptia de Paris

(1) Pronuptia de Paris (Pronuptia) is a French public limited company incorporated in 1958 which has a registered capital of FF 3.3 million. Pronuptia specialises in the sale of bridal wear and accessories. On 9 December 1985 financial difficulties forced the company to apply to the

Paris Tribunal de Commerce, for temporary protection from its creditors, during which it was allowed to continue its operations.

(2) Pronuptia carries on business mainly in France and other European countries, but is also represented outside Europe in countries such as Canada, Japan, Lebanon and the United States.

(3) In France, its distribution network numbers 148 of which 135 are franchised, five are subsidiaries and eight are branches.

(4) In the other Member States (Germany, Belgium, Spain, Greece, Ireland, Luxembourg and the United Kingdom) in which Pronuptia uses franchising to distribute its products, it has a little over 100 franchised outlets. In Germany, Spain and the United Kingdom it also has subsidiaries.

(5) The total turnover of the Pronuptia network throughout the world in 1985 was about FF 250 million.

(6) Pronuptia claims to have the biggest chain of shops offering formal wear in the world, and to be the only network specialising in bridal wear in France, where there is no similarly organised competition. In France, Pronuptia holds about 30% of the bridal wear market. Against this, it holds only more modest shares in other Member States.

B.   The relevant products and market

(The services offered by the Pronuptia chain (honeymoons, photographers, receptions, etc.) are disregarded as they are at present only offered in France and only if the franchisee wishes. Their economic impact is therefore probably insignificant.)

(7) The Pronuptia network sells and hires not only wedding dresses but also wedding attire for attendants and guests, including men's formal wear, and a full range of accessories such as hats, veils, tights, gloves, shoes, handbags, garters, scarves, and lingeries. Its collection in any year numbers around 1 000 items of all types.

(8) The articles offered from Pronuptia outlets fall into three categories which also differ as to their sourcing:

(a) fashion goods, of Pronuptia's own design, which are manufactured for it by subcontractors, such as its wedding dress designs which are registered and bear the 'Pronuptia' trade mark;

(b) other fashion goods, not of Pronuptia's design but of designs commissioned or selected 'off-the-shelf' from other suppliers, which Pronuptia buys in and on which it also puts its trade mark;

(c) goods not designed by or for Pronuptia which are purchased by franchisees directly from the supplier of their choice and invoiced to them by the supplier.

The articles in categories (a) and (b) which are supplied and invoiced to franchisees by Pronuptia itself account for about two-thirds of the goods traded through the network. Pronuptia sells at the same prices to all franchisees.

(9) There are many other manufacturers of bridal fashions in France and other EEC countries. In France, there are, to name but a few, 'Les Mariées de Christina', 'Les Mariées de Marcelle', (Maggy Rouff), 'Les Mariées de France', 'Les Mariées de Reve', Claude Hervé, and 'Les Mariées Laura'; in Germany, there are Vera Mont, Pagels and Horrn, and the Team Brantude International chain. These manufacturers generally do not use the franchising route to sell their products. There is also competition from small dressmakers' shops and from the large fashion houses, all of which also design wedding dresses.

C. The Pronuptia franchise agreement

(10) Pronuptia proposes to sign the notified franchise agreement with all its franchisees both in France and in other EEC and non-EEC countries. It wishes the Commission to take a formal decision on its application for exemption of the agreement.

(11) The main provisions of the standard form agreement are as follows:

— The franchisor, Pronuptia, grants the franchisee the exclusive right to use the 'Pronuptia de Paris' trade mark in a defined sales territory, where the franchisee agrees to run a retail outlet dealing primarily in bridal wear and accessories under the Pronuptia name and logo or a derived logo approved by the franchisor. The franchisor undertakes to credit the franchisee with 10% of any mail-order sales it makes to customers in the territory involving products normally sold by the franchisee (clause 1).

— The franchisor undertakes to assist the franchisee with, in particular, selecting the site and the premises, shopfitting and stocking, regular training of the franchisee and his staff, promotion and advertising (for which the franchisor will provide point-of-sale material and will check that the franchisee's advertising is consistent with the network's brand image), and with continuing information and advice on innovations, promotions, market analysis, purchasing, etc. (clause 3).

— The franchisee undertakes not to use the Pronuptia trade mark and logo other than in conjunction with his own business name followed by the words 'Franchisee of Pronuptia de Paris' (clause 2).

— The franchisee agrees to carry on the franchise business in the particular manner developed by the franchisor and to use the know-how and expertise the franchisor has made available (clause 4, second paragraph, first indent).

— The franchisee is required to carry on the franchised business exclusively from the premises approved by the franchisor and fitted and decorated according to its instructions (clause 4, second paragraph, second indent).

— The franchisee must obtain the franchisor's approval for his local advertising (clause 4, second paragraph, third indent).

— In consideration of the rights and services received, the franchisee agrees to pay the franchisor an initial non-recurring fee and monthly royalties of between 4 and 5% of his total turnover from the direct sale of the franchise goods to customers from the franchised shop (clause 5). (The initial entry fee depends on the population of the allotted sales territory and varies between FF 0.15 and 0.20 per resident. The average population of a territory is about 300 000. The average entry fee is thus between FF 45 000 and 60 000.)

— The franchisee agrees to contribute a further sum, equal to his monthly royalty payment, to an advertising and promotional fund. This fund is managed by the franchisor, who however consults with franchisees on how to obtain the maximum benefit from the advertising budget (clause 6).

— The franchisee agrees to pay a minimum amount of royalties each year (clause 7).

— The franchisee agrees to order the goods traded from the franchised business exclusively from the franchisor, and may be required to obtain them exclusively from the franchisor if the franchisor is able to supply all the franchisee's requirements (clause 9, first and third paragraphs). However, the franchisee may obtain goods not connected with the essential object of the franchise business from the supplier of his choice, subject to the franchisor's right to vet such goods afterwards and to forbid the franchisee to market them from the franchised outlet if it judges them to be out of keeping with the brand image (clause 8, fourth and fifth paragraphs).

The franchisee undertakes to order at least 50% of his estimated sales, based on those of the previous year, in advance according to a fixed timetable and to have the articles shown in the catalogue in stock (clause 8, seventh and eighth paragraphs).

The franchisee is free to obtain Pronuptia products from any other franchise in the network (clause 8, ninth paragraph).

— The franchise is free to set his own retail prices, the prices circulated by the franchisor in internal literature being only suggestions. However, the franchisee is recommended not to exceed the maximum prices quoted by the franchisor in advertising and promotions (clause 9).

— The franchisee may not assign the franchised business in law or in fact to another person without the written consent of the franchisor. In the event of the sale or assignment of the management of the franchised business, or the death or incapacity of the franchisee, or any other circumstance which prevents the franchisee from carrying on the franchise normally, the franchisor is entitled to terminate the contract (clause 10). The contact may also be determined if the franchisee files for bankruptcy, goes into liquidation, ceases trading, or if either party breaches its obligations (clause 13).

— The agreement has a term of five years, which is automatically renewed for further one-year periods unless terminated upon at least six months' notice before the end of any period (clause 11).

— The franchisee agrees not to engage, directly or indirectly, during the currency of the agreement and for one year after its expiry or termination, in any similar business in the same area or in any other area where he would be in competition with another Pronuptia outlet. However, the franchisee may continue to carry on the business in the allotted territory after the agreement has ended if he

(i) has exercised the franchise for more than 10 years,

(ii) has discharged his contractual obligations, and

(iii) does not put the know-how and experience he has accumulated at the service of a competing network (clause 12).

(12) At the Commission's request, Pronuptia has amended the standard form agreement to put into writing certain rights which the franchisee allegedly had in practice already, namely the rights

(a) to purchase Pronuptia products from other franchisees,

(b) to purchase goods not connected with the essential object of the franchise business from suppliers of their choice, subject to *ex post* qualitative vetting by the franchisor, and

(c) to set their own retail prices, the prices circulated by the franchisor being only suggestions and the franchisee merely being recommended not to exceed the maximum prices quoted by the franchisor in advertising and promotions. Pronuptia has abolished the clause which requires the franchisee not to harm the brand image of the franchisor by his pricing level.

D. The legal proceedings between Pronuptia and one of its German franchises

(13) Following a legal proceeding in 1981, on the subject of a franchise contract and taken by Pronuptia's German subsidiary, Pronuptia GmbH, against one of its franchisees, the Federal Supreme Court asked the Court of Justice of the European Communities for a preliminary ruling on the following questions (*inter alia*):

(i) whether, franchise agreements such as those before it fell within the scope of Article 85(1), and, if so,

(ii) whether such agreements could be covered by Commission Regulation 67/67/EEC, and, if so,

(iii) whether particular clauses found in the agreements before the Court were covered by Regulation 67/67/EEC.

The Court of Justice gave judgment on 28 January 1986.

(14) In this judgment the Court of Justice defined retail franchises, with which the case and the present proceedings are concerned, as systems whereby 'a firm which has established itself in a certain business in one market, and has developed a system for carrying on that business, licenses independent traders, in return for payment, to use its name and proven formula for the business in other markets. Rather than a method of distribution, the system is a way of exploiting a body of expertise financially without having to invest the firm's own capital' (ground 15 of the judgment).

(15) The use of the same name and a uniform business system, and the payment of royalties for the advantages received, were typical features which set franchise agreements apart, the Court said, from exclusive distribution agreements or dealerships in a selective distribution system (ground 15).

(16) The Court acknowledged that for such a retail franchise operation to work the franchisor had to be able to

(a) 'make its know-how available to the franchisees and give them the assistance they require to be able to apply its business system', without running the risk of the know-how and assistance benefiting competitors (ground 16), and to

(b) 'take measures to preserve the common identity and reputation of the network trading under its names' (ground 17).

(17) After having noted in ground 15 that a retail franchise operation

'does not in itself restrict competition', the Court held in the operative part of the judgment that 'the compatibility of retail franchise contracts with Article 85(1) is a function of the clauses such contracts contain and the economic context in which they occur.'

(18) It further held not to be restrictions of competition falling within Article 85(1) 'clauses that are indispensable to prevent the know-how made available and the assistance given by the franchisor from benefiting competitors' and 'clauses that provide for the control essential to preserve the common identify and reputation of the network trading under the name'.

(19) It held on the other hand that 'clauses that involve market sharing between franchisor and franchisee or between franchisees constitute restrictions of competition within the meaning of Article 85(1) . . . and are capable of affecting trade between Member States'.

(20) The Decision in the present proceedings is inspired by the principles established and guidance given by the Court in the above judgment.

(21) Following the publication of a notice pursuant to Article 19(3) of Regulation No 17, the Commission has received several comments from third parties. These ask the Commission, before adopting a favourable decision, to be particularly careful in its examination of the legal and factual background of this standard agreement. In addition, they express concern over certain clauses of the contract, notably those that concern indicative prices and the prohibition of competition, and those which result in a partitioning of the market. In this respect, it is sufficient to point out that these clauses have been considered in the light of the principles set out in the judgment of the Court in the 'Pronuptia' case, already discussed, and taking very careful account of the factual background.

II. Legal Assessment

A. Article 85(1)

(22) Article 85(1) prohibits as incompatible with the common market all agreements between undertakings, decisions by associations of undertakings and concerted practices which may affect trade between Member States and which have as their object or effect the prevention, restriction or distortion of competition within the common market.

(23) The standard form of retail franchise agreement that Pronuptia proposes to sign with all its franchisees is an agreement between business undertakings within the meaning of Article 85.

(a) *Clauses not falling within Article 85(1)*

(24) First, the obligation on the franchisor to assist the franchisee with selecting the site and premises, shopfitting, promotion and advertising, training, news of products, innovations, etc. (clause 3 of the contract) does not fall within the scope of Article 85(1) because it forms part of the basic services the franchisor provides to the franchisee.

(25) The clauses in the contract that serve the following purposes are also not restrictions of competition falling within Article 85(1) according to the Court's judgment (see also paragraph 18), in which many of these clauses were specifically mentioned:

(i) clauses that are essential to prevent the know-how made available and the assistance given by the franchisor from benefitting competitors, namely (*inter alia):*
— the prohibition on the franchisee from engaging, directly or indirectly during the currency of the agreement and for one year after its expiry or termination, in any similar business in the same area or in any other area where he would be in competition with another Pronuptia outlet (clause 12).

The ban on competition during the period of the contract is necessary to protect the know-how and other assistance supplied. These benefits lend themselves to use with other products which would benefit competitors, if only indirectly. Other ways of preventing this risk might not be as effective.

The period of one year after the ending of the contract during which the franchisee continues to be bound by the non-competition covenant can in the present case be regarded as reasonable, within the meaning of the Court's judgment (ground 16), both for the purpose stated above and to allow Pronuptia to establish a new outlet in the territory of the former franchisee, which it is unable to do during the term of the contract because of the franchisee's exclusivity. It should also be noted that the post-term competition ban is relaxed in certain circumstances (clause 12, second paragraph).

Therefore, in this particular case, it should not be considered as restricting competition within the meaning of Article 85(1). The assessment of the clause in question does not prejudice any relief available to franchisees under national law at the end of the contract,
— the prohibition on the franchisee from selling the franchised business or assigning its management to another person, under penalty of termination by the franchisor (clause 10);

(ii) clauses that provide for the control essential to preserve the common identity and reputation of the network trading under the franchisor's name, namely (*inter alia*):

— the obligation on the franchisee to carry on the franchised business in the manner prescribed by Pronuptia and to use the know-how and expertise it makes available (clause 4, second paragraph, first indent),

— the obligation on the franchisee to carry on the franchised business from the premises approved by the franchisor and fitted and decorated according to its instructions (clause 4, second paragraph, second indent),

— the obligation on the franchisee to obtain the franchisor's approval for his local advertising (clause 4, second paragraph, third indent); it should be said that this control only concerns the nature of the advertisements with the object of ensuring conformity with the Pronuptia chain's brand image,

— the obligation on the franchisee, owing to the nature and quality of the products traded in the franchise business (fashion goods) and in order to preserve the consistency of the brand image, to order the goods connected with the essential object of the franchise business exclusively from the franchisor or suppliers nominated by the franchisor (clause 8, first paragraph). It is emphasised that the franchisee may purchase such goods from any other franchisee in the network (clause 8, ninth paragraph),

— the right of the franchisor to vet, *ex post*, the quality of products not connected with the essential object of the franchise business that the franchisee may purchase from the supplier of his choice and to forbid the franchisee to market them from the outlet if they are damaging to the brand image (clause 8, fourth and fifth paragraphs),

— the prohibition on the franchisee to assign their contract without the written agreement of the franchisor (clause 10).

(26) The Pronuptia standard form agreement also contains a number of other clauses which do not, by reason of their object, nature or effect, fall within Article 85(1). They include:

— the prohibition on the franchisee's using the Pronuptia trade mark or logo except in combination with his own business name followed by the words 'Franchisee of Pronuptia de Paris' (clause 2), which merely serves to identify the franchise relationship,

— the obligation on the franchise to pay the franchisor an initial non-recurring fee and monthly royalties of between 4 and 5% of his total turnover from the direct sale of the franchise goods to customers from the franchise shop (clause 5), because this is the franchisee's consideration for the rights and services obtained from the franchisor; it should be noted that no royalties are payable on goods that the franchise sells to other franchisees in the Pronuptia network.

— the obligation on the franchisee to contribute a further sum, equal to his monthly royalty payment, to an advertising and promotional fund (clause 6), this obligation, while it restricts the commercial freedom of the franchisee as regards how much to spend on advertising, how to advertise and whether to advertise at all, does not appear in the present case likely appreciably to affect competition on the relevant market,

— the circulation of retail prices to franchisees and the recommendation to franchisees not to exceed the maximum prices quoted by the franchisor in his advertising and promotions (clause 9).

With regard to the circulation of retail prices by the franchisor, the Commission has no evidence of any concerted practice between the franchisor and franchisees or between franchisees *inter se* to maintain these prices. In these circumstances the mere suggestion of prices for the guidance of franchisees cannot be regarded as restrictive of competition, as is acknowledged by the Court in its judgment (see in particular paragraph 1(e) of the operative part of the judgment).

There is no more evidence of abuse or ground a conclusion other than that reached for the circulation of retail prices, *mutandis mutandis*, in the recommendation to franchisees not to exceed the prices quoted by the franchisor in advertising and promotions, since the recommendation to observe certain prices is not itself likely to restrict the licensee's freedom to determine his prices. The Commission reserves the right to intervene if the franchisor should seek to limit the franchisees' freedom to set their resale prices.

(27) Retail franchise agreements, as the Court acknowledged in its judgment (see paragraph 15), are different in nature and in content from the bilateral obligations accepted by the parties, both in cases of exclusive distribuion contracts and dealerships in a selective distribution system.

This being so, the obligations on the franchisee

— to pay a minimum amount of royalties each year (clause 7),
— to order in advance according to a fixed timetable at least 50% of his estimated sales, based on those of the previous year (clause 8, seventh paragraph), and
— to hold stocks (clause 8, eighth paragraph),

do no constitute in the present case, restrictions of competition falling within Article 85(1).

In a selective distribution system, such obligations could be regarded as restricting competition when they exclude from the network firms that fulfilled the uniform qualitative selection criteria but were unwilling to accept such further obligations, and when their effect was that distributors would be forced to push certain products to the detriment of other items. It is a different matter, however, in the systems of distribution franchises operated by Pronuptia in this particular case. In effect, the characteristics of such a system are such that the franchisor grants to the franchisee the exclusive right to use his brand marks and his commercial know-how in a defined territory, and that the franchisor is free to choose his franchisees. The exclusion of any others from the territory allotted to the franchisee is therefore a consequence which is inherent in the very system of franchising. Likewise, one may consider as a consequence inherent to this franchise system the fact that the franchisee, because of the use of the franchisor's exclusive mark and brand which identifies the franchised sales outlet, and because of the obligation not to compete, will in fact concentrate his promotional efforts on the particular products franchised.

In the circumstances, the real competitive situation in the market should not be influenced by the obligations in question as such.

(b)   *Clauses falling within Article 85(1)*

(28) As the Court held in its judgment (ground 23 and 24 and operative part, paragraph 1(d)), 'Clauses that involve market sharing between franchisor and franchisee or between franchisees do constitute restrictions of competition within the meaning of Article 85(1). This is the case with the following clauses, which were specifically mentioned by the Court:

— the exclusivity granted to the franchisee to operate under the franchisor's name in a given sales area (clause 1, first paragraph),
— the obligation on the franchisee to carry on the franchise business exclusively from the premises approved for that purpose (clause 4, second paragraph, second indent).

The combined effect of these clauses is to protect each franchisee against competition from other franchisees. Moreover, the further clause (clause 1, fifth paragraph) whereby the franchisor undertakes to pay the franchisee 10% of any mail-order sales to customers in the franchisee's territory, on products normally sold by the franchisee, implies that the franchisor may not directly operate in the allocated territory.

(29) The Court also held that 'retail franchise agreements containing clauses that involve market sharing between franchisor and franchisee or between franchisees are inherently likely to effect trade between

Member States, even if they are between parties resident in the same Member State, because they prevent the franchisees setting up in another Member State' (ground 26). An effect on trade is all the more likely in the present case as Pronuptia holds a significant share of the French market for the relevant products and its network covers several EEC countries (*see* paragraphs 4 and 6).

(30) Consequently, the clauses referred to in paragraph 28 are restrictions of competition falling within Article 85(1) and are likely to affect trade between Member States.

B.   Article 85(3)

(31) Article 85(3) allows the provisions of Article 85(1) to be declared inapplicable to any agreement or category of agreements between undertakings which contributes to improving the production or distribution of goods or to promoting technical or economic progress, while allowing consumers a fair share of the resulting benefit, and which does not:

(a) impose on the undertakings concerned restrictions which are not indispensable to the attainment of these objectives;

(b) afford such undertakings the possibility of eliminating competition in respect of a substantial part of the products in question.

(32) The Court rule in the judgment that Regulation 67/67/EEC was inapplicable to retail franchise agreements such as those concerned in the present case. After noting that retail franchise agreements displayed features which distinguished them from exclusive distribution agreements (see paragraph 15), the Court stated that Article 2 of the Regulation expressly referred only to exclusive distribution agreements and did not include among the obligations that could be imposed on the exclusive distributor either an obligation to pay royalties, obligations designed to preserve the common identity and reputation of the network, or obligations to transfer know-how and provide assistance. The standard form agreement is therefore not covered by the block exemption granted by Regulation 67/67/EEC.

(33) On 1 July 1983 a new block exemption for exclusive distribution agreements, Commission Regulation (EEC) No 1983/83, entered into force, replacing Regulation 67/67/EEC for such agreements. The content of the new Regulation is such that the same reasons as the Court gave for holding that Regulation 67/67/EEC was inapplicable to agreements like that concerned in the present case could be adduced for saying that Regulation (EEC) No 1983/83 was also not applicable. Like the old regulation, Regulation (EEC) No 1983/83 only refers to exclusive distributorships and does not mention any of the above clauses that are typical of retail franchise agreements.

There are then grounds for examination of the standard form agreement in question to see if an individual exemption under Article 85(3) can be given.

(34) The standard form of franchise agreement that forms the basis of the Pronuptia distribution network contributes, through the combined effect of all its provisions, to improving the production and distribution of the products concerned, for the following reasons. It enables:

— the franchisor to extend its distribution network without the level of investment it would need to open its own retail network, which for a relatively small company like Pronuptia might not be possible, at least not so quickly. The investment involved in setting up the new outlets is undertaken by the prospective franchisees, in return for which they receive the benefit not only of the franchisor's established name and reputation, but also of its expertise, commercial know-how and marketing, which enables them to achieve a larger volume of business at lower cost and with less risk.

The franchise, in which the complementary interests of the franchisor and the franchisee converge, opens up the market to new competitors, intensifying inter-brand competition and increasing the competition faced by firms distributing their products through a branch network using a standard business format and product range;

— the franchisor to set up a distribution network using a standard business format and product range;

— the franchisor to keep in touch, thanks to its close and direct business relationship with the franchisees, with changes in consumer tastes and preferences and to reflect such changes in its production;

— the franchisee to concentrate his sales effort on a given area and to be more active in cultivating a clientèle there, thanks to the exclusivity which the combined effect of the clauses referred to in paragraph 28 gives him for that area, although consumers resident in the area are not prevented from purchasing the product outside the area and franchisees may freely buy and sell the products among themselves;

— the franchisee, thanks to his enjoyment of territorial exclusivity and his closeness to the marketplace, to make confident forecasts of his future sales, which help the franchisor to plan his production better and to guarantee regular supplies of the products.

(35) The standard form of franchise agreement which forms the basis of the Pronuptia distribution network allows consumers a fair share

of the benefit resulting from these improvements in production and distribution.

Consumers may be expected to benefit, first of all, from a coherent distribution network offering uniform product quality and a comprehensive range of the articles and accessories available in the trade. Consumers will also benefit from the efficient and attentive service the franchisee will be encouraged to provide as a self-employed businessman who has a personal and direct interest in the success of his business, since he alone bears the financial risks. Consumers will further directly benefit from the continuity of supplies of products which satisfy their wants and reflect changes in tastes and fashion emerging in the market. Finally, the competitiveness of the market (see paragraph 9), and the freedom consumers have to purchase the products elsewhere in the network, will tend to force franchisees to pass a reasonable part of the benefits of the rationalisation of production and distribution on to consumers. Post-finally, consumers can tell that they are dealing with independent traders (see paragraph 11 above, third indent), who can be held responsible.

(36) The Pronuptia standard form agreement does not contain restrictions that are not indispensable to the attainment of the said benefits. The clauses referred to in paragraph 28, which restrict competition by giving the franchisee territorial exclusivity, can be considered, in the circumstances, to be indispensable in that prospective franchisees would probably be unwilling to undertake the necessary investment and to pay a substantial initial fee to enter the franchise system if they were not provided with some protection against competition from other franchisees and from the franchisor in the allotted territory. It should be noted that franchisees are free to buy and sell the products among themselves.

(37) Pronuptia's standard form of franchise agreement and the resulting self-contained franchising operation do not give the firms concerned the possibility of eliminating competition for a substantial part of the products in question. As noted above (paragraph 9), the Pronuptia network faces competition from a number of other manufacturers and suppliers in the EEC countries who do not use the franchising route to distribute their products.

Franchisees also compete with one another, because they can sell to any customer whether resident in the allotted territory or coming from outside it, and to any other franchisee. Furthermore, they are entirely free to determine their own sales prices.

(38) The agreement therefore meets all the requirements for exemption laid down by Article 85(3).

C. Articles 6 and 8 of Regulation No 17

(39) Under Article 6 of Regulation No 17, the Commission is required to specify the date from which an exemption decision takes effect. This date may not be earlier than the date of notification.

(40) Under Article 8 of Regulation No 17, the Commission is also required to state the period of exemption.

(44) The notified standard form of Pronuptia retail franchise agreement, as it is applied, meets the requirements for exemption laid down in Article 85(3). An exemption may therefore be granted to take effect from the date of notification, 22 April 1983. It is reasonable in this particular case, in view of the five-year term of the agreement and the date on which this decision takes effect, to grant the exemption for eight years.

Computerland

(87/407/EEC)

1. Facts

A. General description of the Computerland franchise system

(1) CLE is a wholly-owned subsidiary of the Computerland Corporation of California (USA). CLE has subsidiaries in France, Spain, the United Kingdom and Italy with varying responsibilities, a subsidiary in Luxembourg which handles the distribution of products for the franchise network, and various branches, called regional offices, which handle marketing, advertising and public relations and provide on-the-spot support to franchisees, such as assistance in recruiting personnel. The Computerland group has approximately 850 retail stores worldwide. Its operations in Europe started in the late 1970s. Since then, 100 outlets have been established in Western Europe, of which approximately 85 in all of the Member States except Ireland; the largest number of Computerland stores are found in France, the UK and Germany. According to CLE's prognosis, the number of outlets will more than double over the next three years. The average turnover of a Computerland store in the Community is 1.5 million ECU. The turnover of the Computerland group worldwide in 1986 was over one thousand million US dollars.

(2) Using the Computerland name, trademarks and the Computerland system, Computerland franchisees sell to end-users (predominantly busi-

ness-users as opposed to home-users) numerous different brands of microcomputer products (hardware, software and peripheral products), and provide pre- and after-sales service and, usually, training facilities. CLE assists franchisees in setting up and running their stores, providing both commercial and technical know-how. Its continuing support services include training, information, advice, guidance and know-how regarding the Computerland methods in store management, operation, financing, advertising, sales and inventory, based on Computerland's extensive empirical experience in the area of retail sales of microcomputer products throughout the world. CLE procures advance information on numerous brands of new products and how they can be used together, and passes this on to franchisees, as well as advice as to which among the many new products are likely to succeed on the market. Franchisees can thus offer their customers a broad range of up-to-date products and well-researched technical advice. In return, franchisees make various financial contributions and are bound by obligations aimed at preserving the uniformity and quality standards of the system.

(3) There are approximately 20 major manufacturers of microcomputer products in the world, of which five are estimated to account for the top five market shares on the European market. They use various ways of marketing these products, some of which overlap. Sales can be divided broadly into direct sales by the manufacturers to end-users, on the one hand, which account for 20% of total sales in Europe, and sales through various types of intermediaries on the other. While some manufacturers use non-specialised outlets such as retailers of consumer electronics, many others, believing that for the time being these sophisticated technical products can only be sold effectively by specialised dealers capable of offering pre- and post-sales service and generally fulfilling certain standards of quality, have chosen to sell through authorised dealers. Such dealers can be independent retailers authorised by one or more manufacturers, or part of a dealer chain offering a broad range of products of different brands, pre-sales advice and after-sales service; some of these dealer chains, such as Computerland, are in the form of franchise networks.

Computerland stores sell the products of approximately half of the major manufacturers, including the five biggest on the European market. Their competitors are thus all retailers of whatever form selling the same or similar products. Leaving aside non-specialised retailers, statistics indicate that there are approximately 10 000 authorised microcomputer dealers in Western Europe, of which less than 1% are Computerland stores. Although Computerland is the only pan-European chain, there are half a dozen multi-country chains (franchised or not), of which the largest after CLE has some 50 outlets in four countries. Furthermore, there are several single-country chains. In the three

Member States in which CLE has its greatest number of outlets (France: 22, United Kingdom: 16, Germany: 12), it is competing with at least half a dozen dealer chains, some having a comparable number of outlets.

In 1985, Computerland stores accounted for less than 3,3% of retail sales in the Community as a whole, while in 1986 the largest market share in any given Member State was approximately 4%. Worldwide, the Computerland group has much larger market shares, for example going even beyond 20% in the United States, Canada, Australia and Japan.

B. Relevant features of the notified standard-form agreement

(4) *Choice and legal form of franchisees.* Franchisees are chosen on the basis of their personal and financial standing and their prior experience in the retail trade, and subject to successful completion of a training programme organised by CLE; employees are also expected to be fully trained in the Computerland system. Every franchisee is obliged to form a corporation for the purpose of running his Computerland store business, and a sign indicating that the franchisee independently owns and operates the business under a franchise from Computerland must be conspicuously posted in the store. The products sold must likewise bear labels indicating the franchisee's name, address and telephone number.

(5) *Use of the Computerland names, trademarks and system.* The franchisee is given the non-assignable right to use the Computerland names, marks and system in connection with the operation of the Computerland store and for no other purpose. In signing the agreement, the franchisee acknowledges the validity of the names and marks and CLE's ownership thereof, but there is no restriction of his right to contest CLE's industrial property rights.

The franchisee agrees to adhere to the standard business operating methods (set out in an 'Operator's Manual') and respect the confidentiality of the information he receives from CLE and to divulge it only, if necessary, to his employees, subject to a written statement in which the latter likewise acknowledge the confidential nature thereof. The franchisee must report to CLE any innovations or improvements he makes, and grants to CLE a worldwide, royalty-free non-exclusive right to use these during the term of the agreement. Upon termination for whatever reason, the franchisee must stop using the Computerland names, marks and system, and return the Operator's Manual and any other copyrighted material, but he may continue using any innovations or improvements he has developed which are demonstrably separable from the operation of the Computerland store and system.

(6) *Best personal efforts.* The franchisee undertakes to devote his best personal efforts to the day-to-day operation of his store; he may not

engage in any other type of business at the store without prior written approval by CLE.

(7) *Location clause and protected area.* The franchisee must operate his Computerland store exclusively at the location approved in advance by CLE, but he is not obliged to make 'over-the-counter' sales, i.e. customers do not actually have to buy the products in the store itself. He must adhere to CLE's instructions regarding the interior and exterior of the premises and may not relocate without its prior approval.

Each location is surrounded by a 'protected area' having a radius of less than one kilometre after the first year of the agreement (during the first year it is double that distance) in which no other Computerland outlet may be established.

The protected area is not one of marketing or clientele exclusivity, which means that any franchisee can sell to any end-user customer, wherever the customers may reside or do business. They can also set up so-called 'satellites', which offer showroom and selling facilities and can be inside or outside the 'mother store's' protected area, but not in the protected area of another Computerland franchisee. For stocking and servicing purposes and other operational support, such satellite outlets remain dependent on the Computerland store to which they are contractually attached.

(8) *Products and services — advertising/pricing policy.* The franchisee may only sell those products and perform those services specifically authorised in the Operator's Manual or in other instructions from CLE, or products and services of equivalent quality, subject to prior approval by CLE, which will not be unreasonably withheld. Franchisees play an active role in establishing the range of products they sell, *inter alia* by participating in regular meetings of the 'European Network Product Council', where proposals can be made to CLE to authorise new products.

Advertising material must be made or approved by CLE, but approval may not be withheld or withdrawn because of the franchisee's pricing policy, for which he bears sole responsibility.

Franchisees may purchase their requirements from CLE, which exercises a central purchasing function, but they are not obliged to do so, nor are there any minimum purchasing requirements. Franchisees are thus free to buy approved products from any supplier they choose.

CLE leaves franchisees free to determine their own resale prices; franchisees may, of course, receive recommended resale price lists from their other sources of supply.

(9) *Training facilities.* Most franchisees provide training facilities at the approved location, although there is no obligation to do so. Customers may sign up for training courses even without purchasing any

of the franchisee's products. In general, the revenue derived from operating these training facilities, over which the monthly royalty must be paid, represents a very limited percentage of the franchisee's overall turnover.

(10) *Sales to end-users.* The Computerland system has been devised and developed to promote sales of microcomputer products at retail level. Franchisees are accordingly required to sell to end-users, unless otherwise authorised. Sales to other Computerland franchisees are expressly allowed. Furthermore, the obligation to sell to end-users does not prevent a franchisee from carrying out his obligations or exercising his rights under agreements he may have with any manufacturer as its authorised dealer.

(11) *Financial obligations/reporting requirements/right to inspect.* In return for being admitted into the Computerland franchise network, the franchisee must pay an initial entrance fee which varies between Lfrs 250 000 (5 800 ECU) and Lfrs 1 250 000 (28 750 ECU), depending on the type of outlet. Subsequently, a monthly royalty payment amounting to 3.5% of the preceding month's gross revenue, which is any income, from which certain items, such as VAT and interfranchisee sales, are deducted. Normally, a monthly payment is also made as an advertising contribution. Franchisees must submit regular financial statements including balance sheets and profit-and-loss statements, and CLE's representatives must be allowed into the premises during working hours in order to inspect the operation of the store, including the quality of the goods being sold, the supplies on hand and the services rendered.

(12) *Non-competition clauses.* During the term of the agreement, the franchisee may not engage or have an interest in any business whose activities include the sale or service, at retail or wholesale level, of computer hardware, software and related products and services offered by Computerland stores. The franchisee must, however, remain free to acquire financial interests in the capital of a competing enterprise, provided such investment does not enable him effectively to control such a business.

Under the agreement as notified, the above non-competition obligation continued for three years after termination of the agreement at a given distance from the ex-franchisee's former outlet, for two years after termination at a given distance from any Computerland store and for one year after termination at any location. Following discussions with the Commission in the course of the notification procedure, CLE decided that a non-competition obligation of one year after termination of the agreement within a radius of 10 kilometres of the ex-franchisee's former outlet would be sufficient to safeguard the confidentiality of the know-how transmitted to the ex-franchisee during the term of the agreement and to allow a new Computerland store to be established and start accumulating good-will and clientele in the ex-franchisee's former zone of business activities.

(13) *Guarantees.* CLE will only agree to sell a manufacturer's products if they are covered by a Europe-wide guarantee of at least six months. Products which franchisees acquire from other sources, for example directly from the manufacturer, must be covered by each manufacturer's respective guarantee, otherwise approval by CLE will be withheld.

(14) *Term and renewal.* The term of the agreement is 10 years, unless terminated by mutual consent. Both franchisor and franchisee have the right to terminate unilaterally 'for good cause', with regard to which a non-exhaustive list of examples is given in the agreement.

Renewal for a further 10-year period is possible subject to certain conditions, including payment of a renewal fee.

Transfer of the agreement to third parties must be consented to by CLE.

On termination for whatever reason, CLE may choose to have assigned to it the franchisee's lease.

C.   Other Computerland agreements

(15) Some Computerland franchisees have chosen not to replace their existing contracts with the notified standard form agreement which was introduced in 1983, for varying reasons, such as the royalty level, the size of the protected area or other reasons not relevant for the present purposes. CLE has undertaken to ensure that to the extent these agreements, which are not standard, contain obligations which might be considered as being more restrictive of competition than their counterparts in the notified standard agreement, the necessary adaption will take place.

(16) The same undertaking applies with respect to the special standard franchise agreement developed in 1986 for the German market in order to facilitate State-backed financing arrangements for the franchisees, which entails prior approval of the agreement by the lending bank.

(17) For Denmark and the Italian province of Tuscany, CLE has devised a slight variation to the standard agreement, 'Development Area Agreements', whereby a single enterprise is granted the exclusive right to open a fixed number of Computerland stores in a designated area over a limited period of time. This form of agreement is chosen for areas in which there are no existing Computerland stores and a franchisee is willing to take on the high economic risk of single-handedly

setting up several stores in an undeveloped market. In return, he receives the abovementioned exclusivity, unless the timetable is not met, in which case CLE is again free to grant third parties the right to open stores in the area. These special agreements are an exception to the rule that a franchisee normally operates only one shop, and also offer a wider protected area to the successful developing franchisee. The Development Area Agreements do not impose any obstacles to exports or imports.

D. Third parties' observations

(18) The Commission did not receive any observations from interested third parties following publication of the notice required by Article 19(3) of Regulation No 17.

II. Legal Assessment

A. Article 85(1)

(19) The standard franchising agreement notified by CLE is an agreement within the meaning of Article 85(1) of the EEC Treaty. The individual franchisees who have entered into the standard agreement with CLE, a corporation under Luxembourg law, are the proprietors of their business and carry out economic and commercial activities at their own risk; the agreement is an instrument legally binding upon the parties.

(20) Both the Court of Justice (*see* the *Pronuptia* case, Appendix IV) and the Commission (*see* the *Yves Rocher* and *Pronuptia* decisions above) have been called upon to assess the applicability of Article 85 to distribution franchises, that is, franchise agreements under which the franchisee offers certain products and ancillary services, using the franchisor's business name and applying uniform business methods developed by the franchisor, usually subject to certain financial contributions. The main principle established by the Court, and followed by the Commission in its subsequent decisions, is that such franchise systems, which on the one hand allow a franchisor to profit from its success and expand into new geographical markets without making significant investments and on the other hand enable interested candidates to use the franchisor's name and reputation to set up a new business more easily and rapidly than if they had to acquire he necessary expertise independently, are not in themselves caught by Article 85(1) where competitive market conditions prevail. The applicability of Article 85(1) can, however, not be determined in the abstract, but depends on the specific provisions concerned.

An effective transfer of the business formula can only take place:

(i) if the franchisor is able to communicate his know-how to the franchisees and provide the necessary assistance without running the risk that competitors may benefit therefrom;

(ii) if the franchisor is able to take the necessary measures for maintaining the identity and reputation of the network bearing his business name or symbol.

All contractual provisions which are necessary to ensure that these conditions are met can be deemed to fall outside the scope of Article 85(1). Other provisions, in particular those which may lead to market sharing between the franchisor and the franchisees, or between the latter, or those which interfere with the franchisees' individual pricing policies, may on the contrary be considered restrictions of competition.

(21) The franchise network set up by CLE by means of the notified standard franchise agreement is a distribution franchise: the franchisor has devised an original method for selling microcomputer products and accessories to end-users, which in the interest of expansion it is willing to share with others, the franchisees. In return for receiving the package of Computerland's specifically developed commercial and technical know-how and the use of the franchisor's business name, trademarks, symbols and business methods, franchisees must make certain financial contributions and adhere to the standards of operation devised by the franchisor. Although franchisees offer pre- and after-sales advice and make product repairs, such services are ancillary to their main task, which is the sale of products to the public. Furthermore, some franchisees may also choose to offer training facilities, not necessarily in connection with the sale of products. This service normally represents a minor part of their activities and can be viewed as a means of developing goodwill.

Having thus established that the Computerland system is a distribution franchise, the following tests can be applied.

PROVISIONS NOT FALLING WITHIN THE SCOPE OF ARTICLE 85(1)

In the specific circumstances of this case, the following provisions are not caught by Article 85(1).

a. *Provisions aimed at preventing the know-how and other assistance given by the franchisor from benefiting competitors*

(22)(i) The franchisee's obligation to respect the confidentiality of the information received and to ensure that his employees do the same;

(ii) The franchisee's obligation not to carry on competing activities during the term of the agreement; at the Commission's request, the scope of the non-competition clause was adjusted so as to allow franchisees to acquire financial interests in the capital of competing undertakings, although not to the extent that such participation would enable them to control those undertakings;

(iii) The franchisee's obligation not to engage in competing activities for one year after termination of the agreement within a radius of 10 kilometres of his previous outlet. The post-term non-competition obligation which was included in the agreement as notified was considered to be unreasonably broad as regards both duration and geographical extent, but as amended the clause is deemed sufficient to prevent the ex-franchisee from using the know-how and clientele he has acquired to the benefit of CLE's competitors. Also, given the time it takes CLE to choose, train and establish a new franchisee and for the latter to start acquiring goodwill and clientele, the clause as modified is a reasonable compromise between the franchisor's concern to protect the confidentiality of his business formula and to open a new outlet in the ex-franchisee's former exclusive territory on the one hand, and the ex-franchisee's legitimate interest in continuing to operate in the same field in the other hand. In view of the fact that, during the term of the agreement, a franchisee is not bound to over-the-counter sales and is furthermore free to sell anywhere, he can develop goodwill and clientele far beyond his own protected area; during the one year in which the post-term non-competition obligation is in force, he can thus continue to reap the benefits of the efforts he has made as a franchisee, only being prevented from competing during that period in the vicinity of his former outlet.

The post-term non-competition clause is thus in the particular circumstances of this case not considered to be restrictive of competition within the meaning of Article 85(1). This assessment does not prejudice any provisions of national law which may bestow certain rights on franchisees upon termination of the contract.

b. *Provisions which allow the franchisor to safeguard the identity and reputation of the network bearing his business name or symbol*

(23)(i) The criteria which CLE applies in selecting franchisees and their obligation to follow training courses and to familiarise employees with the Computerland system are justified means of ensuring that every Computerland outlet is managed in keeping with the business standards developed by the franchisor; the same concern underlies the provision that transfer of the agreement to third parties can only take place with CLE's consent;

(ii) The franchisee's obligation to use the Computerland names, trademarks and system only for the operation of the Computerland store and to stop using them immediately upon leaving the network are aimed at ensuring that the network image is not tarnished by activities not developed specifically by the franchisor; at the Commission's request, however, ex-franchisees are now expressly entitled to continue using innovations or improvements they have developed which are demonstrably separable from the Computerland system;

(iii) The franchisee's obligation to adhere to the franchisor's standard business methods is an inherent part of the franchise system and ensures the standards of uniformity and quality of the network;

(iv) The franchisee's obligation to devote his best personal efforts to the day-to-day operation of his store is necessary to ensure that the business methods developed by the franchisor are properly and fully applied; his obligation in principle not to engage in any activities in his store which are not included in the business formula transmitted by the franchisor, is acceptable in the light of the concern to preserve the reputation and uniform identity of the network.

(v) The franchisee's obligation to obtain the franchisor's prior approval for the location of his store, and to adhere to the franchise's instructions regarding its interior and exterior aspects, is aimed at ensuring the reputation of the network, which is a concern not only of the franchisor but of every franchisee. In the Operator's Manual, CLE outlines the objective criteria it uses in site approval, such as the structure and dimensions of the building, its location in relation to key intersections and business centres, its accessibility for customers and the nature of the surrounding business centres. The main objective in setting up these criteria for site approval is to ensure that the success of the outlet is not hampered because of a possibly unfavourable location.

(vi) The franchisee's obligation to sell only the products and provide the services authorised by CLE, or products and services of equivalent quality, is necessary to preserve the network's reputation as a source of high-quality microcomputer products mainly for the business community; sales of sub-standard products which do not meet the technical norms applied by CLE would damage the reputation of the network, thereby harming not only the franchisor but all other franchisees as well.

The franchisor's prior approval of the goods and services offered in Computerland stores ensures buyers that they will be able to obtain goods of the same quality from all franchisees, regardless of their location. In the case at hand, given the wide product range (there are over 3 000 items on CLE's product list) and the very rapid technological evolution in this product market, it would be impracticable to ensure the necessary quality control by establishing objective quality specifications which franchisees could apply themselves. In fact, laying down objective standards could be detrimental to the franchisees' freedom to sell the most up-to-date products, unless the specifications were constantly up-dated, an overly burdensome if not impossible task. In the present system, franchisees have a substantial voice in proposing products for approval, in bilateral contacts with CLE as well as collectively in the 'European Network Product Councils', which meet regularly; most products aimed at business users will be approved, and such approval covers all relevant accessories and future improvements; furthermore, should a manufacturer introduce new products of a higher standard than an existing range which has been approved, franchisees do not require prior approval to sell such new products. Also, as CLE's main source of income is derived from royalties on sales of all products by franchisees, it is in its interest to allow franchisees to sell products which are expected to be commercially successful, as long as they are technically suitable for the customers for which the Computerland network caters.

One essential element in assessing this provision under Article 85(1) is the fact that once a given product has been approved by CLE, franchisees are free to procure it from any source of supply they wish. Although franchisees may purchase their requirements from CLE, they are not obliged to do so, nor are there any minimum purchasing requirements if they do.

Furthermore, in selecting products which it will itself sell to franchisees, as well as in approving products which franchisees can procure from any source, CLE ensures that a Europe-wide guarantee is given. This policy is in line with the Commission's concern for market integration and consumer protection (*see*, for example, points 77 and 78 of

Twelfth Report on Competition Policy and recital 12 of Commission Regulation 123/85 (Official Journal No L.15 of 18.1.85)).

(vii) The franchisee's obligation to use only advertising material made or approved by CLE.

Advertising plays an essential role in the development of a network's reputation. A franchisor therefore has a legitimate interest in ensuring that publicity undertaken by the franchisees will not adversely affect the reputation established by the franchisor. In the present case, the policy regarding advertising is clearly based on a justifiable concern for quality control and not aimed at interfering with the franchisee's freedom to determine his own prices: the notified agreement expressly states that approval of advertising material will not be conditioned on, or subject to any change in, the pricing policy or the price quotations of the franchisee.

(viii) The franchisee's obligation to submit to inspections of the premises by CLE's representatives and to present financial statements allows the franchisor to verify whether the franchisee is operating in accordance with the Computerland business format and fulfilling his financial commitments.

c. *Other Provisions*

(24) The franchise system includes a number of provisions which are not relevant to competition and can therefore by their very nature in the present case be excluded from the scope of Article 85(1):

(i) The franchisee's obligation to pay entrance fee and subsequent monthly royalty payments and advertising contributions; the financial commitment, which is applied on a non-discriminatory basis, is merely the consideration which the franchisee must pay for being admitted into the network and receiving the resulting rights and benefits; to ensure the possibility of interfranchisee sales, the agreement now specifies that royalties are not payable on such transactions;

(ii) The franchisee's obligation to form a corporation, which is based on the consideration that his business dealings will thus be facilitated;

(iii) The franchisee's obligation to post a sign on the premises indicating that he is the independent owner thereof, operating under a franchise from CLE, which ensures that the public is in no way misled as to the true ownership of and responsibility for each individual outlet;

(iv) The franchisee's obligation to indicate on each product he sells his name and address, which is required solely for the purpose of directing end-users to sales and service assistance;

(v) The provisions relating to the term and renewal of the agreement, and the assignment of the franchisee's lease to the franchisor.

The assessment of these provisions is without prejudice to any relevant constraints under national law.

PROVISIONS WHICH CONSTITUTE RESTRICTIONS OF COMPETITION WITHIN THE MEANING OF ARTICLE 85(1)

(25) The conjunction of the location clause, which obliges the franchisee to operate from the premises specified in his contract and thus prevents him from opening further stores, and the exclusivity clause, which assures him of a protected zone in which no other Computerland outlets can be established, either by the franchisor or by other franchisees, results in a certain degree of market-sharing between the franchisor and the franchisees or between the latter, thus restricting competition in the network in which the Computerland business format is exploited.

In the present case, it is particularly the prohibition from opening further outlets which interferes with franchisee's commercial independence: in this context, it is important to take into account the fact that Computerland outlets are generally not one-man operations, but medium-sized enterprises employing on average ten to twenty persons and sometimes even substantially more. For such entrepreneurs, for whom expansion may be a logical and desirable development, the limitation to one outlet unless otherwise authorised is clearly restrictive.

Although franchisees are allowed to operate 'satellite shops' for display and selling purposes, also outside, their protected areas, this freedom is only relative, in that prior approval by CLE and payment of a fee similar to the usual entrance fee, albeit reduced, are required. Also, such outlets may not be located in another franchisee's protected area.

(26) Under the specific circumstances of this case, the franchisee's obligation to sell only to end-users or to other Computerland franchisees unless otherwise authorised is likewise deemed to be a restriction of competition. In certain franchise systems, for example where franchisees sell products bearing the franchisor's name and/or trademark, the prohibition on resale by franchisees to resellers who do not belong to that franchise network is based on the legitimate concern that the name, trademark or business format could be damaged if the contract products were sold by resellers who do not have access to the franchisor's know-how and are not bound by the obligations aimed at preserving the reputation and unity of the network and its identifying marks.

In the case at hand, however, the Computerland name and trademark cover the business format as such, but not the microcomputer products being sold, which bear the name and trademark of each individual manufacturer. The prohibition on Computerland franchisees to sell the products to otherwise qualified resellers is thus restrictive, both as regards the franchisees themselves, who while being independent entrepreneurs are thereby limited in their freedom in deciding to whom to sell, and as regards third party resellers, who are thereby deprived of a possible source of supply.

In the present case, this restriction is mitigated by a characteristic which is peculiar to sales in the microcomputer field, namely the fact that retailers can be part of a franchise network such as Computerland and at the same time be appointed an authorised dealer in a selective distribution system established by a manufacturer to ensure that his products are handled only by qualified resellers. A Computerland franchisee who thus operates simultaneously in two or more different networks must be in a position to fulfil the obligations and exercise the rights which flow from each one. In this context, the Commission has sought to ensure that a Computerland franchisee who is at the same time authorised by one or more manufacturers, can function both within the Computerland network and within the selective distribution network(s) to which he belongs.

(27) The provisions which lead to market sharing within the network and the obligation to sell to end-users are liable to affect intracommunity trade, because franchisees are not free to expand their operations to other Member States, either at retail or wholesale level. This effect on trade between Member States is liable to be appreciable, in view of:

— the expanse of the existing Computerland network, which is the only one of its kind having outlets in all Member States except Ireland (where two outlets are, however, planned for the near future),
— the growth of the network: although the market share has not yet reached the 5% mark in the EEC, the rate of growth which the network has experienced already in its first years of existence in Europe should lead to substantial expansion in the years to come. Indeed, sales by the network will probably increase more rapidly than the current trend, in view of the expected increase in the total number of outlets before 1990 to more than 150,
— the fact that the products sold by Computerland stores are those of the most important European and worldwide manufacturers.

In view of the above considerations, the notified standard agreement is deemed to fall within Article 85(1).

(28) The 'Development Area Agreements' referred to above under point 17, which contain similar provisions to the standard form agreement regarding location clause, protected area and sales to end-users, are accordingly likewise deemed to be restrictive of competition.

B. Article 85(3)

(29) The block exemption regulations relating to exclusive dealing and exclusive distribution agreements (*see* Commission Regulation 67/67 (Official Journal No 57 of 25.3.67) and its successor, Commission Regulation 1983/83 (Official Journal No L.173 of 30.6.83)) are not applicable to distribution franchise agreements such as the one at hand, which go beyond the category of agreements covered by those regulations (*see* points 15 and 33 of the *Pronuptia* case at Appendix IV above). The characteristics which are typical of distribution franchises, such as the franchisee's right to use the franchisor's business name and symbol in return for certain financial contributions and the obligations to adhere to uniform business standards developed by the franchisor, are not referred to in either block exemption regulation. The notified agreement must therefore be examined in the light of the conditions laid down in Article 85(3) for exemption on an individual basis.

(30) Distribution in the field of microcompter products is improved by the Computerland system, since the franchisor, who acts as a link between the main microcomputer producers and the franchisees, is able to establish outlets throughout the Community without any major financial investments, while franchisees are closely assisted in rapidly setting up and operating retail outlets in which a wide range of products and services are offered. Given the technical nature of the products in question and the fact that they are normally not sold as single items but as part of a range, potential buyers attach particular importance to trying out different systems and receiving pre-sales advice regarding possible applications and configurations and post-sales repair and maintenance services. Furthermore, the franchise system promotes both intra-brand and interbrand competition: the products offered are also sold via specialised dealer networks set up by the manufacturers as well as various other types of outlets, and the Computerland stores thus offer an alternative source of supply which stimulates competition, and thereby distribution, at retail level. Moreover, Computerland franchisees are free to compete with each other, also as regards the prices at which they sell to customers, which equally enhances the distribution of the products concerned.

(31) The Computerland system also contributes to rationalising distribution: CLE takes orders from franchisees, buys the products from manufacturers or other sources of supply and resells them to the

franchisees, thereby rapidly channeling the products concerned to the Computerland outlets. This central purchasing function enables CLE to negotiate favourable terms for its franchisees, with respect to prices and quantities supplied, and often allows franchisees to procure the products in question much sooner than other retail sellers.

(32) The benefits resulting from the improvement and rationalisation of distribution accrue directly to consumers, which in this case are mainly professional end-users.

In the first place, the Computerland stores provide a single location at which customers can compare the prices and characteristics of a wide range of different brands of up-to-date microcomputer products and benefit from the advice of specially trained personnel especially as regards the possibility of using different brands of products together, and the training facilities offered. Customers who decide to buy their products at the Computerland outlet are ensured of further advice, maintenance and repair services and if necessary further training possibilities.

Secondly, the Computerland system offers consumers an expanding network of outlets at which they can buy microcomputer products. Computerland stores compete directly with the numerous other outlets selling the same products, with the result that all retailers should, because of the pressures of heightened competition, offer better quality, services and prices.

(33) The restrictions of competition which the Computerland system entails are indispensable to ensure the existence of the network: potential franchisees would not be willing to make the investments necessary for opening up a new outlet if they were not assured that no other Computerland outlets will be established in their near vicinity. Aside from the restrictions which are thus the necessary cornerstone of the franchise system, franchisees are free as to the sources from which they procure approved products, the prices at which they wish to sell those products, the territories in which they operate, and the clientele they cater to.

(34) The franchisee's obligation to sell to end-users only, unless otherwise authorised by the franchisor, is a direct consequence of the fact that the basic concept underlying the franchisor's business formula is the operation of a network of retail stores in which products and services are offered to final consumers. The training and support services given to franchisees, who are willing to pay a fee in return, are therefore specifically aimed at helping them to become and remain efficient and profitable retail sellers. The Computerland business formula and all the efforts put into making it successful would be diluted if franchisees were free to divert their efforts to activities other than retail sales and

servicing. In order for the benefits relating to improved and rationalised distribution to accrue and be passed on to consumers, in this case business users, it is therefore indispensable that franchisees accept the obligation to operate as retail sellers and not, for example, as wholesalers.

An important relaxation of this rule is the express freedom of franchisees to sell to other franchisees within the network; no royalties are due in the case of such interfranchisee sales.

(35) The Computerland franchising system does not afford its members the possibility of eliminating competition in respect of a substantial part of the products concerned.

Computerland franchisees offer products which are at the same time sold by a very large number of competing outlets. Even in the Member States in which the greatest number of Computerland stores are located, they are faced by competing chains having a comparable number of outlets. Finally, given the overall competitive structure of this market, there is no danger that the Computerland network will reduce or otherwise distort competition between competing brands and distribution outlets.

Furthermore, there is a substantial amount of competition within the network itself: the protected zone surrounding each franchisee is relatively small, and does not entail any marketing or clientele exclusivity, which means that franchisees are free actively to seek and to sell to any customers. CLE does not in any way impose or recommend prices at which the franchisees sell to customers which, combined with the franchisees' freedom as to their sources of supply, results in a substantial degree of price competition within the network.

Under these circumstances, the agreements between CLE and its franchisees do not individually or collectively afford the parties the possibility of eliminating competition with respect to the goods concerned.

(36) Consequently, the provisions of Article 85(1) may, under the terms of Article 85(3), be declared inapplicable to the standard form Computerland franchise agreement. The same arguments referred to in points 29 to 35 apply *mutatis mutandis* to the 'Development Area Agreements' and other existing franchise agreements which are equally or less restrictive of competition than the standard form agreement.

C. Articles 6 and 8 of Regulation No 17

(37) The agreement as notified by CLE on 18 September 1986 contained a number of provisions which stood in the way of a favourable decision, in particular the clauses relating to the non-competition obligation both during the term of the agreement and after termination

thereof, which was considered to be unreasonably broad. Following the discussions with the Commission during the course of the notification procedure, CLE has redrafted the standard franchise agreement taking into account the comments made.

Pursuant to Article 6(1) of Regulation No 17, the commission is required to specify the date from which an exemption is granted. As the notified agreement did not fulfil the requirements for exemption, the date on which the exemption takes effect is not the date of the notification, but the day on which the franchisees were informed by CLE of the amended version of the agreement.

(38) According to Article 8(1) of Regulation No 17, a decision in application of Article 85(3) must be issued for a specified period. Given the 10-year term of the standard franchise agreement, a corresponding period would seem appropriate. In view of the changeable nature of the retail market for microcomputer products as a whole and the expanding tendency of the Computerland network, the exemption should, however, not be more than 10 years either. CLE should be obliged, pursuant to Article 8(1) of Regulation No 17, to communicate any substantial changes in the franchise system to the Commission and furthermore, halfway through the period of exemption, to inform the Commission of the number of outlets per Member State and the market share of the network in the Community as a whole and in each Member State individually.

(39) Finally, to the extent CLE maintains franchise agreements which differ from the standard agreements, provisions which are more restrictive of competition will be adapted to be in line with the standard agreement as amended.

ServiceMaster

(88/604/EEC)

I. The Facts

(1) ServiceMaster has notified a standard form service franchise agreement for use in all the EEC Member States. The agreement concerns the supply of housekeeping, cleaning and maintenance services to both commercial and domestic customers. ServiceMaster has applied for a negative clearance or alternatively an exemption decision under Article 85(3) of the Treaty.

(2) Following observations made by the Commission, ServiceMaster has agreed to make certain amendments to its notified agreement. The amended agreement was communicated to the Commission on 10 May 1988.

(3) Reference is made to the notice published pursuant to Article 19(3) of Regulation No 17, for a more extensive description of the ServiceMaster franchise system and its relevant clauses which are mentioned or discussed hereinafter only in so far as is necessary for the reasoning of the Commission. The facts set out in the Article 19(3) notice form part of this Decision.

(4) The Commission did not receive any observations from interested third parties following publication of the said notice.

II. Legal Assessment

A. Article 85(1)

(5) The franchise network set up by ServiceMaster by means of the notified standard form agreement is a service franchise; it concerns the supply of housekeeping, cleaning and maintenance service to commercial and domestic customers according to the instructions of ServiceMaster and, on an ancillary basis, the supply of goods directly linked to the provision of those services. The ServiceMaster franchise includes a uniform presentation of the contract services based on the use of a common name, a substantial package of technical, commercial and administrative know-how relating to the provision of the services and continuing assistance provided by ServiceMaster. The franchisees are proprietors of their businesses, which they operate for their own account and at their own risk. In exchange for the right to exploit a ServiceMaster franchise and certain ServiceMaster intellectual property rights related to trade marks and copyrights, the franchisees have to make various financial contributions and are bound by obligations aimed at preserving the uniformity and quality standards of the ServiceMaster system.

(6) The Commission considers that, despite the existence of specific matters, service franchises show strong similarities to distribution franchises and can therefore basically be treated in the same way as the distribution franchises already exempted by the Commission (*see also* the *Yves Rocher*, *Pronuptia* and *Computerland* decisions above). The basic premise relies on the fact that the EEC competition rules apply without distinction to both products and services. This does not prevent the Commission from taking into account in individual cases certain specific characteristics relating to the provision of services.

In particular, know-how is often more important in the supply of service than in the supply of goods because each service requires the execution of particular work and creates a close personal relationship between the provider of the service and the receiver of the service. Therefore, the protection of the franchisor's know-how and reputation can be even more essential for service franchises than for distribution franchises where mainly the goods advertise the business by carrying the trademark of the producer of distributor. Also certain services, as for instance the ServiceMaster services, are executed at the customer's premises, while goods are usually sold at the premises of the retailer. Services of this type further reinforce the link between the provider of the services and the customer.

Provisions not falling within Article 85(1)

The following provisions of the ServiceMaster franchise agreements do not fall within Article 85(1).

(a) *Provisions aimed at preventing the know-how and other assistance given by the franchisor from benefiting competitors*

(7) The franchisee's obligation to preserve, before and after the termination of the agreement, the secrecy of all information and know-how and to impose a similar obligation on his employees. The commercial value of know-how is dependent on its secrecy. The obligation not to disclose the know-how is a necessary condition for maintaining such value and for enabling ServiceMaster to grant it to other potential franchises.

(8) The franchisee's obligation to use the know-how and intellectual property rights licensed solely for the purposes of exploitation of the ServiceMaster franchise. This field-of-use restriction is necessary to protect the franchisor's know-how because it lends iself to use with competitive services provided by either the franchisee or other competitors.

(9) The franchisee's obligation, after termination of the agreement, to cease using the know-how package of Service Master unless this know-how package as a whole has fallen into the public domain otherwise than in breach of obligation. This post-term use ban on know-how is essential for the protection of the franchisor's right to this know-how. As long as its know-how has not become accessible to the public, the franchisor has the right to limit the transfer thereof to a fixed period of time, in this case to the lifetime of the franchise agreement. If the franchisor lost the exclusive right to make use of its know-how after expiry of the franchise agreement, it could not prevent competitors from using its know-how.

(10) The franchisee's obligation, during the term of the agreement,

not to be engaged in a competing business, except through the acquisition of a financial interest not exceeding 5% in the capital of a publicly-quoted company. This non-competition obligation is necessary to avoid the risk that the know-how supplied by ServiceMaster to its franchisees might benefit competitors, even indirectly. The limitation of the acquisition of a financial interest in a publicly-quoted company to 5% of the share capital is intended to ensure that the franchisees do not become involved in the operation of such a company, with the risk of transferring know-how to a competing business. Although the prohibition against acquiring non-controlling financial interest in the capital of a competing publicly-quoted company can be a restriction of competition falling within Article 85(1), in this particular case it is not considered to be an appreciable restriction because the franchisees are generally small undertakings for which the prohibition against acquiring more than 5% of a publicly-quoted company does not normally constitute a real hindrance in the development of their own activities. Furthermore, the franchisees are completely free in the acquisition of financial interests in non-competing companies.

(11) The franchisee's obligation, after the termination of the agreement, not to be engaged, for a period of one year, in a competing business within any territory within which he has provided services prior to the termination of the agreement. In addition, the franchisee may not solicit, for a period of one year, customers who have been, during the period of two years prior to the termination of the agreement, his customers.

This post-term non-competition and non-solicitation obligation is acceptable both as regards its duration and its geographical extent. This obligation is necessary to prevent the ex-franchisee from using the know-how and clientele he has acquired for his own benefit or for the benefit of ServiceMaster's competitors. It is further necessary to allow Service-Master a limited time period to establish a new outlet in the ex-franchisee's territory. This assessment does not prejudice any relief available to franchisees under national law upon termination of the contract.

(12) The prohibition on the franchisee against selling the franchised business or against assigning the franchise agreement to a third party without ServiceMaster's approval. This prohibition is clearly indispensable to protect the know-how and assistance provided by the franchisor.

(b) Provisions which allow the franchisor to safeguard the common identity and reputation of the franchise network

(13) The franchisee's obligation to use ServiceMaster's know-how and to apply the trading methods developed by ServiceMaster is an obli-

gation which is inherent in the franchise system and ensures the standards of uniformity and quality of the franchise network.

(14) The franchisee's obligation to communicate to ServiceMaster any improvements he makes in the operation of the business. This grant-back obligation is made on a non-exclusive and reciprocal basis. It will improve the efficiency of the ServiceMaster franchise network by creating a free interchange of improvements between all franchisees.

(15) The franchisee's obligation to obtain ServiceMaster's prior approval for the location his franchise premises. This obligation is necessary to ensure that a bad choice does not damage the reputation of the network which is a concern of the whole franchise network.

(16) The franchisee's obligation to devote the necessary time and attention to the ServiceMaster business and to use his best endeavours to promote and increase the turnover of that business. This promotion obligation is intended to oblige the franchisee to concentrate his efforts on the development of his business. This obligation is acceptable in the light of the concern to preserve the reputation and uniform identity of the network by creating an efficient franchise system devoting all its efforts to the provision of the ServiceMaster services.

(17) The franchisee's obligation to purchase certain cleaning equipment and certain chemicals used in the operation of the business from ServiceMaster or other suppliers nominated or approved by ServiceMaster. This purchase obligation is essential for the efficient working of the business and acts as a form of quality control. The obligation does not prevent franchisees from obtaining supplies of equipment and goods of equivalent quality from third-party suppliers. ServiceMaster will not withhold its approval of suppliers proposed by franchisees if the goods of those suppliers chemicals, the requirements of safety, non-toxicity, biodegradability and effectiveness. The franchisee is also free to purchase the required goods from any other ServiceMaster franchisee.

(18) The franchisee's obligation to obtain the approval of ServiceMaster for the carrying-out of advertising. This control concerns the nature of advertisements, but not selling prices, with the object of ensuring conformity with the ServiceMaster brand image.

(19) The franchisee's obligation to submit to inspections of his premises by ServiceMaster and to present financial statements. This obligation allows the franchisor to verify whether the franchisee is operating in accordance with the ServiceMaster methods of operation and is fulfilling his financial obligations. In so far as this right of inspection is not abused to discipline franchisees in their sales activities outside their own

territory or in the determination of their sale prices, it cannot be considered restrictive of competition.

(c) *Other provisions*

(20) The recommendation of sales prices to franchisees is not a restriction of competition since franchisees remain entirely free to determine their own prices for the supply of services and home-care products.

(21) The franchisee's obligation to resell home care products only with the consent of ServiceMaster and only to customers serviced by the franchisee. This restriction on the resale of home-care products is based on the legitimate concern that the franchisee must concentrate on his primary business which is the provision of services, rather than the resale of goods.

Provisions falling within Article 85(1)

The following provisions of the ServiceMaster franchise agreement fall within Article 85(1).

(22) The combined effect of the clause which prohibits the franchisee from setting up further outlets outside his own territory, and the territorial protection clause which prevents the franchisee from actively seeking customers outside his territory, results in a certain degree of market-sharing between the franchisees, thus restricting competition within the ServiceMaster network.

This territorial protection is, however, limited by two elements: the franchisee holds a non-exclusive right only within his territory with regard to ServiceMaster itself and each franchisee is entitled to provide services to non-solicited customers outside his territory.

(23) Trade between Member States is affected by the prohibition imposed upon franchisees against setting up outlets in other Member States and against actively seeking customers in territories of franchisees of other Member States. These prohibitions lead to market-sharing between the franchisees of the different Member States. This effect on intra-Community trade is likely to be appreciable. ServiceMaster has notified a standard form agreement which it will use for the establishment of a European-wide franchise network. At the present time, ServiceMaster is only developing this network. However, when assessing the appreciable effect on trade between Member States the Commission must also take into account the likely future development of such a network. In this respect it must be considered that ServiceMaster is an important competitor in the market which is capable of setting up a great number of outlets throughout the EEC as it has done before in the United States and Canada where ServiceMaster has over 2 900

franchisees. ServiceMaster already has a 6% market share in the United Kingdom and reckons that its EEC market share will exceed 5% in the near future. Given this context, the Commission considers that there exists a sufficient probability that the restrictions contained in the notified standard form agreement are, at the least, such as to affect intra-Community trade appreciably. The notified standard form franchise agreement therefore falls within Article 85(1). It is thus necessary to examine whether that agreement can be granted an exemption under Article 85(3).

B. Article 85(3)

(24) The ServiceMaster standard form franchise agreement contributes, through the combined effect of all its provisions, to improving the supply of the services concerned for the following reasons:

— it helps ServiceMaster rapidly to penetrate new markets with only limited investments, in this case the markets of all 12 Member States,
— this rapid development of a European-wide service network increases inter-brand competition with other service providers in the various markets concerned,
— it helps a great number of small undertakings to enter a new market by allowing them to set up outlets more rapidly and with a higher chance of success because they receive the benefit of ServiceMaster's name and reputation, and of its technical, commercial and administrative know-how,
— it permits an intensive servicing of customers through the personal commitment of independent traders.

(25) The ServiceMaster standard form franchise agreement allows consumers a fair share of the benefit resulting from the above improvements in the supply of services. First, the network as a whole is intended to provide a better and uniformly high-quality service to consumers. Secondly, as already mentioned in the preceeding paragraph, consumers will benefit from the efficient service which the franchisee will be encouraged to provide as an independent trader who has a personal and direct interest in the success of his business. Thirdly, the freedom which consumers enjoy to obtain services elsewhere in the network will force franchisees to pass on to consumers a reasonable part of the benefits of this intra-band competition. Finally, because of strong inter-brand competition, the franchisees can be expected to offer better services and prices.

(26) The provisions falling within Article 85(1) are indispensable to the establishment and existence of the franchise network: the limited

territorial protection granted to the franchisees is necessary to obtain and protect their investment, comprising *inter alia* the cost of the establishment and maintenance of the business premises, the payment of the initial franchise fee, the acquisition of the necessary means of transport for the carrying out of the services at the customers' premises and the acquisition of special equipment. The limited territorial protection is also necessary to ensure that the franchisees will concentrate their service activity on their own territory. On the other hand, the franchisees retain passive service rights in other territories and remain free in the determination of their sales prices.

(27) The ServiceMaster standard form franchise agreement does not afford its members the possibility of eliminating competition in respect of a substantial part of the services concerned.

The inter-brand competition in the market concerned is both very strong and open: the market for cleaning, housekeeping and maintenance services is highly competitive, with a large number of firms supplying similar or identical services. It is also a market with no barriers to entry, with the result that new suppliers can at any time challenge any attempt by ServiceMaster or its franchisees to increase their prices.

Intra-brand competition within the ServiceMaster network itself is also preserved: the limited territorial protection does not grant the franchisees any marketing or customer exclusivity. Franchisees are free to provide services to non-solicited customers resident outside their own territory. This brings about a certain degree of price competition between franchisees, who are free to determine their sales prices.

(28) The notified agreement therefore meets all the requirements for an exemption under Article 85(3).

C. Articles 6 and 8 of Regulation No 17

(29) The agreement as notified by ServiceMaster on 3 June 1987 contained a number of provisions which did not fulfill the conditions for an exemption, in particular provisions relating to the territorial protection which originally excluded any inter-brand competition between franchisees. Following observations made by the Commission, ServiceMaster agreed to make a certain number of amendments to its agreement. ServiceMaster communicated the amended agreement to the Commission on 10 May 1988. Therefore, the date on which the exemption can take effect is the date of communication of the amended agreement.

(30) It is appropriate in this case, in view of the highly competitive nature of the market concerned and the absence of any barriers to entry to that market, to grant the exemption for a period of 10 years.

Charles Jourdan

(89/94/EEC)

I. The Facts

A. The undertaking

(1) Charles Jourdan Holding AG is a company constituted under Swiss law whose registered office is situated at Spielhof 3, 8750 Glarus (Switzerland). It is itself owned by the Swiss holding company Portland Cement Werke (PCW). Charles Jourdan AG with its affiliates, hereinafter referred to as the Charles Jourdan Group, owns, in whole or in part, a large number of companies in France, in the rest of the Community and outside the Community. These include in particular 'Société Anonyme des Chaussures Seducta Charles Jourdan et Fils' and 'Société Anonyme Xavier Danaud', which, together with Charles Jourdan AG, have notified the agreements which are the subject of this Decision.

- Société Anonyme des Chaussures Seducta Charles Jourdan et Fils notified the franchise and franchise-corner agreements relating to the Charles Jourdan trade mark (shoes and handbags) in France,
- Société Anonyme Xavier Danuad notified the franchise agreements covering the Xavier Danuad trade marks (shoes and handbags) in France and the franchise-corner agreements covering the Xavier Danaud trade mark (shoes and handbags) in France,
- Charles Jourdan Holding AG notified the franchise agreements covering the Charles Jourdan trade mark (shoes and handbags) and the Xavier Danaud trade mark (shoes and handbags) outside France.

(2) The Charles Jourdan Group mainly manufactures and distributes shoes and leather goods (some 80% of its turnover) and handbags (9% of its turnover). It also distributes ready-to-wear clothing and accessories under its own trade mark, and these account for the remainder of its turnover.

In 1984, the Group achieved 55% of its turnover in France and sold 1 685 000 pairs of shoes and 136 000 handbags. In 1987 the Group sold 1.1 million pairs of shoes.

The Group's turnover amounted to FF 896 943 000 in 1984 and FF 941 774 000 in 1985. In 1987 the turnover amounted to about FF 700 000 000.

The turnover of Portland Cement Werke amounted to SwF 568 000 000 in 1985.

B. The product and the market

(3) The Group's main activity is the production and sale of shoes, in particular medium and top quality shoes. The articles in the middle of the range lie roughly within a retail price range of FF 400 to FF 700, while the top quality articles cost over FF 700. On the basis of this distinction, although approximate, articles bearing the Seducta trade mark may be regarded as top category and those bearing the Charles Jourdan, Christian Dior or Xavier Danaud trade marks as falling within the second category. A proportion of the Group's shoe production (around 10%) is subcontracted. The shoe trade marks distributed by the Charles Jourdan Group are Charles Jourdan, Seducta, Christian Dior and Xavier Danaud.

Another of the Group's activities is the production, partly through subcontracting, and the sale of leather goods (handbags, but also belts, luggage, gloves, etc.).

The accessories marketed by the group are generally produced through subcontracting. These include umbrellas, scarves, glasses, perfumes, tights, socks, ties, hats, watches, pens and jewellery. They are designed by the Charles Jourdan Group's stylists.

Lastly, the Charles Jourdan Group distributes under its trade mark a collection of ready-to-wear clothing for men and women that is produced entirely through subcontracting.

(4) The shoe market:

Community production amounted to some 1 200 million pairs of shoes in 1986, almost half of which were manufactured in Italy and some 200 million of which were manufactured in France. In 1986, Community imports amounted to 345 million pairs and exports to 260 million pairs. In the case of France, manufacturers exported a quarter of their production, but more than one in every two pairs of shoes (54%) worn in France is imported.

The Community market, and in particular the French market, is therefore amply open to exports and imports.

There are a large number of smaller producers: out of a total of 423 French firms in 1982, only 15 employed more than 500 persons. However, the latter firms accounted for 25% of total French production, with Eram and GEP heading the field.

Charles Jourdan's European competitors in the production of top-of-the-range shoes include Bally, Kelian, Carel, Manfield, Pinet, Clergerie, Maud Frison and Céline.

Its European competitors in the production of middle-of-the-range shoes include Mirelli, France Arno, Salamander, Heyraud, Raoul and Dressoir.

Competition from producers within the Community (Italy and Spain) though also from non-Community countries (Hong Kong, Taiwan, Singapore and South Korea), is very strong.

These comments also apply to distribution, where competition is fierce not only among sales outlets, but also among distribution networks.

In France, the bulk of footwear products is still distributed by independent retailers. Some independent retailers have formed themselves into joint buying pools (e.g. Cédaf, UCF, etc.) or operate on a franchise basis (e.g. Eram, GEP, Labelle, Charles Jourdan).

Shoes are also sold through the subsidiaries of manufacturing firms (e.g. Bata, Bally, Eram, Myris, André and Charles Jourdan) and purely distributive firms (e.g. Raoul, France Arno and Manfield).

Lastly, shoes are also sold through a number of non-specialist outlets, such as supermarkets, mail order firms and department stores.

In the case of leather goods the number of individual French and European manufacturers is even larger, since this sector includes craft industry as well as industry proper. Competition from Asian countries is very keen in the case of medium quality products. Distribution is widely scattered amongst specialised shops, bazaars, supermarkets, etc.

In the case of leather goods, the Charles Jourdan Group is the third largest French producer.

(5) The Charles Jourdan Group's share of the French shoe market as a whole is around 1%. Its share of the Community market is negligible.

However, if one takes the market in medium and top quality shoes, the Group's market share may be estimated at nearly 10% of the French market and around 2% of the Community market. This market definition is not rigorous but it allows non-leather shoes and cheap shoes to be excluded.

The market share of the other products marketed by the group is insignificant both in France and at the Community level.

C. Distribution of the Group's products

(6) The distribution of the Charles Jourdan Group's products has to meet a number of requirements specific to the products and to the Group. Firstly, it is carried out by traders capable of dealing with a demanding clientele having above-average purchasing power. Secondly, close links are kept up between retailers and the Group so as to maintain a uniform style and approach to customers.

(7) Distribution is carried out through four types of shops:

— branches: these are owned and managed by the Group and display the Charles Jourdan or Xavier Danaud shop sign. They constitute the shop window of the group's activities. In general, they also market all the products in the Charles Jourdan range,

— franchised shops: these are independent of the Group, but have signed a franchise distribution agreement with it, allowing them to display the Charles Jourdan or Xavier Danaud shop sign on the outside of their shop premises in respect of the whole of the shop and allocating them a specified territory,

— franchise-corner retailers: these are independent traders who have signed a distribution agreement with the Group, allowing them to represent the Charles Jourdan or Xavier Danaud trade marks within a specified territory in a separate part of the shop premises, the articles in question being in competition with those of other brands. The shop sign must be displayed within the shop and not on the outside, as in the case of franchised shops.

Because of the franchise-corner retailer's more limited commitment to the Group compared with franchised retailers, there is a difference in the rights and duties of each of the partners. The franchise-corner formula, which combines certain characteristics of franchise retailing and conventional retailing, is intended either, if chosen by the retailer, to allow the franchise-corner retailer to maintain greater independence from the group or, if chosen by the Group, to test the franchise-corner retailer's personal and professional capacity before giving him a franchise,

— traditional retailers: they have no legal link with the Group apart from agreements to sell articles bearing the trade mark. Such retailers are selected by the Charles Jourdan Group on the basis of objective considerations, namely the shop in which the activity is carried out, the quality of the products distributed and the retailer himself, his competence and reputation.

D. Main features of the standard-form agreements notified

(8) *Procedure for choosing the Group's franchisees and franchise-corner retailers*. The agreements are concluded *intuito personae* on the basis of the candidate's personal and professional qualities. The agreement may not be transferred to a third party without the approval of the Group. Any manager employed to run a shop must be approved in advance by the Group.

(9) *Legal independence of franchisees and franchise-corner retailers*. Franchisees and franchisor-corner retailers are the owners of, and legally and financially responsible for, their business and fittings.

However, any change in the geographical location or in the internal or external fittings of the shop must be approved in advance by the Group.

(10) *Exclusive territory*. Each agreement defines the exact territory of the franchisee or franchisor-corner retailer.

Within the franchisee's territory, the franchisee is allowed to operate his shop, under the external shop sign of one of the Group's trade marks and may distribute the relevant products only on the premises defined in the agreement. There may be several traditional retailers and/or franchise-corner retailers within the territory of a franchisee. However, there cannot be more than one franchisee within one and the same territory.

(11) *Transfer of know-how from the Charles Jourdan Group to franchisees and franchise-corner retailers*. Franchisees receive know-how and continuous assistance from the Charles Jourdan Group in the following areas:

— purchasing (season's collection; standard order; trends; colours and materials in fashion), with information being provided to the retailer on the latest fashion trends,
— supply of the general decoration concept, with help being provided on the decoration or redecoration of the shop,
— establishment and maintenance of stock and management information, with assistance being provided on the internal management of the shop,
— provision of information on the sale of products in the 'affiliates and franchisees' networks, with information being given on the business activity of sales outlets distributing the same products,
— advertising, with material help or advice being provided on the advertising policy of franchisees.

The know-how thus made available is primarily commercial although it also covers management aspects. It is substantial and gives the trader a clear advantage over competitors. It is this, in addition to the prestige of the trade mark, which prompts actual or would-be independent traders to conclude such agreements with the Charles Jourdan Group.

Franchise-corner retailers only receive information on purchasing and fashion trends from the Charles Jourdan Group. Such information is both more limited and covers fewer fields than that provided for franchisees. No provision is made for management assistance.

All the information supplied to franchisees or franchise-corner retailers is confidential.

(12) *Industrial property rights*. The Charles Jourdan Group remains the owner of its registered trade marks and of its designs, trade names, signs, emblems, symbols and other distinctive commercial marks. It alone may decide on the use made of them.

(13) *Right of inspection by the Charles Jourdan Group*. Franchisees and franchise-corner retailers must make their accounts available to the Group and must each month send in a statement of sales and quantities

sold for the previous month. They must allow inspections to be carried out of their staff and business premises, including premises for storage. The inspection may also relate to whether the franchisee is meeting the quality standards associated with the name and reputation of the goods.

(14) *Financial obligations to the Charles Jourdan Group.* In exchange for the franchisor supplying the general decoration concept, the overall building plan, samples of materials, the specification, and the assistance of the decorator, the franchisee has to pay an entry fee of FF 20 000 to FF 30 000 depending on the trade mark involved. The costs of fitting out and equipping the shop are borne by the franchisee or the franchisor-corner retailer. No entry fee is required from franchisor-corner retailers who have to pay only a guarantee deposit.

In return for the rights granted and the services supplied, the franchisee must also pay the franchisor, depending on the trade mark involved, a franchise fee of 1.5 or 2% of the total amount of net sales, excluding tax, for the shop. In the case of franchisor-corner retailers, the fee is set at 1% of the shop's total sales, excluding tax. In practice, at least 50% of such sales are accounted for by products bearing the Group's trade marks.

(15) *Non-competition clause.* In the case of franchise agreements, the non-competition clause prohibits the franchisee from operating within the allocated territory any other shop franchised by companies other than those of the Charles Jourdan Group, unless such other shop sells articles which because of their price and style cannot be regarded as competing with Charles Jourdan products.

Within the shop itself, the franchisee may distribute only products bearing the trade marks covered by the agreement and the Group's other trade marks. The franchisee may, however, be authorised by the Group to distribute other articles originating outside the Group.

In the case of agreements with franchise-corner retailers, there is a clause prohibiting them from displaying or selling products which, because of their trade mark, name or presentation, would be likely to detract from the Charles Jourdan Group's brand image.

Upon expiry of the agreements, the trader is not subject to any restrictions in his subsequent activities. Where a franchised shop is to be sold, the first offer must be made to the franchisor, who has a period of one month in which to decide whether to buy it.

(16) *Supply arrangements.* The trader may obtain direct supplies of products bearing the Charles Jourdan Group's trade marks either from the group itself, or from a Group branch shop, or from another member of the network, whether such a member is a franchisee or franchisor-corner retailer, or even from a traditional retailer of products bearing the Group's trade marks, whether or not such suppliers are established

in the same Member State. As a general rule, cross-supplies between distributors of products bearing the Group's trade marks are allowed, provided that the principal activity of the franchisee or franchisor-corner retailer is not that of wholesale. This possibility was granted to these Charles Jourdan Group retailers at the Commission's request.

(17) *Purchase prices.* Within one and the same Member State purchase prices are the same for all franchisees, franchise-corner retailers and traditional retailers. However, quantity rebates may be granted.

Variations in purchase prices from one Member State to another are due to the costs of distribution, transit, exchange, etc. involved in export operations.

(18) *Selling prices.* The Charles Jourdan Group draws up price lists every season. The price lists are intended for guidance purposes and retailers are not required to abide by them. This freedom for retailers to determine their selling prices was expressly specified in the agreements at the Commissions's request.

(19) *Duration of the agreements.* All the agreements are concluded for an initial term of five years.

(20) *Termination of the agreements.* The Charles Jourdan Group may terminate a franchise agreement or an agreement with a franchise-corner retailer if the trader's assets are placed in the hands of the receiver or the trader goes into liquidation, if the shop is transferred to other premises or altered, or if sales are insufficient. In the event of breach of any of the clauses of the agreements, the Charles Jourdan Group or its partner, the franchisee or the franchise-corner retailer, may terminate the contract.

(21) *Effects of termination or expiry of the agreement.* Franchisees or franchise-corner retailers are not subject to any restrictions on the exercise of their future activities. They may continue to distribute similar or competing products within the same geographical area and in the same shop.

They are merely required to remove all shop signs and advertising displays from their shops, to modify the fittings associated with the activity of franchisee or franchise-corner retailer and to hand over to the Charles Jourdan Group all printed matter, labels, packing materials, etc. bearing the trade marks, excluding any supplies necessary for the disposal for remaining merchandise in stock.

(22) *Observations from third parties.* The Commission received no observations following its publication of a notice in accordance with Article 19(3) of Regulation No 17.

II. Legal Assessment

A. Article 85(1)

(23) Through the standard-form distribution agreements notified, the Charles Jourdan Group:

— grants to its franchisees and franchise-corner retailers, within a territory specified in the agreement, the exclusive right to use in a retail shop its identifications (shop signs, trade mark, business name) and its designs and models for the purposes of selling. This results in a uniform presentation of the products marketed within the network. The exclusive right applies to the shop sign on the outside of the shop and to the shop sign inside the shop in the case of franchise-corner retailers,

— transfers to its franchisees and its franchise-corner retailers know-how consisting of a body of commercial and management knowledge previously tried and tested by the Charles Jourdan Group itself and not divulged to third parties and of continuous assistance. The technical and business know-how is updated in the light of the results of the experience acquired by the Charles Jourdan Group.

(24) The Charles Jourdan Group is able to develop a coherent and efficient sales network without massive investments, while at the same time maintaining control over the activity of the sales outlets.

This formula allows franchise retailers not already experienced in the distribution of articles bearing the trade mark to benefit from the franchisor's know-how and experienced franchise retailers, in addition to this advantage, to concentrate all their efforts on marketing the products of the Charles Jourdan Group, whose reputation is enough to guarantee them a clientele.

The formula enables franchise-corner retailers to benefit from the Group's know-how and from the reputation of the Charles Jourdan Group's trade marks, while at the same time maintaining a large degree of business autonomy thanks to the distribution of competing trade marks in their shops.

(25) The standard-form franchise agreements or franchise-corner retailer agreements which the Charles Jourdan Group has signed or intends to sign with its franchisees or franchise-corner retailers are agreements between undertakings within the meaning of Article 85, the Charles Jourdan Group and each of its partners remaining independent undertakings.

(a)   *Clauses not covered by Article 85(1)*

Franchise agreements

(26) The Court of Justice in the Pronuptia judgment (*see* the *Pronuptia* case at Appendix IV above), and the Commission in the Pronuptia, Yves Rocher and Computerland Decisions, took the view that clauses which are essential to prevent the know-how supplied and assistance provided by the franchisor from benefiting competitors and clauses which provide for the control that is essential for preserving the common identity and reputation of the network, operating under the shop sign do not constitute restrictions of competition within the meaning of Article 85(1).

(27) The clauses that are essential to prevent the know-how made available from benefiting competitors are the following:

— the clause providing for non-competition during the term of the agreement prohibits the franchisee from operating any other franchised shop within the allocated territory, unless such other shop sells products that are unrelated to the products of the Charles Jourdan Group. This clause is justified for the franchisee by the fact that the know-how provided could easily be used for the benefit of other products and other trade marks under another franchise system. The franchisee is not bound by any non-competition clause once the agreement has expired. Such a non-competition clause would not be justified first as the know-how provided includes a large element of general commercial techniques, and second, as this type of franchise is primarily granted to retailers who are already experienced in selling shoes,

— the provision prohibiting the franchisee from transferring its franchise contract, subletting its shop, setting up a sub-franchise, placing its business under management by a third party or appointing a salaried shop manager without the express approval of the Charles Jourdan Group enables the Charles Jourdan Group to ensure that the franchisee possesses the professional qualities necessary for the exercise of its functions, but also that persons not belonging to the Charles Jourdan network do not benefit from the advantages inherent in the distribution system being examined here.

(28) The clauses that provide for the control essential to preserve the common identity and reputation of the network trading under the franchisor's name are as follows:

— obligation on the franchisee to carry on his business activity from premises fitted out according to the indications and advice of the group. This makes it possible to ensure the consistency, commer-

cial homogeneity and reputation of the sales outlets of the Charles
Jourdan Group's network.

— obligation on the franchisee to cooperate with the Charles Jourdan
Group. This obligation relates principally to advertising, which
must be carried out in agreement with the Charles Jourdan Group
so as to maintain the Group's broad image and the quality of the
management of the sales outlet, so as to prevent bad management
from harming the interests of the trade marks represented,

— ban on the franchisee reselling the Charles Jourdan Group's goods
to traders other than franchisees, franchise-corner retailers or
retailers supplied by the Group. This clause is intended to maintain
the unity of the network and the link, in the consumer's mind,
between the Charles Jourdan Group's product and the place where
it is sold,

— obligation on the franchisee unless otherwise authorised by the
Group, in view of the nature of the products concerned (fashion
goods) and in order to preserve the consistency of the brand
image, to order the goods connected with the essential object of
the franchise business exclusively from the Charles Jourdan Group
or from suppliers designated by it. The franchisee may purchase
the goods in question from any other franchisee, franchise-corner
retailer or traditional retailer belonging to the Charles Jourdan
network,

— obligation on the franchisee to submit to checks by the Charles
Jourdan Group. The Group's right of scrutiny of the management
of its retailers is a counterpart to the responsibilities delegated by
the Charles Jourdan Group to its partners.

(29) As regards retail prices, which are only recommended, it should
be emphasised that the mere communication of recommended prices by
the group to its retailers cannot be regarded as restricting competition,
provided that it does not result in concerted practices between retailers
in the network or between retailers and the Charles Jourdan Group.

(30) The lack of any obligation on the Group to define and abide by
selection criteria in choosing its franchisees is due to the desire to
establish an integrated and interdependent distribution network to which
each trader, with his professional and personal capacities, has chosen
to belong. The continuous assistance which the franchisee receives
during the term of the agreement implies a significant involvement of
the Group's representatives with each of the traders. The members of
the distribution network must therefore be limited in number. Consequently, the Group can of its own accord choose the traders which seem
to it most suitable for maintaining the cohesion of the network.

Franchise-corner retailer agreements

(31) The clauses not covered by Article 85(1) are firstly those which provide the Group with the essential control needed to preserve the common identity and reputation of the network symbolised by the shop sign within the shop: the franchise-corner retailer must carry out his activity in the part fitted out in accordance with the Group's directives. He must also cooperate with the Group in matters of advertising and management. He cannot purchase the goods from or resell the goods to traders other than those who are already members of the Group's distribution network. Lastly, the franchise-corner retailer must submit to checks by the Charles Jourdan Group.

The franchise-corner retailer is not subject to any non-competition obligation. Nevertheless he cannot display or sell in his shop products liable to detract from the Charles Jourdan Group's brand image. He is free to market other trade marks. This clause is justified by the quality of the Charles Jourdan Group's products, necessitating proper presentation. In view of the highly competitive situation in the sector, this restriction is not likely to have any significant effect on competition.

The agreement is automatically terminated in the event of transfer, management by a third party, control of the company by a third party or appointment of a salaried shop manager without the express approval of the Charles Jourdan Group, so as to ensure that the franchise-corner retailer has the necessary qualities and the advantages of the formula do not benefit a third party.

(b)   *Clauses covered by Article 85(1)*

Franchise agreements

(32) The clauses that involve market sharing between the Charles Jourdan Group and its partners or between its partners themselves constitute restrictions of competition within the meaning of Article 85(1). This applies to:

— the exclusivity granted to the franchisee to operate under the franchisor's trade marks in a given sales area, and
— the obligation on the franchisee to carry on his business activity exclusively from the premises approved for that purpose.

The combined effect of these clauses is to afford each franchisee relative protection against competition from other franchisees within its sales area. However, such protection is restricted by the fact that, while there may be only one franchisee within a given area, there may be several franchise-corner retailers and traditional retailers within the area.

(33) The franchise agreements may affect trade between Member

States as they constitute the basis of a network which is bound to spread over the whole Community and as the franchisees are not allowed to become established in another Member State.

Franchise-corner retailer agreements

(34) The exclusive right to display an internal shop sign within the shop, does not, within the territory, exclude either branch shops or franchise shops, which have, in addition, an external shop sign. Nor does such exclusive right exclude the display of Charles Jourdan Group trade marks in traditional retail shops. The contracts only restrict the retailer a little and, on a highly competitive market, offer very limited protection against competition within the network.

(35) Since, in addition, the number of franchise-corner retailers was very low on the date when the agreements were notified and since the number of franchise-corner retailers is not, according to the Charles Jourdan Group, going to increase significantly, they are not likely to affect trade between Member States, or significantly to prevent, restrict or distort competition within the common market. The provisions of Article 85(1) do not therefore apply to the franchise-corner agreements.

B. Article 85(3)

(36) Commission Regulation (EEC) No 1983/83 on the block exemption of exclusive distribution agreements does not apply to the standard-form franchise agreements in question, since their legal nature is different (*see* points 15 and 33 of the *Pronuptia* case at Appendix IV above). In addition to being distribution agreements they are agreements under which the franchisor grants the franchisee the right to operate a shop using an original and evolving distribution formula. It should therefore be examined whether the agreements in question are eligible for individual exemption under Article 85(3).

(37) Through the combined effect of their provisions as a whole, the standard-form franchise agreements governing the Charles Jourdan distribution network contribute to improving the distribution of the products concerned within the meaning of Article 85(3). They enable:

— the Charles Jourdan Group to extend its distribution network without carrying out investment in the material fitting out of new branches, investment which it would perhaps otherwise not be able to carry out, or to carry out as rapidly, since it is the prospective franchisees which are responsible for the necessary investment,
— the Charles Jourdan Group to make available to consumers a distribution network which is uniform in the business methods

used and the range of products offered. Such uniformity makes it possible to rationalise business methods by standardising them,
— the Charles Jourdan Group, given the close and direct links which it has with its partners, to be rapidly informed by them of any changes in consumers' habits and tastes and thus to be able to take account of this in its forward plans on sales and production,
— the franchisee, who enjoys exclusive rights to use the external shop sign within the allocated territory, to concentrate his sales efforts on that territory and on the Group's trade marks,
— the franchisee to enjoy the commercial benefits of the brand image of the products and the tried and tested know-how and continuous assistance of the Charles Jourdan Group.

(38) The agreements governing the Charles Jourdan distribution network allow consumers a fair share of the benefit resulting from these improvements in distribution:

— consumers can acquire products from the Charles Jourdan Group's range in a larger number of sales outlets and countries,
— the know-how transmitted and the assistance provided by the Group to its partners ensure that consumers receive high-quality service,
— the fact that the retailers remain the owners of their businesses ensures commercial dynamism and diligence on the part of the trader.

The pressure of competition within the sector and the freedom which consumers have to purchase the products at any shop within the network will tend to force franchisees to pass on to consumers a reasonable share of the advantages resulting from the rationalisation of distribution.

(39) The Charles Jourdan Group's standard-form agreements do not contain restrictions that are not indispensable to the attainment of the said benefits. The restrictive clauses that provide for some territorial exclusivity may be considered, in the circumstances, to be indispensable in that few prospective franchisees would be willing to undertake the necessary investment, to pay an initial lump-sum fee or a guarantee deposit and to pay royalties in proportion to their turnover in order to belong to such a distribution system, if they did not enjoy some territorial protection against competition from other franchisees and from the Charles Jourdan Group itself. It should be noted that the franchisees are free to buy and sell the relevant products among themselves or to sell them to and buy them from other independent retailers of the trade mark.

(40) The Charles Jourdan standard-form agreements and the system resulting from their implementation are not such as to afford the under-

takings concerned the possibility of eliminating competition in respect of a substantial part of the products in question. With regard to producers and distributors that are competitors of the Charles Jourdan Group, the Charles Jourdan network cannot produce any significant horizontal anti-competitive effects outside of the trade mark, given the dispersal of the supply of products both at production level and at distribution level.

(41) The production and distribution of Charles Jourdan Group shoes, which is the Group's main activity, account for only a modest share of the French market and an even smaller share of the Community market. On the submarket for medium and top quality shoes, the Charles Jourdan Group accounts for some 10% of the French total and only around 2% of the Community market. Its turnover, which amounted to less than FF 1 000 million in 1985, is relatively modest compared with that of its European competitors. In addition, the footwear market, like the market for leather goods, accessories or ready-to-wear clothing is buoyant and very keenly competitive.

(42) The franchisees are, in addition, in competition with one another, since they are allowed to sell to any consumer resident within or outside the alloted territory and to any other franchisee, franchise-corner retailer or retailer of the trade mark, subject to the condition of not acting as a wholesaler by way of principal activity. Furthermore, they are entirely free to set their selling prices. The distribution network, which covers several different systems of marketing, creates a healthy rivalry between retailers, thus allowing the consumer the widest choice and hence the best purchasing conditions.

Lastly, there is no provision for any non-competition clause upon expiry or after termination of the agreements, and this enables any franchisee to continue to carry on his business activity in his own shop without any restriction once he has ended his relationship with the Group.

(43) All the conditions for the application of Article 85(3) are thus met.

(44) The exemption decision will take effect as from the date on which the most recent amendments were made to the standard-form agreements, i.e. 17 December 1986. Exemption may be granted for a period of 10 years. This period seems justified given the limited restriction of competition resulting from the agreements and the competitive context in question.

Appendix VI

'Concerted Practices'

The following extracts are taken from an article, 'Franchisees and "Concerted Practices" ', by Bryan Harris, published in *The Journal of International Franchising and Distribution Law*, December 1988.

The article quotes paragraph 25 of the judgment in the *Pronuptia* case (*see* Appendix IV), in which the Court speaks of the obligations of franchisors and franchisees in respect of concerted practices.

'In an early case before the Court of Justice it was held that a concerted practice was established if it was shown that there was a form of co-operation between undertakings which, without having reached the stage where an agreement properly so called has been concluded, knowingly substitutes practical co-operation for the risks of competition. By its very nature, then, a concerted practice does not have all the elements of a contract but may arise, *inter alia*, out of co-ordination which becomes apparent from the behaviour of the participants'.

The case referred to was the so-called 'Dyestuffs Case' (*ICI v Commission*, 48/69). It was reaffirmed in the subsequent cases discussed in the article, which points out that concerted practices are in the last event matters of proof and circumstances.

Given the special relationship between franchisors and franchisees,

'it would be wrong for the EEC authorities to attribute collusive motives to business meetings and communications of the kind which are characteristic of the relationship between franchisors and franchisees.

However, if franchisees, with or without the franchisor, agree either personally or in writing between themselves that they can all charge a certain price, there may well be evidence of a concerted practice and hence a breach of the EEC rules. If the evidence also shows that the franchisor in question has a large market share, and can therefore hold the consumer to ransom, the infringement may well be aggra-vated. Again, if some franchisees decide to operate at less than the recommended price, and other franchisees (with or without the fran-chisor) apply pressure on those franchisees to conform with the recommended price, there may well be *prima facie* evidence of a concerted practice.

To sum up: where franchisees, using their individual judgment and not being subject to any pressure from the franchisor or other fran-chisees, accept and apply the prices recommended or indicated by the franchisor, there is little likelihood that they will be in breach of the EEC rules of competition, even if all the other franchisees in the network happen to do the same.'

Appendix VII

Checklist of clauses

The effect which the provisions of the Regulation have on the terms of the franchise agreement is considered by category.

Territorial restrictions

(a) The grant by the franchisor of exclusive territorial rights, coupled with undertakings by the franchisor not to appoint another franchisee or itself to carry on business within the territory, is permitted (art 2(a)).

(b) The franchisor may also undertake not to supply goods manufactured by it, to its specification or bearing its trade mark to third parties within the territory allocated to the franchisee (art 2(a)).

(c) The franchisee may be restricted to trading only from the premises identified in the contract (ie a location clause) (art 2(e)).

(d) The franchisee should also be permitted to move to alternative premises with the franchisor's consent. The franchisor cannot withhold its consent to such a move if the alternative premises match the franchisor's normal criteria for trading premises (art 3(2)(i) and 8(e)).

(e) The franchisee can be prohibited from soliciting or touting for custom from those whose residence is or business premises are outside any allocated territory but the franchisee cannot be required to refuse to do business with a non-solicited customer from outside the territory (art 2(d) and 8(c)).

(f) A master franchisee can be prohibited from selling franchises outside his territory (art 2(b)).

Goods the subject of the franchise

(a) The franchisee can be prohibited from manufacturing, selling or using in the course of the provision of services, goods competing with the franchisor's goods (ie goods produced by the franchisor or according to its instructions and/or bearing the franchisor's name or trade mark) (art 2(e)).

(b) Without prejudice to the above the franchisor must not refuse, for reasons other than protecting the franchisor's industrial or intellectual property rights, or maintaining the common identity and reputation of the franchised network, to designate as authorised manufacturers third parties proposed by the franchisee (art 5(*c*)).

(c) The franchisee can be required, so far as is necessary to protect the franchisor's industrial or intellectual property rights or to maintain the common identity and reputation of the franchise network,

   (i) to sell, or use in the course of the provision of services, exclusively goods which match minimum objective quality specifications laid down by the franchisor (art 3(1)(*a*));

   (ii) to sell, or use in the course of the provision of services, goods manufactured only by the franchisor (art 3(1)(*b*));

   (iii) to sell, or use in the course of the provision of services, goods manufactured by nominated third parties where it is impracticable owing to the nature of the goods which are the subject matter of the franchise to apply objective quality specifications (art 3(1)(*b*));

   (iv) to sell the goods only to end users, other franchisees and others within the manufacturer's distribution network (art 3(1)(*e*) and 4(*a*));

   (v) to use his best endeavours to sell the goods (art 3(1)(*f*));

   (vi) to offer for sale a minimum range of goods (art 3(1)(*f*));

   (vii) to achieve minimum sales targets and plan orders in advance (art 3(1)(*f*));

   (viii) to keep minimum stocks (art 3(1)(*f*));

   (ix) to provide customer and warranty services (art 3(1)(*f*));

   (x) to honour guarantees whether the goods have been obtained from the franchisor, nominated suppliers, other franchisees or other distributors of the goods which carry similar guarantees in the common market (art 4(*b*)).

(d) The franchisee cannot be prevented from

   (i) buying the goods from other franchisees or other distributors thereof (art 5(*e*));

   (ii) fixing his own prices, although the franchisor may recommend prices (art 5(*e*)) — it should be noted that the Commission can withdraw the benefit of the exemption given by the Regulation if 'franchisees engage in concerted practices relating to sale prices of the goods or services which are the subject-matter of the franchise' (art 8(*d*));

   (iii) obtaining spare parts or accessories for the franchisor's goods other than from the Franchisor (art 2(*e*));

   (iv) supplying goods or services to non-solicited end users because of their place of residence (art 5(*g*) and 8(*c*)).

The provisions relating to products taken as a whole indicate that the position on tied supplies of goods may be summarised as follows.

1. The franchisee can be required to sell or use in the provision of services only franchisor's goods (as defined) and no others. This requirement cannot be imposed in respect of accessories or spare parts for these goods.
2. The franchisee must be permitted to obtain franchisor's goods from other franchisees or other distributors of such goods.
3. Insofar as it is necessary to protect the franchisor's industrial or intellectual property rights or to maintain the common identity and reputation of the franchised network, (a) the franchisor can require the franchisee only to sell goods obtained from nominated suppliers where it is impracticable owing to the nature of the goods to formulate objective quality specifications, and (b) to sell exclusively goods which match minimum objective quality specifications laid down by the franchisor.
4. The franchisee cannot be prevented from obtaining supplies of goods of a quality equivalent to those offered by the franchisor without prejudice to 1 and 3(a) above.

The combined effect of 3 and 4 is that the franchisee may be obliged to deal in goods supplied by a nominated supplier where it is impracticable to formulate objective quality criteria. In the *Pronuptia* case the Court gave two examples to illustrate what this means. The first was the nature of the products, such as fashion goods (not a surprise since the case involved a fashion goods franchise) and the second was where the cost of monitoring compliance with the specifications would be too expensive as could be the case if there were a large number of franchises.

To resolve these issues (apart from any others which may be relevant) the following questions will have to be addressed.

(a) Is what is proposed necessary to protect the franchisor's industrial or intellectual property rights or to maintain the common identity and reputation of the franchised network?
(b) Is it impracticable to formulate objective quality criteria by reason of:
   – the nature of the goods; or
   – the cost of monitoring compliance in the light of the numbers of suppliers involved?

Competition

The franchisor can require the franchisee

(a) not to manufacture, sell or use in the course of the provision of services, goods which compete with the franchisor's goods. This requirement cannot be extended to spare parts and accessories for such goods (art 1(*e*));

(b) insofar as it is necessary to protect the franchisor's industrial or intellectual property rights or to maintain the common identity and reputation of the franchised network not to engage directly or indirectly in any similar business in a territory where the franchisee would compete with:
   (i) a member of the franchised network; or
   (ii) the franchisor
at all during the agreement and for a reasonable period not exceeding one year after the agreement ends in the territory where the franchisee has exploited the franchise (art 3(*c*)). This prohibition can extend to non-solicited customers who reside or have their place of business outside the franchisee's allocated territory;

(c) insofar as it is necessary to protect the franchisor's industrial or intellectual property rights or to maintain the common identity and reputation of the franchised network not to acquire financial interests in the capital of competitors which would give the franchisee power to influence the economic conduct of the competitor (art 3(*d*)).

Know-how

The franchisor is entitled to protect its know-how and can impose an obligation on franchisees:

(a) not to use the know-how other than for the purpose of exploiting the franchise, during or after the end of the agreement, but only until the know-how becomes generally known or easily accessible other than by breach of an obligation by the franchisee (art 3(2)(*d*) and 5(*d*));

(b) not to disclose the know-how to third parties during or after the termination of the agreement (art 3(2)(*a*); and

(c) to require staff of the franchisee to keep confidential the know-how imparted to them to enable them to discharge their duties as employees of the franchisee.

Generally

(a) The franchisor must oblige the franchisee to indicate his status as an independent undertaking (art 4(c)).

(b) Insofar as is necessary to protect the franchisor's industrial or intellectual property rights or to maintain the common identity and reputation of the franchised network the franchisee can be required to make advertising contributions and not to advertise unless the nature of such advertising shall have been approved by the franchisor (art 3(1)(g)).

(c) The franchisor must not prohibit the franchisee from challenging the validity of the industrial or intellectual property rights which form part of the franchise. However if a franchisee does mount such a challenge the franchisor can provide for the termination of the agreement (art 5(f)).

(d) The franchisor must not use its right
   (i) to inspect the location (or vehicle),
   (ii) to veto a move to new premises, or
   (iii) to withhold consent to an assignment of the franchisee's rights and obligations under the franchise agreement (ie sell the business)

for reasons other than

1. protecting the franchisor's industrial or intellectual property rights,
2. maintaining the common identity and reputation of the franchise network, or
3. verifying that the franchisee is performing his obligations under the agreement.

(Art 8(e)).

The franchisor can require franchisees to introduce modifications of the franchisor's commercial methods (art 3(2)(f)).

Index